BREAKING
THE SPELL

The truth about money, success, and the pursuit of happiness

DEBBIE LACHUSA

IlluminatePress

A service of DLC Marketing, Inc.

PMB 310, 9625 Mission Gorge Road, Suite B2

Santee, California, 92071

www.DebbieLaChusa.com

ISBN-10: 0615590780

ISBN-13: 978-0-615-59078-3

Library of Congress Control Number: 2012901566

Limits of Liability and Disclaimer of Warranty

The author and publisher shall not be liable for your misuse of this material. This book is for strictly informational and educational purposes. The views expressed in this book are solely those of the author and those interviewed. Because of the dynamic nature of the Internet, any web addresses or links contained in the book may have changed since publication and may no longer be valid.

CONTENTS

PREFACE

When I decided to write this book I was angry. I had invested seven years and $200,000 to become more successful in my business and achieve my ultimate goal of becoming a millionaire. I had done everything I had been coached and taught to do. And yet, seven years later, there I sat, thousands of dollars in debt, my business in a shambles, and facing a foreclosure on my previously stellar credit report. I was nowhere near the epitome of success I had been seeking to be. I felt duped. I was angry at the personal development industry. I was angry with the professionals I had trusted and sought help and advice from. I was angry at the world. But most of all, I was angry with myself for becoming so mesmerized by the promise of fame and fortune and spending so much time and money trying to achieve both. I didn't start out seeking them, but somewhere along the way, everything changed. I wanted to find out where, and more importantly, why.

Although I was angry, I was very certain I did not want to write this book from that perspective. I wanted this book to be informative and enlightening. I knew that would not be possible if I wrote it from a place of anger and blame. And deep down I knew others weren't to blame for my situation. I had created it myself. What I didn't understand was why.

I wanted desperately to know why I, and millions of other people, had gotten so caught up chasing money, success, and happiness. I began doing research. I read books. I surveyed five hundred people. I interviewed people from around the world and all walks of life: people with jobs; people who were unemployed; students; retirees; entrepreneurs; mothers; fathers; those who had faced financial hardship, foreclosure, and bankruptcy. I interviewed success experts and professionals specializing in personality type, psychology, and addiction. Through it all, the fog began to lift. I began to understand what had happened to so many others and me. I began to feel better. The anger subsided. I was ready to share what I had learned in the hope it would help others wake up, heal, and move on.

On the following pages you will find my story and the stories of the people I interviewed. I was amazed at how openly they shared their personal experiences, thoughts, fears, and perspectives on money, success, and happiness. While I would have loved to share the totality of the interviews I conducted, there simply was not enough room to do so in the pages of this book. However, if you visit www.BreakingTheSpellBook.com/bonuses, you will find recordings and transcripts of those interviews. I encourage you to check them out, as they add great depth to the stories and information shared in the book.

I have also included a references section with a complete list of the research I consulted, books I read, and resources cited throughout the book. Additionally, you will find links to all of the references as well as a summary of the survey I conducted at www. BreakingTheSpellBook.com/bonuses. If a particular topic or resource interests you, I encourage you to consider further reading from the reference list.

Lastly, at the end of each chapter you will find a list of questions to help you determine whether you have become spellbound, along with a list of ten steps you may want to consider to help break the spell. You will also find these "Spellbound" and "Breaking the Spell" lists in PDF at the above web address, in case you'd like to print them or use them as worksheets.

Researching and writing this book was a journey for me. I encourage you to approach reading it in the same way. Each chapter investigates a different way we have been conditioned and encouraged to seek money, success, material possessions, and happiness.

I won't pretend to be an expert on any of these topics. Rather, I am simply someone who chose to step back, ask questions, investigate, illuminate a problem, and then share some potential solutions.

We begin with my story—the story of how I became spellbound. It's where my journey started, and I believe sharing it is the best way to set the stage for the rest of the book.

INTRODUCTION:
SPELLBOUND

". . . Caught in a trap. I can't walk out . . ."

~from the song "Suspicious Minds,"
made popular by Elvis Presley

This is a story about success, money, and the pursuit of happiness. It's also a story about failure and disappointment. It's my story. But it's not only my story. It's also the story of millions of people, many of them probably a lot like you. My goal in sharing this story is that you will understand the dangerous path that so many people have been on for the past five to ten years. You may see some of yourself in this story; if you do, I hope you will be motivated and inspired to create change for yourself, those you care about, and the world.

Chasing Success

"If at first you don't succeed, try, try again."

~unknown

That's what we're taught isn't it? Success is the ultimate goal, and we must keep trying until we achieve it. On the surface, it's an admirable ambition, and when faced with the alternative—giving up on our dreams—it certainly appears to be the better choice. However, as with anything, too much of a good thing can mean trouble. Being consumed by a goal, regardless of how noble, can blind even the most levelheaded person.

I've chased success most of my life. I set big goals and worked hard to achieve them. I subscribed to the personal development empowerment mantra of "you can be, do, or have anything." It's certainly not a bad concept, unless, of course, you sacrifice everything else in the constant pursuit of being, doing, and having more. Unfortunately, that's exactly what happened.

In my pursuit, I read books, hired mentors and coaches, attended seminars and conferences, invested in real estate and other promises of passive income, and dropped a boatload of money. All in search of more success, more achievement, more recognition, and more money—and all the things it can buy. Until I realized that, despite all the time and money I had invested, I wasn't happier, I wasn't fulfilled, I wasn't richer, and, in fact, I was still seeking more. I was on the hamster wheel of success, with no beginning and no end, just constantly running and trying to keep up.

I Wasn't Raised This Way . . . or Was I?

"I'm on the right track, baby. I was born this way."

~from the song "Born This Way" by Lady Gaga

I grew up in a middle-class family, a twin daughter of a teacher and an artist. As a family of six living on a teacher's salary, we were far from wealthy, yet we always had what we needed. My parents raised us to work hard, get good grades, go to college, and make good lives for ourselves. Like any family, we had our problems, but they were always kept behind closed doors. From the outside we looked like the perfect family, and in many ways we were.

At age nineteen, I made the decision to drop out of college, get a full-time job, and marry my high school sweetheart, much to the dismay of my father. For the next year, I worked as an accounting clerk in a payroll department. But I remember looking at my boss and thinking the only thing separating me from his superior position and higher paycheck was a college degree. So, I made the decision to go back to school and get my degree. I graduated two years later and landed my first job in advertising.

Climbing the Corporate Ladder

"We are taught to consume. And that's what we do. But if we realized that there really is no reason to consume, that it's just a mindset, that it's just an addiction, then we wouldn't be out there stepping on people's hands climbing the corporate ladder of success."

~River Phoenix, actor

Over my first thirteen years in advertising, I did what most college graduates do. I worked my way up the corporate ladder, eventually achieving vice president status. I remember thinking, "Wow, I've finally made it!" Yet, despite having the job I had always dreamed of, a fancy VP title, a good salary, a nice house, two kids, a dog, and a husband who loved me, I still wasn't satisfied.

About this time, I realized I was suffering from burnout—the result of constantly trying to be, do, and have it all. It showed up in the form of chronic stress and illness and an overall feeling of dissatisfaction, even though on the outside my life looked like the epitome of success, the fulfillment of the American dream.

I decided to leave the security of my job and start my own business. I felt it was the only way to balance my career and family. What I didn't know was that I was opening up an entirely new can of worms in the "world of more." Over the next six years I ran a marketing consulting business out of my home. By all accounts, I was successful, just as I had been in my career. Yet, once again, I didn't feel successful. I found myself constantly striving for more and wondering when the time would come that I could relax and enjoy the fruits of my labor.

Caught in the Web of Success

"The toughest thing about success is that you've got to keep on being a success."

~*Irving Berlin, composer*

Six years into running my own business, I started a second, Internet-based business. While I was doing OK, as I looked around, I saw others who were making multiple six figures—some were even making seven. They talked about no longer trading hours for dollars, making passive income, and the freedom and flexibility to do what they wanted, when they wanted. Here I was with a six-figure business, but for the most part I was still trading hours for dollars. Everywhere I turned I was reminded that trading hours for dollars was *bad.* That's not what *successful* people do. Successful people work *on* their businesses not *in* them. So even though I was making good money, enjoyed what I was doing, and was home with my kids, my takeaway was, "I'm still not good enough. I'm not really successful. I'm not doing it *right.*"

The overachiever in me set out to create a million-dollar lever-aged business in which I made money while I slept and had total freedom and flexibility. Knowing how coachable I am—I work hard and do whatever I'm taught—I figured if I could learn how to do it, I could make it happen. I spent the next seven years and more than $200,000 in search of this new level of success. In the process, I started eight businesses. I invested in, learned, and tested virtually every marketing strategy and business model available. I became a real estate investor. I tried FOREX. I sank $60,000 into an infomercial. I attended seminars. I bought information products. I joined high-priced masterminds. I hired coaches and mentors—at one point I had four coaches and wore it like a badge of honor. Through it all, I did everything I was taught. I implemented every "secret to success" and followed every "proven blueprint." Every time something didn't work, I told myself I just needed to find that one missing puzzle piece and million-dollar success would be mine. After all, I was smart and I was doing all the right things, all the things other people had done to create million-dollar businesses. If it worked for them, it would work for me too, right?

The Elusive Quest

> *"Happiness is like a butterfly which, when pursued, is always beyond our grasp, but, if you will sit down quietly, may alight upon you."*
>
> ~Nathaniel Hawthorne, novelist

Despite investing all that time and money, I never achieved the level of success I was seeking. Although I became a millionaire on paper, I never actually arrived at the place I was searching for. I never got "there." Where is "there"? For me, "there" was the place I would feel equally successful with all those people I was aspiring to be like. "There" was a million-dollar business with passive income and total freedom and flexibility. "There" was the place I believed all of these people I was modeling lived. "There" was utopia: a world of fame, fortune, and true happiness.

In reality, I didn't know how famous, successful, wealthy, or happy the people I was modeling actually were. All I knew was how famous, successful, wealthy, and happy they appeared to be. I was basing my quest for success on a perception. After spending years chasing more and more success, I realized that, rather than growing my business and becoming more successful, I actually had run my business into the ground and was in debt from all the mentoring I had invested in. The real estate investment business my husband and I started in an attempt to generate passive income was draining our bank account and causing stress in our marriage.

We made the difficult decision to let one of our properties go into foreclosure, and we sold the others. Because of the foreclosure, our formerly stellar credit rating was history. If all that wasn't humbling enough, American Express cancelled my credit card account. But maybe worst of all, I was completely lost. So many voices were telling me what I should be doing to become more successful that I couldn't hear my own. I had gone from being a confident, successful woman to a total basket case. All because I thought success had to look a certain way.

Waking Up

"Through the blackest night, morning gently tiptoes, feeling its way to dawn."

~*Robert Brault, freelance writer*

Thankfully, at the end of 2009, I came to my senses. I realized I had lost myself in this quest for success and I desperately needed to find *me* again. I took a month off from my business and gave myself time and space to get grounded. I closed or sold all of my business ventures except one. I declared myself in a "no-buy zone" and stopped investing in personal development, coaches, and mentors. I got back in touch with the knowledge and expertise I had accumulated over the previous twenty-five years and used it to rebuild my business, *my* way. I began following my heart and doing what I felt inspired to do, instead of chasing money and success and trying to build a business that looked like someone else's. I started blogging about my experiences and was met with overwhelming support. It turns out I was not alone.

The Other Side

"It is the chiefest point of happiness that a man is willing to be what he is."

~Desiderius Erasmus, philosopher

I'm happy to report I found myself again. I have redefined success for myself. I now know I am successful, and it has nothing to do with my bank balance, how many properties I own, or my business looking a certain way. I'm successful because I'm doing work that fulfills me, serves others, and makes me happy.

In the end, grounding myself and recognizing that success can't be bought wasn't about selling all my worldly possessions and taking a vow of poverty. I still run my business. I still live in a nice home. I still drive a Lexus. I still indulge in regular massages and manicures and pedicures. Not because these things demonstrate my success, but because I enjoy them. I'm living within my means. I have a more balanced life and operate from a totally different mental space and attitude.

I admit I'm a work in progress. Money still has a grip on me at times. I often worry about not having enough (no matter how much I have). I still grapple with believing I'm OK right where I am. I constantly remind myself life is not always about getting somewhere else. Through all the doubts, I strive every day to make decisions from an inspired place instead of being driven by money and achievement.

Life, Simplified

"Our life is frittered away by detail . . . simplify, simplify."

~Henry David Thoreau, author

While on the outside my life looks pretty much the same, it is simpler these days. Getting rid of all the businesses and investment properties has a lot to do with that. My experience was that this so-called "passive income" does require work. It also involves risk, constant mental energy, additional tax bills, insurance, expenses, and a multitude of professional and legal services that aren't cheap. Even though I'm no longer a millionaire (selling all the real estate eliminated that claim to fame), there is much less stress in my life today. I'm more at peace. I worry less. I also care less about what other people think or do. Instead, my focus is on me, my business, and my family and doing what serves all three. My relationship with my husband is stronger. I'm healthier and fitter than I've been in a long time. And, I believe I'm setting a much better example for my children.

The $64,000 Question: Why?

"The truth is, you don't know what is going to happen tomorrow. Life is a crazy ride, and nothing is guaranteed."

~Eminem, recording artist

I can't help but wonder why I got so caught up in the constant quest for more. I also know I'm not alone. It's a global problem. In the past ten years, countless Americans have spent money on things they couldn't afford. People purchased homes that were too rich for their incomes, and the mortgage industry enabled them to do so. Others became real estate investors in an effort to finance their way to easy street, only to find themselves out of money and upside down. Still others maxed out credit cards and tapped into their home equity to finance lifestyles beyond their means and now find themselves in homes that are worth less than the mortgages. Others found themselves chasing the promise of entrepreneurial success, investing thousands of dollars, and still not fulfilling their dreams.

In the meantime, The Great Recession hit and threw a wrench into many people's plans. Let's face it—it's not a big deal to spend and invest freely when money is flowing and everything is escalating in value. However, when the money flow slows and investment values nosedive, it's an entirely different ballgame. For many people, things went south, fast.

Because the average American spends nearly all of what he or she earns and has little savings, there was no cushion to fall back on. In fact, in the United States, personal savings rates have dropped dramatically over the past twenty years, going from an average of 7 percent of the gross domestic product in the 1960s, 1970s, and 1980s to 4.5 percent in the 1990s, and just 1.1 percent by 2005.

Overconsumption and overspending also have created an epidemic of bankruptcy filings and foreclosures, both of which have increased significantly in recent years. U.S. bankruptcy filings doubled from 2007 to 2010. Foreclosures more than quadrupled between 2005 and 2010. We are paying the price for all the striving for more.

How Did We Get Here?

"One's destination is never a place but rather a new way of looking at things."

~Henry Miller, novelist

What possessed so many people to keep spending more money than they were earning, to keep striving for more, to keep trying to fill up their tanks with achievements and acquisitions? Were we trying to buy happiness? Achieve success? Keep up with the proverbial Joneses? Perhaps. Whatever it was, clearly it was contagious.

The Spell

As I look back, the only explanation I can find is that we were spellbound—under the illusion that more material possessions, achievement, and money would make us happier. In my observation, there are many factors that precipitated this vicious spell. It's not that these things are inherently bad. However, in analyzing their cumulative effect, I believe they all played a role.

Competition. We live in a society in which winners are celebrated and being number one is the goal. How can that not create a culture in which we're constantly striving for more?

Popularity. In school, we learn success is about popularity. It plays out in who gets voted homecoming queen and king. The football players and cheerleaders are the cool kids. We bestow titles such as "best smile" and "most likely to succeed" on the popular students. If that's the environment we're raised in, it's no wonder we strive for success in the real world.

Advertising. Every day we're bombarded with messages telling us that, for a price, we can look younger, more beautiful, or more fashionable. Our children will love us more if we stock our pantry with foods they like. We'll be better moms if our homes pass the white-glove test and our kids' clothes are spotless. We can express our success by the homes we live in and the cars we drive or show how thoughtful we are by going hybrid. The common theme in all of these messages is that appearances matter and material possessions will make our lives better and us happier.

The Media. The media have a knack for sensationalizing stories. If you've ever watched the teasers for the evening news during prime-time television, you know what I mean. Anything happening in our world grows in magnitude simply by getting reported in the news. Fears are instilled. Ideas are perpetuated. People begin living their lives and making decisions based on their perceptions of what's happening in the world instead of reality or what is most important to them.

The Personal Development Industry. Since its birth in the 1800s, the field of personal development has exploded into an $11 billion dollar industry. The original concept of selling help has evolved into one of selling success. We're constantly told we can be, do, or have anything. It's no wonder we're continually striving to achieve more, because we've been told if we're not growing, we're dying. It makes me wonder, what ever happened to just *living*?

Social Media. With the introduction of social networking websites such as Facebook, we are all living out loud. Our lives and accomplishments are now on display for the world to see. It's by choice, of course, but as of this writing, more than 800 million people worldwide have made that choice. We have a built-in audience and vehicle for sharing our successes. (After all, who wants to share failures?) And, because of the influence of competition and popularity, the natural tendency is to strive for more in order to look good.

Reality Television. Whether we're watching everyday people "outwit, outplay, and outlast" competitors on *Survivor* in an effort to win a million dollars; budding pop stars vie for fame, fortune, and a recording contract on *American Idol*; or toddlers parade around in full glitz makeup and bedazzled dresses on *Toddlers & Tiaras* in their quest for a beauty pageant crown, it's clear competition—and winning—is the name of the game.

These are just a handful of ways we're surrounded daily by the message that money, acquisition, accomplishment, and success are what we should be striving for. We're seduced by the idea that if we have these things, we will be happy.

In the movie *Bruce Almighty*, Bruce Nolan (played by Jim Carrey) says, "I'm not OK with a mediocre job. I'm not OK with a mediocre apartment. I'm not OK with a mediocre life." I think there are probably a lot of people with whom this statement resonates. We want more than an average life. We want to contribute. We want to leave a legacy.

While we were trying to build our fortune, my husband and I used to joke that our parents probably thought we had joined a cult. From our perspective, we were simply on a quest to make life better for our children and ourselves. But it's been said there's a seed of truth in every joke. Looking back, I see there was one in ours. The cult of success is a seductive one, but then most cults are. You hear what you want to hear. You believe what you want to believe. It's exciting. You can't understand why everyone isn't jumping on board. In this case, millions of people actually were.

Don't get me wrong, I'm all for self-improvement. In fact, I have worked in the industry for the past seven years as a business mentor and coach. I've seen the industry from both sides. I'm the first to admit it put me in a precarious position when I realized I had gotten totally caught up in it. Was it the industry's fault?

Were the self-improvement gurus preying on people's wants and desires and making big promises just like the legendary snake oil salesmen? After all, many promise quick and easy riches in just a handful of simple steps, but if it really were that easy, wouldn't we all be millionaires already?

If the whole industry really is just a sham, as purported by Steve Salerno in his 2005 book, *SHAM: How the Self-Help Movement Made America Helpless*, and I'm part of the industry, what does that say about me? This prompted a lot of introspection on my part. I debated leaving the industry, but I enjoy my work and I do believe it helps people. So instead, I started blogging about my experiences and speaking out about some of the practices in the industry I didn't like. It was a bit scary at first, stepping out publicly in this way, but I felt compelled. Thankfully, the reception was very positive. It turns out I was not alone with these feelings, doubts, and questions.

That's when I decided to write this book. Rather than just getting angry, making accusations, or switching industries, I chose to learn more and gain a better understanding of what happened to me and to others who have shared their similar experiences with me. I wasn't quite ready to give up on self- improvement. I do believe learning is a good thing. It expands our minds. It opens us up to new possibilities. It helps us create our lives in a way that can potentially maximize our experience on this earth. There are more than 125,000 books on Amazon on how to become successful. It's a billion-dollar industry that's predicted to continue growing. But clearly there is a dark side as well. I wanted to find out why we are so drawn to it and, in some cases, completely spellbound by it.

When I woke up in December 2009 with a giant self-improvement hangover and my business in a shambles, I made the decision to stop chasing success, begin rebuilding my life and business, and try to understand what happened. I began doing research and reading books on psychology, happiness, success, achievement, the self-help industry, and even addiction.

I share all of what I discovered in the following pages. We're going to look at the psychology of success and why our brains appear to be programmed to continually seek it. Why what we have never seems to be enough and we're always seeking more. We'll examine the connections among money, success, and happiness and how they appear to be changing. We'll look at the societal influences and cultural programming I believe have trapped so many of us in the web of success, often to our own detriment. We'll look at addiction and ask and answer the question "Is it possible to become addicted to success, just as one becomes addicted to drugs?" We'll study overachievers. We'll look at the roles our educational system, competitive sports, and even reality television play in the quest for success. We'll look at personality types to ascertain whether certain people are predisposed to becoming spellbound by success. And, we'll take a look deep inside the self-help industry and how it has evolved and ask ourselves whether the changes are for the better or worse.

In addition to reviewing existing research and reading books on the topics of money, success, and happiness, I also conducted a survey and personally interviewed people from around the world. You'll find the results of that survey and candid stories from the people I spoke to throughout the book. You'll read about people like Anthony, a forty-seven-year-old disabled appraisal coordinator from Philadelphia who firmly believes that without a large sum of money, he will never be happy. You'll meet Camille, a twenty-eight-year-old Stanford grad and single mother who is torn between living up to her parents' expectations and making herself happy. You'll find out how James, a fifty-four-year-old business owner from Ohio—through mentoring high school students, a prison ministry, and a retail consulting business—is making it his personal mission to change attitudes about money and success. And you'll meet many more.

Sprinkled throughout the book, you will also find blog posts I wrote as I struggled to let go of the hold success had on me. They capture many of the challenges I faced and questions that arose along the way. I've included them to provide a snapshot of my transformational journey. It has not been a smooth or easy path. After all, it's not as if you decide one day to stop being so focused on success and your life immediately changes and you live happily ever after. It's a process, to be sure. If you choose to embark on this journey yourself, you too will likely find yourself bumping up against your old ways over and over again, just as I have. I want you to know you are not alone. I want to share how I dealt with these challenges in the hope it will light the way along your journey.

True Self-Help

> *"I went to a bookstore and asked the saleswoman, 'Where's the self-help section?' She said if she told me, it would defeat the purpose."*
>
> ~George Carlin, comedian

What you won't find in this book is a step-by-step process or blueprint to help you break the spell of money and success, because that's exactly the mentality I believe cast the spell in the first place. This book is not a self-help book in the traditional sense, because as I see it—and as George Carlin quipped—if it's someone else's help, it's not *self*-help. I believe true self-help comes from finding your own way. While I agree there are always things to learn, we must ultimately look within for the answers. Therefore, my intention with this book is to help you step back and re-evaluate—and perhaps expand your awareness and help you see things in a new light. Awareness, after all, is the first step toward creating change.

My goal is to provide thought-provoking information for you to consider, along with questions you may ask yourself to diagnose, if you will, where you fall on the spellbound scale. And, I will share

Breaking the Spell action steps that have worked for me as I've traveled this path from materialism to meaning. In the end, I encourage you to come up with your own answers. For they need to suit you and your goals, not mine. This is about finding *you*, not about finding a "secret to success," because, in my opinion, there are no such secrets.

The Following Inspiration Experiment

When I started writing this book, I had many opportunities to face my attachment to money and success head on. I began the journey by making a conscious decision to stop being led by money and to instead follow my heart and intuition. I embarked on what I called "The Following Inspiration Experiment." I knew that to successfully complete it, I could not let my actions be driven by money, no matter what. As a business owner who has always been focused on the bottom line, I knew this would be a challenge. However, I knew if I wanted to confirm my hypothesis that living from a place of inspiration would indeed make me happier and richer (in more ways than just monetarily), I had to totally commit.

As a result of this decision, things began to shift almost immediately. I found myself feeling less engaged in my business. As someone who, in many ways, was also selling success, I began to ask myself whether I was part of the problem that had created such a mess in my own life. Instead of focusing on my business, I spent the majority of my time researching and writing this book. As clients began wrapping up their engagements, I found my income declining. The fear and doubt began creeping in. I began to realize how much I defined myself by what I do, how successful I am, and how much money I make. I felt pressure to go out and build up my business even though my heart wasn't in it.

It became very clear this experiment was about more than just writing a book; it was a necessary step in my own personal growth. I had defined myself by income and success for so long that I didn't know how to value myself any other way. I needed to relearn that my self-worth is not rooted in how much money I make, how many clients I have, or how successful my business is. This was a huge epiphany. I took it on as a personal challenge, knowing I would likely encounter many more battles along the way. I can tell you, I was not disappointed!

The True Meaning of Wealth

"Wealth is not his that has it, but his that enjoys it."

~*Benjamin Franklin*

I've always said my goal was to live a happy, healthy, wealthy life. I recently learned the word "wealthy," which is derived from the Old English word *wela*, actually means "well-being." Well-being isn't defined by money or success. Well-being means leading a rich, satisfying, and happy life.

I hope this book enables you to do exactly that.

CHAPTER 1

SHOW ME THE MONEY

". . . one of the most defining, demanding aspects of being engaged in the human experience is our struggle, our challenge, and our interactions with money."

~Lynne Twist, in her book The Soul of Money

For the most part, when I was younger I followed my heart, not money. When I interviewed for one of my first jobs after college, I discovered several of my classmates had also interviewed for the position. I got the job and was told one of the reasons was that the others had demanded too high a salary. Even though the job didn't pay very well, I saw it as a stepping stone, and a few years later I was indeed doing very well financially in my chosen field. Was it a case of "follow your heart and the money will follow"? I don't know. But what I do know is that the decisions I made back then weren't driven by money, and yet money was never a problem.

In 2003 I was introduced to the world of personal development. A friend invited me to an event put on by an organization called the Enlightened Millionaire Institute. Shortly thereafter my husband and I attended another event called the Millionaire Mind Intensive. Prior to this I had never even entertained the thought of becoming a millionaire. Suddenly I saw it as a possibility, and something inside me shifted. Over the next seven years I would find myself constantly chasing that million dollars and what I believed it represented: financial freedom and validation of my success. My income grew. Our net worth rose, and, on paper at least, we hit that magic million-dollar goal. However, I never felt financially free. Regardless of our net worth or how much money I made, it never felt like enough.

I kept investing more, trying to achieve more. Coaches along the way doled out advice that continued to fuel my quest. I heard things like "The more you invest, the more serious the universe will see you, and you will be rewarded accordingly" and "You must invest in yourself to the degree you want others to invest in you." For example, if I wanted to charge clients $20,000 to work with me, I must first pay a mentor $20,000. I bought it all at face value. I later realized I was trying to buy success. It had become about the money. Not in terms of all the things the money could buy—while the money was nice, it was never about material possessions. The money represented accomplishment. It was a sign I was successful and had "made it." My self-worth had become totally entangled in how successful my business was and how much money I was making. I even created a business called 6-Figure Work-at-Home Mom. If that wasn't proof I had crossed over to the other side, I don't know what was!

By 2009 I was throwing money at pretty much anything that moved, desperately trying to reach my goals. And, after running a profitable business and carrying no business debt for ten years, I found myself for the first time with a net loss and a huge mountain of debt. It was a great big wake-up call.

I know now the universe doesn't keep financial score and that being able to charge a client $20,000 has a lot more to do with my self-confidence than the amount I invest in coaching. Ironically, looking back, I realized that not only was my business considerably more profitable, my client fees were higher *before* I invested all the time and money to learn how to earn more.

In the Grip of Money

"For a small piece of paper it carries a lot of weight. Oh that mean, mean, mean, mean green . . . almighty dollar!"

~from the song "For the Love of Money" by The O'Jays

So what happened? How did I become so driven by money? I've discovered it's a fairly common problem. Lynne Twist shares an explanation in her book *The Soul of Money*: "In the grip of money, those wonderful qualities of soul seem to be less available. We become smaller. We scramble, or race to 'get what's ours.' We often grow selfish, greedy, petty, fearful, or controlling, or sometimes confused, conflicted, or guilty. We see ourselves as winners or losers, powerful or helpless, and we let those labels define us . . . ."

I certainly saw myself as a winner when things were going well and was quick to brand myself a loser when they weren't. I had let myself become defined by my level of success and income. Don't get me wrong—I have nothing against money. It's certainly nice to have. In many ways it makes life easier; however, I've learned that more doesn't necessarily make life better. The issue I have, and the one Lynne Twist illuminates in her book, is the hold we've allowed money to have on us. The enormous amount of power and energy we've given it. The way we've let it take over lives, rule our decision-making, and define who we are. I believe it's time to put money back in its place and remove our emotional attachment to it. It's time to reframe money as what it really is: currency created to facilitate the exchange of goods and services.

In her book *Secrets of Six-Figure Women*, Barbara Stanny writes that numerous psychologists told her that the amount people earn indicates how they feel about themselves, like a mirror reflecting back their level of self-worth. She shares that most of the 150 six-figure women she interviewed admitted that as their earnings soared, their self-esteem increased. One woman said, "When I made money it changed the way I thought about myself." Another added, "I made $150,000 so far this year, which tells me people think I'm talented. When I wasn't making money, I would say . . . 'you're so talented you should have more clients.' But it wouldn't help. I didn't feel worthy. Making this kind of money feeds my self-esteem." Stanny also found that for the high-earning women she interviewed, money was not the motivator; rather, it was what the money represented: recognition, security, challenge, and inde-pendence. She also discovered that, despite the fact these women were earning more than 99 percent of the people in the world, very few felt rich. Instead, most felt that even though they were earning six figures, they still didn't have enough money. It turns out I was in good company.

Money and Status

> *"Money has never made man happy, nor will it, there is nothing in its nature to produce happiness. The more of it one has the more one wants."*
>
> *~Benjamin Franklin*

In today's culture it is common to define oneself by financial status and external achievements. As a society we're driven by the American dream and bettering our situations for our children and ourselves. Yet, for all the abundance money represents, it is also notorious for bringing up fears and shining a spotlight on inadequacies. We feel as bad for what we don't have as we feel good about what we do. I was watching an interview on television one day with Oprah Winfrey and J.K. Rowling, author of the *Harry Potter* books. Both of these women are billionaires with more than enough money to last a lifetime, yet both admitted at times they fear losing it all. Both still work extremely hard in their respective fields. In fact, as of this writing, the final *Harry Potter* movie had just pushed the franchise past the $7 billion mark. Lynne Twist found the same fears in her work with the affluent. She discovered "where wealth and privilege are the prevailing conditions, and money defines life and character, the fear of losing it is often profound."

Imagine being a billionaire and not feeling like it is enough. I admit it made me feel better about my constant pursuit for more. Perhaps it is simply human nature.

📷 Blog Snapshot

Do I Have to Sell My Lexus?

I began to wonder, to really follow my heart. Do I have to sell my house and my car and totally change my life? Is that what it takes to let go of the hold money seemed to have on me and to be in sync with this new path of following inspiration I had stepped onto? Although I admit I live a pretty simple, middle-class life—not an extravagant one by any means—the question haunted me.

As I'm navigating this journey from materialism to meaning, I'm very conscious that I don't know exactly what it means. While I'm very clear my experiment, and ultimately my message, is not about selling all my belongings and moving to an ashram, I also don't know exactly how to start living in this new way. It's a daily question, sometimes a battle between heart and head, and ultimately a choice about what feels right to me. And my guess is, I'm not the only one facing this question.

The other day, as I was driving to an appointment, the question of "Do I need to sell my Lexus?" was on my mind. It's important to note that when I originally bought my Lexus, it wasn't for the status of owning a Lexus. After years of driving reliable and practical Nissans, Toyotas, and Hondas, I really wanted a Lexus. I liked them. And, I had worked hard to build a successful business and I felt I deserved a little reward. So on Mother's Day 2005 I bought myself that Lexus. And, it felt good every time I got into it and drove it. It felt like a reward for my hard work. I'm not always good about rewarding myself—historically, when I've accomplished something, I've been more focused on raising the bar and shooting for another goal than celebrating the achievement of the current goal.

So these questions, "Do I need to sell my Lexus?" and "Do I need to buy a Prius?" (for some reason, that seems like the acceptable car for a person on a journey of following meaning), were on my mind as I drove to my appointment. I pulled into the parking lot and proceeded to back into a parking spot next to a wall. And guess what happened? I hit the wall and *bruised* my Lexus! Thankfully, it was only a surface scratch and not a dent, and my Lexus and I will both be just fine. What was my reaction to this debacle? I thought, well, of course I hit the wall! I was so focused on the car, and what you focus on expands, right?

What I Walked Away With

The Lexus is not about excess for me. It doesn't define who I am. That's not why I bought it. That's not why I drive it. That's not why I love it. It just makes me feel good. Also, I didn't die when I scratched it, a sign that I'm not too attached to it. After all, it is just a car. But it was a good lesson for me and an important signpost along this new path I'm navigating. And that is, money and things are not inherently bad. There's nothing wrong with them if they make us happy. It's when they rule our lives, cause us to do things just to acquire more of them, and throw our perspective out of whack that they're a problem.

So, while some people may choose to sell their homes and other belongings, I don't need to go to that extreme. I can still walk this inspired path, being led by my heart and creating the kind of world I want my children to grow up in. A world that is not about MORE, MORE, MORE just to prove we're good enough, or better than, or worthy, but a world in which we do what makes us happy.

By the way, I've decided keep the Lexus, scratched fender and all.

Source: www.FollowingInspiration.com

Money and Emotion

"Money won't make you happy . . . but everybody wants to find out for themselves."

~Zig Ziglar, author

While we jokingly call it "cold, hard cash," there's nothing cold about it. It's definitely an emotional substance, at least in terms of what it represents for most people. We've seen the television commercials showing Publisher's Clearinghouse awarding million-dollar prizes to unsuspecting winners. They jump for joy. They smile from ear to ear. In 2011, ABC aired a television series called *Secret Millionaire,* in which millionaires spent a week with those less fortunate and donated thousands of dollars from their own bank accounts to needy individuals and charities. The generous financial gifts were received with hugs, tears, and gratitude for the difference they would make in the lives they would touch.

We remember the joy we felt as children when the tooth fairy left a shiny coin under our pillow. As working adults, most of us have experienced the validation that goes along with getting a pay raise and a promotion. Millions of people play state lotteries, hoping to win big and be able to embark on their dream lives. Make no mistake; money holds great power over us. It's power we've chosen to give to it, whether it's been a conscious choice or a subconscious one.

While money can bring great joy, it is also one of the most common causes of friction in relationships. It's responsible for divorces and stress. It can make us feel inferior to others with more. Money and material possessions are the key components in the comparison trap so many people fall into.

Our emotional attachment to money is real. It affects how we live our lives and treat others. Money controls us through attitudes such as "it takes money to make money" and "the rich get richer."

We live by these beliefs and allow them to take away our power and put it squarely in the hands of money. While it might only be paper and metal, it can be so much more in terms of the impact we allow it to have on our lives.

Money and Security

> *"I equate money with security, not success or happiness. My drive to make more money is based solely on taking care of myself and my family."*
>
> *~respondent in my survey on money, success, and happiness*

In 1954 a psychologist named Abraham Maslow surveyed research in psychology about what motivates people. He discovered that humans seek to satisfy their basic needs in a hierarchical manner.

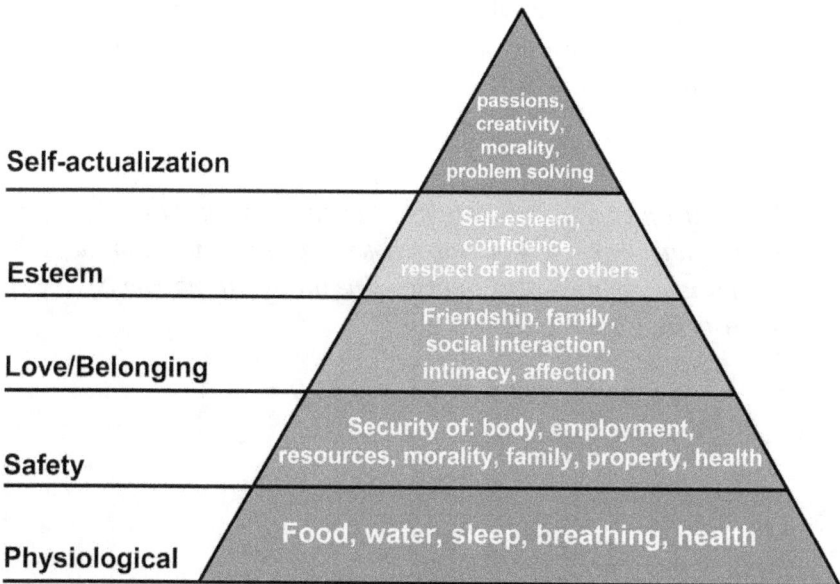

Self-actualization — passions, creativity, morality, problem solving

Esteem — Self-esteem, confidence, respect of and by others

Love/Belonging — Friendship, family, social interaction, intimacy, affection

Safety — Security of: body, employment, resources, morality, family, property, health

Physiological — Food, water, sleep, breathing, health

Maslow's Hierarchy of Needs

As Maslow states, we start at the bottom of the ladder and move up as each need is satisfied. We seek to fulfill our physiological needs first (food, water, shelter), and once those are taken care of, we move up to safety (security, stability, freedom from fear), and so on up the ladder, with self-actualization being the final step. While we may want to achieve what's at the top of the ladder, we recognize the lower rungs are more essential to our existence.

There's no denying in the twenty-first century that money plays a large role in satisfying our needs as we progress up the ladder, at least through the safety level. In my research, 95 percent of the people I surveyed said their income or the amount of money they have is "directly related" to their sense of security. A full third said it is "totally related," and another 44 percent said it is "very related." Knowing we are self-reliant and have the financial means to take care of our families and ourselves is important. We live in a world that encourages independence, and financial security is definitely a part of that independence. I know it's true for me, and it was a common theme in my research.

Following are some of the comments people shared when asked about the connections they make among money, success, and happiness.

> *"Even if I had a fascinating job, I would be unhappy if I didn't make enough money to feel financially secure. For me, money isn't about status or expensive things. It represents security and having choices in life."*

༄ ༄

"It isn't the money that is important but the security at this time of my life."

❦

"I understand that money isn't everything, but I would appreciate a little more 'cushion' to ease my thoughts on my financial future."

❦

"Money helps secure your health, which in turn makes you happier."

❦

"Don't tell me that happiness is only because of your own mindset. Most joys and tears are related to your available resources. When you have too little, you cannot generate the basic security, optimism, and comfort you need."

❦

"Money doesn't make me happy, but I don't wish to be dependent on anyone else, so it keeps me independent, which indirectly makes me less stressed."

Money and Happiness

"All I ask is a chance to prove that money can't make me happy."

~Spike Milligan, actor and comedian

We've all heard the adage that money can't buy happiness. That's easy to say when you have money. Many people who feel they don't have enough believe more money will make them happier. In my research, I certainly found this to be true. Nearly 80 percent of those surveyed said their level of happiness was directly related to how much money they had. Additionally, 68 percent believed they would be happier if they had more money. Anthony, one of the many people I interviewed, was no exception.

Meet Anthony, the $46 Million Man

Anthony, a forty-seven-year-old appraisal coordinator from Philadelphia, is clear about what success means to him: money. Forty-six million dollars, to be exact.

This former addict—who once homeless, has been shot twice, and is now disabled—has completely turned his life around in the past seventeen years. But despite his triumphs and occasional moments of fun and enjoyment, he says he will not be happy until he has enough money that he never has to worry about money again. Anthony has experienced abundance twice in his life, but it was short-lived. However, when he had money, life was good and he was happy, if only for a few months.

Between the ages of fourteen and twenty-nine, Anthony embarked on a path of self-improvement in hopes of finding happiness. As he candidly shares, if it promised happiness, "he joined it, read it, participated in it, smoked it, bought it, and had sex with it." He read books like *Dianetics, The Power of Positive Thinking*, and *Think and Grow Rich*. He studied Jose Silva's *The Silva Method* and how to buy real estate with no money down with Carleton Sheets. He explored various religions and even burned candles and tried to cast spells to get money and be happy. Yet, he feels happiness has eluded him.

Anthony is quick to point out that, while he's a bit of a show-off, for him money is not about status or stuff. He wants it to buy experiences and for the peace of mind he believes it will provide. If he ever gets that $46 million, he fully intends to share, give back, and further his education for the sheer joy of learning. He says that, while his desire for success and money is largely fueled by inner drive and determination, being surrounded by people flaunting their riches is certainly another factor in his quest. Turning on the television and seeing shows such as *MTV Cribs* and *Lifestyles of the Rich and Famous* makes him feel resentful, as does seeing celebrities who are rich simply because they are attractive. He openly admits that seeing others with nice homes and nice cars spurs a jealousy within him. Living without a car (after a drunk driver totaled his) and in what he calls a "crappy Philly row home," Anthony believes if he had what these other people have, he would be happy. He believes it would make his life, including dealing with his disability and medical issues, easier.

This former addict admits his desire for money is like the need for a drug, and the high is in wanting it probably more than getting it. Anthony says that for him, success has always been about the money, but in recent years it has become more consuming. Every day he hopes for a miracle. He feels he will never be whole without the money, and he's haunted by the fear he will die and never experience it.

While Anthony's story may be extreme, he's not alone in believing money will make him happier. A 2005–2006 Gallup survey of 136,839 people worldwide found life satisfaction was "directly and strongly correlated with income." According to a *Washington Post* report on the survey, earning more money makes people more likely to say they are happy with their lives overall. These findings were consistent across age, gender, social class, or country. Ed Diener, leader of the study and professor emeritus of psychology at the University of Illinois, said, "Yes, money makes you happy—we see the effect of income on life satisfaction is very strong and virtually ubiquitous and universal around the world."

A 2004 survey by Princeton researchers similarly found that "people with above-average income are relatively satisfied with their lives but are barely happier than others in moment-to-moment experience." According to Princeton professor and economist Alan B. Krueger, "If people have high income, they think they should be satisfied and reflect that in their answers. Income, however, matters very little for moment-to-moment experience." The study also referred to what's called "the focusing illusion": in some cases, people act in ways they believe will increase their income in the belief it will make them happier, when in fact they may be sacrificing time spent on the activities that truly bring enjoyment.

A 2009 Princeton study also concluded that money does buy happiness—but no more than $75,000 worth of happiness a year. The study found that the lower a person's annual income falls below $75,000, the unhappier he or she becomes. However, regardless of how much more than $75,000 a person makes, he or she doesn't report feeling any happier. The study also discovered there are two types of happiness. The first is day-to-day mood, and the second is overall satisfaction with life. Apparently, making $75,000 or more per year doesn't seem to impact day-to-day mood. It does, however, improve the satisfaction people feel about the way their lives are going. The study, conducted by economist Angus Deaton and psychologist Daniel Kahneman, who won a Nobel Prize for Economics, also found 85 percent of Americans felt happy each day regardless of their income. Additionally, they found that the more money people made, the more they felt their lives were going well. The study authors concluded, "High incomes don't bring you happiness, but they do bring you a life you think is better."

In the end, it may come down to this: if you believe money will make you happy, then it just might.

Meet Brian and His Epiphany

Brian, a forty-nine-year-old photographer from Ontario, Canada, jokes, "Money doesn't buy happiness, but it sure buys any misery you like." While he laughs about this, he believes we need to be careful about throwing around the saying "money can't buy happiness."

"To someone who doesn't have money, can't keep a roof over their head and can't afford to feed their children, money will buy that kind of happiness. You never know what will make another person happy." Unfortunately, Brian believes too many people are peddling their own versions of happiness and failing to take into account each individual's point of view, "How can someone else say I'm not in the right headspace or successful enough? Or that I don't have enough money to buy happiness?"

Still, quantifying success has remained a bit of a mystery to Brian. He's quick to point out that if Warren Buffet is a success and Buffet's the yardstick, "then maybe I'm not successful." He sees the measurement of success as an important distinction and a very individualized one. When someone says he or she isn't successful, Brian's immediate response is, "compared to what?"

Brian admits he can see why some people might define him as successful. "I took a great leap of faith and quit a government job with full benefits that paid really well," he says. "Sure, I've had my bumps and lumps along the way, but I guess I've made it pretty good." Admitting it may not be the best way to define success, he goes on to say that he hasn't gone bankrupt, still has a roof over his head, can feed himself and his wife, can take vacations, and can even buy a good bottle of wine or take himself out to dinner once in a while. He acknowledges this may be viewed as "small" to some people, but it works for him. Yet, while he feels successful on some level, he believes he can and should always strive for more. He's never going to be complacent, because to him, that is stagnation. He likes to keep things fresh and interesting.

He admits he still struggles with being influenced by society. He knows it's wrong, but it's hard to escape. He still wants the bigger and better house, because at times he doesn't think his is good enough. Even though he has let go of viewing the kind of car he drives as a status symbol, he admits there's still a little voice in the back of his head that wonders if he drove a Lincoln Navigator whether people would see him as more successful. (He drives a Kia.) He wonders if he appears successful or if he is successful enough. But he also believes much of what drives his pursuit of success comes from within his own head. Is he where he should be at this stage in his life, based on the goals he set years ago?

He acknowledges chasing success and comparing yourself to others can be tiring. "At some point you just say, 'That's it. I'm done. I'm out.'" Getting tired is one of the things that prompted a recent epiphany. Brian asked himself, what would happen if he just decided to be happy? Instead of looking for happiness in the future, what if he just made a decision to be happy today, where he is right now? It's a different perspective for Brian, as someone who has always pursued success, but it's a welcome one he is ready to embrace. Although, he does admit he's not going to just stop and "fly level"—he'll still keep striving for more.

The Role Money Plays in Our Lives

"Money is not the only answer, but it makes a difference."

~President Barack Obama

In the sampling of people I surveyed for this book, the majority did admit money plays an important role in the way they live their lives. In fact, 95 percent said money—making it, saving it, or avoiding losing it—plays a role in their day-to-day decisions. Fifty-six percent say it plays a large role in their decisions about how to spend their time. They also reported money is directly related to their level of personal fulfillment, happiness, sense of identity, self confidence, level of success, health, fitness, and freedom. It appears that money is thoroughly entangled in every aspect of our lives.

The good news is, attitudes appear to be changing. My research also showed that five years ago, 41 percent felt the amount of money they made was "very related" to their definitions of success; today it's down to 35 percent. People also rated things such as "how much they enjoy what they do for a living," "their contribution to society and the world," "their level of happiness," and "freedom to do what they want when they want" as playing greater roles in their definitions of success today than five years ago. While 43 percent reported they were better off financially five years ago, the majority also said they are happier and their lives have more meaning today.

Meet Dale, a Lucky Senior from San Francisco

For Dale, a retired fundraiser from San Francisco, money is not about declaring to the world that she has it. It's not about status seeking or living an opulent lifestyle. She admits it took her a while to realize this. She says she never gave it much thought when she was younger. She did what she wanted when she wanted. She believes she was probably happier back then, not because of the money, but because she was young and healthy, life was fun, she had lots of friends, and the opportunities seemed limitless. She didn't have to think about things.

Now she has too much time to think. At 66, single, and without a job, she feels isolated and believes that contributes to her lower level of happiness more today than in years previous. At the same time, she also believes she's finally realized what it takes to be happy. She's gotten a lot clearer about what's important, and her values have changed. She's simplified her life. She's matured.

As she walks down the streets of San Francisco and sees all the homeless men, women, and children, Dale reminds herself of all the things she has to be grateful for. She admits she didn't give a lot of time to self-reflection and gratitude when she was younger. Today she does. She has enough money to feel secure, and she has perspective. She considers herself lucky.

Two Sides of the Coin

"Women, can't live with them, can't live without them."

~Desiderius Erasmus, philosopher

Just as the philosopher Erasmus quipped about women, money, too, is an integral part of our lives. We can't live without it. On a basic level it pays for essentials like shelter and food. It provides security. By financing education it pays for opportunity. It finances experiences, fun, and entertainment. We're surrounded by messages that money equals "the good life." In 2010 the song "Billionaire" peaked at number three on the Billboard Hot 100, with its aspirational lyrics, "I wanna be a billionaire so fricking bad, buy all the things I never had." We are conditioned to believe money will make our lives better and us happier. And, as we all know, perception is reality. Our beliefs color our lives, for better or worse.

For years, I carried the belief that more success—measured by more money—would make me happier. Regardless of what the research says, I have come to my own conclusions, and I believe in the end that's what we all must do. For me, more doesn't necessarily mean happier. Yes, money makes life easier in many ways, but as I discovered, it can also bring with it stress and a more complicated life. That may not be true for everyone, but in my case it was. As I mentioned previously, I'm not about to take a vow of poverty, as I believe that still attaches my happiness to money—just the lack of it in that case. I've discovered upon closer introspection that many of the things that make me happy—that day-to-day happiness that some of the research referred to—cost little to nothing.

Recently a friend encouraged me to embark on an exercise featured in the book *Wishcraft* by Barbara Sher. The exercise involves making a list of 20 things you like to do, and for each one, asking yourself the following questions:

- How long since you last did it?
- Does it cost money or is it free?
- Is it something you do alone or with someone else?
- Is it a planned or spontaneous activity?
- Is it related to your job?
- Is there any physical risk involved?
- Is it a fast-paced or slow-paced activity?
- Is it a mind, body, or spiritual activity?

Once you complete the list, the challenge is to look for patterns to identify what you can learn about yourself and the kind of life you're living. I discovered the majority of things I like to do don't cost a lot of money and, in fact, I am doing many of them regularly. Looking back to a time when I would describe myself as spellbound by money and success, I can't say the same. It's liberating just to become aware that so many things that make me happy are within reach regardless of how much money I'm making.

In his book *The 4-Hour Workweek*, Timothy Ferriss writes, "People don't want to be millionaires—they want to experience what they believe millions can buy." He points out that most people are working to finance a retirement so they can enjoy life at some point in the future. Ferriss suggests, and exemplifies in his own life, that financing the experiences we believe will make us happy probably costs a lot less than we think. He advocates finding out what your dreams actually cost and then working to finance those dreams now, instead of deferring them to retirement. While he's done it to an extreme that many people may not choose to follow, his point is a good one. The concept of retirement and working forty years just so we can enjoy life at some point is a waste of our lives. Whether or not you're happy with the amount of money you're making today, it's up to you whether you choose to let that dictate your overall happiness and enjoyment in life.

As I mentioned in the introduction, rather than provide a system or blueprint to help you break any attachment you may have between money, success, and happiness, my goal is merely to get you to step back and evaluate your life. If you're happy where you are, great. If, however, you recognize your happiness is contingent on money, and you'd like to untangle the two, following are some questions you can ask yourself to facilitate this process. If upon further introspection you determine you are indeed spellbound, I've also included a few suggestions, which have helped me break the spell, for your consideration.

Spellbound

1. Are you letting other people influence your income goals?

2. Do you believe you must make a certain amount of money to be happy?

3. Do you find that no matter how much money you make or have, you're still not happy?

4. Are you placing your happiness in the future, contingent upon hitting a certain income level?

5. Do you measure your success based on how much money you make compared to others?

6. Do you look to money to validate what you are doing?

7. Have you been trying to buy success by investing in various forms of support, believing that if you invest, your investment will be rewarded in kind (i.e., the universe is a bank that's keeping score)?

8. Do you believe you need to live in a nice house, drive a nice car, etc. to be respected in your field and seen as successful?

9. Do you find yourself branding yourself a winner or loser based on how much money you're making?

10. Does your life feel like an emotional roller coaster, with your ups and downs tied to how well you're doing financially?

Breaking the Spell

1. Stop listening to what other people say about how much money you need to make to be successful, and instead set your own income goal, based on the lifestyle you want to live.

2. Recognize that money in and of itself will not make you happy, and choose to be happy today, with whatever you have.

3. Stop comparing yourself and your income to other people and what they make.

4. Acknowledge that you are valuable and that money is merely one tool of measurement. Know that if you enjoy what you're doing and you're happy with your life, that's all that matters.

5. Invest to learn and expand your knowledge and recognize you cannot buy success. Realize one person's keys to success may or may not work for you. Take what fits and be willing to let go of the rest, not judging it as bad or ineffective, just as not right for you.

6. Do an inventory of what makes you happy and how much these activities cost. Begin incorporating these activities into your life regularly.

7. Identify times in your life when you were happy and ask yourself if there is any correlation to how much money you were making at the time. Discern whether it was the money or what you were doing that made you happy.

8. Choose to live your life in a way that makes you happy instead of worrying about what others think. Stop labeling yourself as a winner or loser based on other people's criteria.

9. Recognize that perception may not be reality—just because others appear to have more money and be happy doesn't mean they actually are. Be sure you're basing your aspirations on reality.

10. Separate your enjoyment of life and happiness from your bank account and paycheck. Recognize that what you do for a living, and how much money you make doing it, is just one aspect of your life, and it needs to be balanced with all the others.

CHAPTER 2

I'LL BE HAPPY WHEN . . .

"If only we'd stop trying to be happy we could have a pretty good time."

~Edith Wharton, author

When I started my second business—an information marketing venture—I thought if I could make $5,000 a month, I would have it made. It would allow me to close my consulting business, and in my mind I would have "made it." But once I hit $5,000 a month, it was no longer enough. My goal became $10,000 a month. After all, I had heard successful information marketers talking about how easy it was to make $10,000 a month. I dreamed of waking up to an e-mail inbox full of sales notices and money in the bank. I thought when I achieved that, I would truly be financially free. When I hit $10,000 a month, I was happy, but it didn't last long. I heard others talking about making $30,000 a month, a goal that previously would have seemed unattainable. Naturally, it became my new goal. The idea of making more money in one month than many people make in a year (the way it was marketed by those promising to teach me how) was extremely seductive. Who wouldn't want that?

I still remember my first $30,000 month. It was exhilarating to see that five-digit number when I ran my monthly sales report—in fact, it was a high. But, like most highs, it didn't last. And it brought with it an unexpected side effect: the pressure to do it again. It also raised the financial bar. My new goal? One million dollars. Once again, what had never seemed possible now seemed like the logical next step. And why not? Others were doing it, so why not me?

The Never-Ending Chase

"Happiness in this world, when it comes, comes incidentally. Make it the object of pursuit, and it leads us on a wild-goose chase, and is never attained. Follow some other object, and very possibly we may find that we have caught happiness without dreaming of it."

~Nathaniel Hawthorne, novelist

When you live your life or run your business this way, at some point you have to step back and realize you're on a never-ending chase. In hindsight, no amount of money or success at that time would have been enough to satisfy my hunger. I was fighting an internal battle I simply could not win. The achievement of one goal only led to the creation of new goals. I was so busy chasing, there was no time to be happy. I kept telling myself, "I'll be happy when . . . ." Unfortunately, it became a constant quest, a vicious cycle, an exhausting treadmill.

The sad part is, too often this quest is based on outside appearances and perception instead of reality. You are basing your future happiness on an illusion, on what you think your life will be like when you accomplish the goal. The trouble is, none of us really knows what it looks like on the inside of someone else's success and achievement. Just as the family I was raised in didn't air its dirty laundry and thus looked perfect on the outside, most people don't go around talking about their struggles or disappointments. Those selling the dream of financial success don't talk about expenses, they only talk about revenue. We don't have the full picture. We're making decisions based on the rosy picture that's been painted. And in some cases, the real picture may indeed be rosy. But what if those making millions are so caught up in achievement that they're spending almost as much as they're making just to get to the financial goal?

Is It Worth It?

> *"The end may justify the means as long as there is something that justifies the end."*
>
> ~*Leon Trotsky, revolutionary*

A friend of mine was at a business-building conference when a prominent business coach stood up and shared with the entire crowd, "Sometimes it costs a million to make a million." Really? I don't think that's the kind of business I want. Seems like a lot of hard work just to break even.

A few years ago another business coach in the Internet marketing arena shared very publicly that she had hit the million-dollar mark in her business. Then she added, perhaps as justification, that she'd been working seventy to eighty hours a week for the past year to make it happen. She was quick to point out she loved her work and, therefore, it didn't feel like work. I couldn't help thinking that doing anything for seventy to eighty hours a week is not healthy nor sustainable. It's bound to put a damper on personal relationships and crowd out other things that make life enjoyable and fulfilling. As the proverb says, "All work and no play makes Jack a dull boy."

Another coach who publicized hitting the million-dollar mark in her business was asked why she was still working so hard. She shared in her newsletter that, while she had technically made a million dollars the previous year, much of that money was not in her bank account. She also implied that the costs involved to reach one million in revenue were such that she needed to keep working to support herself. (Maybe it actually did cost a million to make a million.) Here's a news flash: a million-dollar gross income does not mean you have a million dollars in your bank account. It also does not guarantee happiness or even satisfaction.

A few years ago my husband and I owned a million-dollar real estate business. Translation: if we had sold all of our properties, we would have netted one million dollars. (And there are times I wish we had!) Our million-dollar business was all on paper. My husband still had his day job, and I was still working in my primary business; we needed to in order to support our family. We couldn't live off that million, so our life didn't look much different from what it looks like today. Yet, I could *say* I was a millionaire (even though I didn't go around saying that). That's why I believe it's so important to be careful what you let influence and drive you. Realize what you see may not be reality. Be cautious. The year I overindulged in personal development trying so hard to make my business more successful, I brought in six figures in revenue—a successful year in many people's eyes but not in mine or my accountant's. Not because six figures wasn't enough, but because my expenses were greater, resulting in a net loss. Combine that with all of my frustration and a mountain of debt, and it was a far cry from a happy or successful business year. But I was the only one who knew that. On the outside, I *looked* successful.

Simply put, things are not always as they appear. Maybe even more important, sometimes what it takes to achieve something is not worth the prize. Yes, the grass may look greener, but is it really? You owe it to yourself to find out before you wrap up your happiness in the acquisition of it.

📷 Blog Snapshot

Are You Chasing the Wrong Goal?

If you ask most people what they are striving for, they'll probably answer "success." Most personal or business development programs are selling success. I'd like to suggest that success is not the goal and that if you're chasing success, you're likely to be disappointed. You're missing out on life because everything is about getting to some point in the future when you will be successful and, therefore, happy.

Think about it for a moment. What is it you think you'll be, do, or have, once you are successful?

The problem with chasing success—or chasing anything—is that usually what we chase eludes us. It's just like when my dog, Cheyenne, runs farther away when we chase her after she has escaped the confines of our home or yard. We get frustrated because we can't catch her. Yet, when we just let her go, she usually returns home quickly on her own.

Secondly, I'd argue that success is not what you're really after. Success does not necessarily bring happiness, especially if you're not enjoying the journey. Life is about the journey, not the destination, and success is almost always a destination. When and if you reach it, you often just want more, so it's an endless chase.

Instead of making success your goal, I'd like to suggest a few alternative goals to consider:

- satisfaction
- living
- adding value
- expressing yourself fully
- growing
- learning

- fulfilling your purpose
- enjoying life

You'll notice a common thread among all of these goals: they're all about being in the moment. Magical things happen when you learn to be present and enjoy the moment. You get inspired ideas. You *really* serve people. You get to fully experience life, and, ironically, you become successful.
Source: *www.DebbieLaChusa.com/blog*

Delayed Gratification

> *"The great Western disease is, 'I'll be happy when . . . . When I get the money. When I get a BMW. When I get this job.' Well, the reality is, you never get to 'when.' The only way to find happiness is to understand that happiness is not out there. It's in here. And happiness is not next week. It's now."*
>
> ~Marshall Goldsmith, author

The attitude of "I'll be happy when . . ." starts young. Even as children we are often focused on the future, wanting what we don't have. We want to be older so we can do everything the big kids get to do. We want to be taller so we can ride the amusement park rides. We want to go to school like our big brothers or sisters. We look forward to holidays and birthdays for the parties and presents. From the time we can think for ourselves, we are looking forward. We look forward to:

- turning sixteen so we can drive
- finishing high school
- turning eighteen so we can vote
- turning twenty-one so we can legally drink alcohol
- graduating from college
- getting a boyfriend or girlfriend

- getting engaged
- getting married
- getting divorced and starting over (for half of those who marry)
- getting a raise
- getting a new job
- getting a new house
- getting a nicer car
- having a baby
- seeing the kids move out
- taking that dream vacation
- retiring

This may sound ridiculous, but I ask you to reflect honestly on your own life. Perhaps you do live in the moment, appreciate what you have, and never want for more. However, if you're like most people, you spend much of your time looking forward and betting your happiness on the future. It's how we've been conditioned.

Future Focus

"Gotta find me a future, move out of my way. I want it all, I want it all, I want it all, and I want it now."

~from the song "I Want it All" by Queen

This future orientation sets us up to constantly strive for more. While we may experience a certain degree of happiness in the here and now, often it's not quite enough. There's always that little voice inside whispering, "You'll be happier when . . . ." But it's a dangerous trap, because no matter what you achieve, there's always more. There's always a next step, another goal, a grander desire. So we end up always chasing and looking for the next high.

Years ago, before I went into business for myself, I landed what I thought was my dream job. Marketing was my career. Fitness was my passion. I was lucky to combine both into a job when The American Council on Exercise hired me to head its marketing department. After years of being frustrated and unhappy in my advertising agency job, I was ecstatic about the opportunity. And at first, I *was* happy. But it was a non-profit organization with a big mission and a small staff. I quickly found myself completely overwhelmed and doing the job of several people. I remember telling myself one spring, "When August gets here, things will slow down and I can enjoy this." When August arrived and nothing had changed, I set my sights on November. After months of continually believing things would get better "in just a few months" and placing my happiness on hold, I realized things weren't going to change. This was the job, and while I loved it, it was overwhelming. After three years, too much stress, and eventual burnout, I made the decision to leave.

I learned an important lesson: you can't put your happiness on hold—happiness exists in the here and now. There's nothing wrong with setting goals, but you've got to be happy while you're moving toward those goals. Otherwise, you may never be happy.

On some level we know this future focus is not the way to happiness. We hear about the importance of living in the present and being grateful for what we have. Intellectually, we get it. We *want* to live it. Yet even for those of us with the best of intentions, future focus often seduces us. It's easy to put all our energy into achievement, gaining approval, and acquiring more goals. I wanted to understand why. Turns out, we learned it in school.

Making the Grade

> "Grades are almost completely relative, in effect ranking
> students relative to others in their class. Thus extra
> achievement by one student not only raises his position, but in
> effect lowers the position of others."
>
> ~James S. Coleman, sociologist

At the ripe old age of five or six most of us were introduced to the concept of success for the very first time. Remember the coveted gold star the teacher put on our homework when we did a good job? Remember the big black "A" written at the top of the page celebrating achievement or the giant red "F" signaling failure? We've been conditioned from a very young age to achieve and seek approval. Accomplishment feels good. Approval is validating. I'm not suggesting either is bad, but it becomes a question of priority and balance. There's no arguing that education plays an important role in our lives. It helps us grow and prepares us to go into the world and live productive and fulfilling lives. In my opinion, it becomes a problem when succeeding becomes more important than learning.

With the passing of the No Child Left Behind legislation in 2001, much of the focus in K–12 education shifted to "test success." Standardized tests are the metric for successful education. Critics argue this forces teachers to "teach to the test" to ensure good scores for their school district. They cite studies that indicate some students simply perform better on tests than others and higher test scores do not necessarily mean a higher quality education. Others argue that instead of being excited about going to school and learning, kids are stressed about passing their annual math and reading tests. And, because each state sets its own pass/fail bar, there really is no standard level of proficiency. Some even suggest that states and schools "game the system" by lowering their standards. Without a standard bar, what do the test scores really mean? And yet they have become the driving force behind our children's education.

My children have always been good students, earning A's and B's throughout elementary, middle, and high school. They received A's in their middle school English classes yet struggled with writing in high school. As the "editor" of many of their high school reports, I was shocked at the grammar and writing basics they lacked. My daughter didn't get her writing chops until she attended a prestigious liberal arts college known for turning out great writers—despite a high school grade point average (GPA) that was above 4.0. One has to wonder about the way we measure success in our schools and how well we are actually educating our children. High GPAs, test scores, awards, and accolades are admirable, but are we preparing kids for college and the real world? Are we teaching them how to prepare for tests instead of teaching them how to think? Are we embedding the idea of future focus instead of teaching them to make the most of where they are?

The Rising Educational Bar

> *"Education is not the filling of a pail, but the lighting of a fire."*
>
> ~William Butler Yeats, poet

My niece graduated from high school with a 4.6 GPA yet still wasn't able to crack the top ten in her class—she was number twelve. At her high school graduation I listened to the exhaustive list of accomplishments and extracurricular activities of the class valedictorian and two salutatorians. I was astonished by all these students had done in addition to earning stellar GPAs. I couldn't help but wonder what drove such high levels of overachievement. It certainly didn't exist when I was in high school. And I'm not sure it's a good thing.

The educational arena has become extremely competitive. It takes more than just good grades to get into college. In fact, the entire focus in high school is on getting into college (future focus at its finest) and earning a scholarship to pay for it. Scholarships and other forms of financial aid are becoming increasingly important as the cost of a college education rises—tuition increases have outpaced inflation for the past ten years. According to the College Board, the average in-state cost of a four-year education at a public institution in 2010–2011 topped $30,000. The average private college or university cost nearly $30,000 *per year*. If you're considering a top-notch private college or Ivy League school, the cost is closer to $50,000 per year. Given the economic downturn, flat salaries, declining savings rates, and dwindling investment accounts, paying for college is more challenging than ever for many families.

When I went to college, scholarships and financial aid weren't even on my radar. I worked my way through school and paid for my own education, no student loans required. Today, you can't have a conversation about college without cost being a part of it. According to a 2007 ABC News poll, 90 percent of parents said it was likely their children would attend college, yet 48 percent said they were behind where they should be in terms of saving money to pay for it. So, added to the burden of getting into college is the burden of paying for it. This puts significant pressure on teens.

I saw it firsthand with my children and their friends. The pressure to excel in high school and the various other endeavors paving their path to college was immense. It was not only about getting good grades. It meant taking challenging honors and Advanced Placement classes, excelling in sports, doing well on SATs and ACTs, earning accolades and awards, participating in extracurricular activities, and performing community service. That's a lot to juggle as a teenager. And it doesn't even guarantee acceptance into college. I'm not suggesting high school should be all fun and games, but with the entire focus being on getting somewhere else (i.e., college), what message are we sending?

Is the Pressure to Succeed Killing Our Teenagers?

> *"Forty-four percent of teens feel strong pressure to succeed in school, no matter the cost."*
>
> ~2006 Junior Achievement Teen Ethics Poll

According to the fourth annual Teen Ethics Poll released by Junior Achievement, 44 percent of teens say they feel either a lot of pressure or overwhelming pressure to succeed in school, no matter the cost. Also, more girls than boys feel this burden. The vast majority (81 percent) of those who feel this pressure to succeed don't expect it to go away; they believe it will remain the same or get worse when they enter the workforce. Sadly, more than one in ten students also think they must cheat to be successful.

But if you're concerned that cheating is the most unfortunate downside of all this pressure, consider this: according to the Centers For Disease Control, suicide is the third leading cause of death among fifteen- to twenty-four-year-olds, accounting for 12 percent of all deaths annually. In 2007, 14.5 percent of US high school students reported they had seriously considered attempting suicide, while 6.9 percent reported they had actually attempted it one or more times.

Just as teen girls feel more pressure to succeed, they also are more likely to attempt and commit suicide. In 2007, 18.7 percent of teen girls considered suicide during the twelve months preceding the survey, compared to 10.3 percent of teen boys. For every teen suicide, there are approximately one hundred to two hundred attempts, compared to four attempts for every suicide among those sixty-five and older. Either teens aren't as proficient as seniors at committing suicide or there are a lot of teens crying out for help. According to the National Institutes of Health, unsuccessful suicide attempts are very often a cry for help.

While there's no data to support a direct correlation between the pressure to succeed and suicide, the stats are startling nonetheless. And the fact remains, happy people do not try to kill themselves.

Just as girls lead the way in suicide, it appears they also lead the way in striving for academic excellence. In her book *Perfect Girls, Starving Daughters*, Courtney E. Martin reveals that women have outnumbered men on college campuses since 1979 and on graduate school campuses since 1984. In a 2006 *New York Times* op-ed piece, Jennifer Delahunty Britz, dean of admissions for Kenyon College (the college my daughter attended) in Gambier, Ohio, wrote about the challenges girls face in the college admissions process. She writes about the competitiveness, recalling a female applicant from Kentucky who was the "leader/president/editor/captain/lead actress in every activity in her school," had taken six advanced placement courses, had been selected for a prestigious state leadership program, and had performed more than three hundred hours of community service in four different organizations. Yet, because of her test scores and GPA, the admissions team debated before finally accepting her. Delahunty Britz laments, "We have told today's young women that the world is their oyster; the problem is, so many of them believed us that the standards for admission to today's most selective colleges are stiffer for women than men. How's that for an unintended consequence of the women's liberation movement?"

While it may plague girls more than boys, this is the overwhelming challenge many of today's teens face. They are all steered toward college whether or not it's a good fit, while the hurdles they must jump through educationally and financially keep getting higher. As much as I am a proponent of education, I do not believe college is the right path for every teen. I think high schools could do a better job of showing teens and their parents all of the post-high-school options and helping them pick the ones that best suit them.

Growing Up Too Fast

"Youth is wasted on the young."

~*George Bernard Shaw, dramatist*

In too many ways, today's kids don't get to be kids. With such a strong emphasis on preparing for the future, the days of youth being wasted on the young, as Shaw quipped about, may be close to extinction. As we have seen, teens face pressures older generations never could have imagined.

James, a fifty-four-year-old businessman from Ohio, has seen this firsthand with the high school kids he mentors, and it concerns him. Despite the fact that today's teens seem to be suffering from future focus when it comes to education, James also believes teens place too much emphasis on instant gratification and material possessions. They're preoccupied with video games, cell phones, and iPads. He's concerned they place too much value on quick success. He says they're in a hurry to get to the top of the ladder, because that's what they believe society expects. He tells them there's nothing wrong with wanting to get to the top but reminds them that once they get there, there's no place but down. And there will still be plenty of people expecting more. He encourages kids to take their time and enjoy the rewards of the journey so when they do get to the top, they can sit back and realize how they got there. Then, if they do fail or if the expectations are set even higher, they will be better prepared to cope with it.

James counsels his teens to measure success by internal, not external, standards. Can they look in the mirror and know what they did that day was in the best interest of everyone around them? Can they honestly say they didn't cheat or hurt anyone? Do they personally feel good about themselves? He believes answering these questions is the way to measure success. It has nothing to do with what he calls "visible scales." Then he adds, "I wouldn't want to be a kid today no more than the man on the moon." I think I would have to agree.

📷 Blog Snapshot

Teen's Death Reminds Me Why Being Present Is So Important

As much as I focus on trying to stay in the present moment, I admit I'm human and often find myself worrying about the future.

The idea of being present has been drilled into my head, and I fully appreciate it. I understand that worrying about something that may or may not happen is futile . . . it's wasted energy. Yet the planner in me persists. And, unfortunately, more times than I care to admit, instead of simply enjoying where I am, I'm all too often focused on where I'm going.

A recent incident provided a great reminder to keep fighting the good fight. Several weeks ago an eighteen-year-old softball player who lived in San Diego and played for the same softball franchise as my daughter was tragically murdered. While we didn't know her personally, she was part of a community we belonged to for years.

Like my daughter, who recently graduated from college after playing softball all four years, this young woman had received a scholarship and was heading off to college to study and continue her softball career. She was a beautiful young woman whose life was cut tragically short.

Additionally, just this past week her local softball team participated in the national championship tournament, a tournament teams must qualify for, and that's no easy feat.

It got me to thinking that if this young woman had focused all of her attention on getting to nationals and getting to college, and did not just enjoy playing and competing along the way, it would have all been for naught. She never got to play at nationals and she will never go to college.

I don't wish to sound morbid, but my point is, none of us knows what tomorrow will bring. So if we're not enjoying what we're doing today, on the path to those bigger dreams, what's the point? If, however, we enjoy the journey, then we win, even if we never achieve the bigger dream, because we've enjoyed our life.

Source: www.FollowingInspiration.com

Parental Pressure

"Parents can only give good advice or put them on the right paths, but the final forming of a person's character lies in their own hands."

~Anne Frank, writer

As teachers, my parents always stressed grades. A's were the goal. I'm not sure how much they actually verbalized this, but it was understood. As a girl who always wanted to please, I worked hard to get A's. I became a perfectionist. I was always striving to do well in school and everything else I did.

This pursuit of perfection and pleasing my parents did not end when I moved out of their home. I found myself still wanting to please them, perhaps in part because I felt I had let my father down when I dropped out of college at nineteen and got married. He made it clear he did not support my decision. In fact, up until a month before the wedding, he had no intention of being part of my nuptials or walking me down the aisle. Thankfully, shortly before the wedding—I think when he realized it was happening with or without him—he came around. On my wedding day, when my father handed me over to my future husband at the altar, the words out of his mouth—albeit somewhat under his breath—were "lucky dog." I'm not sure if I had pleased my dad that day, but there was an air of approval in those parting words.

I'm pretty sure my parents were pleased when, a year later, I decided to return to college. After I graduated and embarked on my career, I regularly reported my accomplishments to my parents. In fact, it was not until I was in my forties that I realized how much I was "reporting" and that, in fact, what I was really doing was seeking approval and maybe even redemption. Now that I've arrived at the half-century mark in my life, I still share with my parents, but not as much. For the most part, I no longer seek their approval, although I admit it's still nice when I get it. My dad, an avid reader, agreed to edit this book. I admit I was a bit anxious to know what he thought of my writing. It was validating when he told me he thought I was an excellent writer. I guess old habits die hard!

From Stanford Grad to Social Worker

Camille is a twenty-eight-year-old Stanford graduate and single mother living in Hawaii. She knows all too well the pressure to do well in school, be successful, and live up to other people's expectations. Ever since college she's fought an internal battle between what makes her happy and what others expect. Growing up in a small Japanese community and being raised by parents who wanted more for their children than they had for themselves, educational success was a top priority. Children were groomed to become doctors or lawyers. Parents sacrificed to send their kids to the best schools. As Camille puts it, she was expected to go off to college and come back and do something great. But after attending Stanford, her definition of "something great" didn't align with that of her parents.

Stanford proved to be an eye-opening experience for this small-town Hawaiian girl. She was shocked by the racial and social stratification she saw, the freeway dividing the rich and the poor, and the focus on the haves and have-nots. It all rubbed Camille the wrong way. She came away from the experience knowing that success for her was not what it had been laid out to be. She had no desire to live in a million-dollar home. The more she tried living up to the expectations placed on her, the unhappier she became. Her struggle between pleasing herself and pleasing others eventually led to depression, therapy, and medication. She says it's especially hard to admit you're struggling with mental health issues when others view you as successful (something people tend to do when you're a Stanford graduate). But she's glad she was willing to seek help. She fears she's not alone. At Stanford she frequently saw other students not being given the chance to value themselves simply for themselves.

What makes Camille happy today is a simple life. She works in what she describes as the painfully underpaid profession of social work and loves it. She defines success as reaching her full potential intellectually and doing work that makes a difference. Five years ago she gave birth to a son, which she describes as the happiest thing that's ever happened to her. Becoming a mom caused her to re-evaluate her life. Today she makes only a small connection between money and success. She doesn't want or need much, just enough money to support her family and maybe go shopping every once in a while. She admits it's not always easy following her heart. The pressures from outside are always there. But with the help of friends and others who support her, she is persevering.

And the Winner Is . . .

"It's not whether you win or lose; it's how you play the game."

~unknown

Ask anyone who plays sports, and they'll agree it's more fun to win than lose. Certainly how you play the game is important, but whom are we kidding when we say it's not about winning? Of course it is. That's what the spirit of competition is all about. Can you imagine the Olympic games with no winners? The Super Bowl? World Series? It defeats the purpose. For many, winning a sports contest is the epitome of success.

My kids have always played sports. My son played Little League and was on his high school tennis team for four years. My daughter started playing softball at age five and continued until she was twenty-one, including competing at the collegiate level for four years. At age five she was just learning the game, and the focus was on having fun and building skills. However, by the time she moved up to the eight-and-under division, it had definitely become about winning. At the end of the season, there was a tournament to determine the first place team. Additionally, the most talented players were voted onto an all-star team to compete countywide and potentially (if they won) at the regional and state levels. This process is repeated in every age division, all the way up to high school. In high school, teams aim to become league champions. For kids who play club sports, the goal is qualifying for nationals, where college scouts can see them. In college, it's about conference titles, and for an elite few, making it to a bowl game or national championship.

Yes, organized sports are about fun, fitness, and teamwork. But make no mistake—they're absolutely about winning. The fact that we tell our children they're not is incongruent with the way the entire system is set up and, quite frankly, with the way many parents behave at children's sporting events. I'm not saying sports should or shouldn't be about winning or competition. I'm merely pointing out that from an early age the message is very clear—winning is the goal. This entrenches the concept of striving for success firmly into the minds of our impressionable youth. Because, after all, if you're not a winner, then you must be a loser.

Keeping Up with the Joneses

"Before you try to keep up with the Joneses,
be sure they're not trying to keep up with you."

~*Erma Bombeck, humorist*

A few years ago several of my neighbors began remodeling their homes and updating their kitchens. At seventeen years old, my house is not that old, but there are definitely updates and improvements that would make it more current. Kitchen remodels, however, are expensive. And any extra cash we had at the time was going into the rental properties we owned and our children's college educations. I remember feeling a bit jealous that I couldn't get a new kitchen with beautiful granite countertops, sleek new cabinets, and stylish stainless steel appliances. Mind you, to this day my appliances work just fine, and the cabinets and tile countertops are still in good condition. Of course, that didn't change the fact that because I saw everyone getting *new* kitchens, I wanted one too.

"Keeping up with the Joneses" is a concept we're all familiar with. It came up often in the interviews I conducted for this book. In a society that in many ways defines social standing by who we are and what we have, we compare notes (another form of competition), and if we don't have as much as others have, we feel shortchanged.

Christie, a sixty-eight-year-old retiree living in San Francisco, admits it's been a lifelong struggle trying not to compare herself to others. She believes it's unavoidable. "Do I look better?" she asks. "Am I smarter? Am I richer? Am I more attractive? We do that with each other, and I think it's based on a larger cultural standard that we all look to."

Mary, a fifty-four-year-old administrative professional from Pennsylvania, says there were times in her life that she wanted more—she wanted to be like the Joneses. Until she came to the realization that those Joneses may be in debt "up to their eyeballs."

Lesley, a fifty-seven-year-old mother of six, admits that when she was in her thirties and living just outside of Washington, DC, the emphasis was on getting the right house in the right neighborhood and all the "external things." But once she had acquired all the material possessions and appeared to have it all, she found herself asking, "Is this all there is?" She realized something was missing, and it wasn't something money could buy.

Brenda, a fifty-three-year-old entrepreneur and mom of two, admits she wants people to look at her and say, "Wow, she's really successful." She believes this stems from being one of the unpopular kids in high school. As a result, she was always trying to get better and adopted a "keeping up with the Joneses" attitude toward success. As the oldest of seven children, she was the one expected to take care of things if Mom wasn't around. Add to that a type A personality, and Brenda always felt she had to be doing something and had to be doing it well. Years later, as a single parent, Brenda worked hard to support her family, at times working two or three jobs. A few years ago she would have told you success meant having a lot of money, the best car, the nicest house, and everything her kids wanted. Unfortunately, it was that very attitude that sank Brenda deep into debt.

Now that her kids are grown and she's happily married, she views things differently. She no longer feels she has anything to prove—a pressure she felt as a young single mother trying to show others she could support her family. She's more comfortable in her own skin, and she's not as worried about appearances. She doesn't need to drive a brand new car to make her neighbors think she's doing well. Recently, Brenda spent a day at the spa with her thirty-year-old daughter, and as they were talking about the past, her daughter admitted she didn't remember a lot of details from when she was younger. Brenda thought, "Good God, if I'd known you weren't going to remember, I might not have worked so hard to keep things perfect."

When it comes down to it, will that remodeled kitchen or new car really make us happier? Maybe in the short-term. I'm the first to admit I want my house to look nice; it makes me feel good. But in the big scheme of things, it's a bit shallow and fleeting. I don't believe belongings bring us the same degree of happiness as relationships and experiences. Psychological research supports this. A 2009 study conducted at San Francisco State University found that in the long run, experiences make people happier than possessions. According to psychologists, the pleasure we get from possessions fades within a few months. Psychologists also point out that experiences tend to involve other people—family and friends— and that may be a reason they generate more happiness.

Learning to Appreciate the Ebb and Flow

"Action and reaction, ebb and flow, trial and error, change— this is the rhythm of living."

~Bruce Barton, author

Money, material possessions, grades, and success (however you define it) come and go. They ebb and they flow. That's the journey of life. Whether you choose to let your happiness be dictated by these comings and goings is up to you. What if instead you learned to appreciate the ebb and flow? That's what Margaret, a sixty-year-old mother and family harmonizing expert from Australia has chosen to do.

While Margaret considers herself successful, she acknowledges success is relative. Even though she can say she's a success, that success can be easily undermined when she sees other people who are "out there more, or are bigger and brighter." She admits she probably devalues her own self-worth by comparing herself to others and to how society defines success. When asked why she does this, she openly admits it's probably a self-esteem issue. She adds that she grew up in a very religious household and often compared herself to her brothers and people in the "real world." While Margaret feels valuable when she is achieving and helping people, she acknowledges receiving external validation makes her feel valuable too. Despite sometimes comparing herself to others, she's quick to point out it's the internal validation that's most important. She adds, "If I can't validate myself internally and know I am good at this no matter what people are saying, I'm not going to really feel it or hold onto it."

When asked if she believes there is a connection between money and success, she says people can be highly successful without earning a lot of money. She shares the example of Robert Kiyosaki (a multimillionaire and successful author) and points out he has a sister who is a highly successful Buddhist monk, with absolutely no money. Margaret also believes more people are waking up to the fact that there is more in life than just physical things: "It's not so much about your shiny car anymore. It's not about how big your house is anymore. People are waking up and realizing those things may not be making them happy."

What makes Margaret happy these days? Her relationship with her daughters is at the top of her list. "My daughters are now twenty and sixteen, and we really get on extraordinarily well. We're constantly telling each other that we love each other. I just have a very pleasant, harmonious life." Margaret also attributes her happiness to being surrounded by like-minded people and friends who support one another. She also enjoys a country lifestyle in a lovely little coastal town near Melbourne with a beautiful view of the ocean and the city in the distance. "It's very nice," she says.

When Margaret talks about happiness, she talks about life's ebbs and flows. She admits there are times when the doubt creeps in and the money may not be coming in the way she'd like. Yet in Margaret's experience, if you're in harmony with yourself and know you're serving others, even if it's only your immediate family, the flow always comes back. So, she's learned not to panic. She's learned to appreciate the ebbs and flows. In fact, appreciation is a big part of Margaret's approach to life and happiness: "Appreciating absolutely everything certainly helps success to move forward and the happiness scale to rise."

Margaret has been keeping an appreciation journal for years. Every day she lists five things she is grateful for. If something is not working out, she includes it. For example, if the money flow is a little slow she makes sure to appreciate the money that *is* coming in, even if it's just coming in "in drips and drabs." In her daily journal she also notes five things she is going to be grateful for the next day. She's noticed a big difference in her life since beginning this practice. When she first began, she started appreciating a person she was having difficulties with. Over time she watched the attitude of this person change. Now she's quick to find a way to appreciate whatever is going on in her life, whether it appears good or bad on the surface.

Margaret is the first to admit that when business is booming and finances are good, she likes it. She still dreams of the day she might have a million dollars. Yet she's also very aware that a million dollars may not change her level of happiness. She finds it's more important to be centered and in harmony, and when she is, her finances and situations around her tend to increase.

Happy Here and Now

*"With the past, I have nothing to do; nor with the future.
I live now."*

~Ralph Waldo Emerson, author and poet

There is nothing wrong with setting goals. When we take a closer look at happiness in chapter 8, we'll see that psychologists say there are three components to happiness: pleasure, engagement, and meaning. Goals provide engagement, and achievement provides meaning. In his book *The Happiness Advantage,* Shawn Achor refers to the term Aristotle used to define happiness: *eudaimonia,* translated as "human flourishing." This too implies some level of achievement. Achor, who conducted one of the largest studies on happiness and potential at Harvard University, defines happiness as "the joy we feel striving after our potential."

I don't believe the antidote to "I'll be happy when . . ." syndrome is denying our thirst for more. I think we can follow the advice Brian shared in chapter 1 and choose to be happy with what we have while continuing to challenge ourselves and set goals. It's when we make our happiness contingent upon achieving those goals that we're shortchanging ourselves.

Spellbound

1. Are you focusing on what everyone else has instead of being grateful for what you have?

2. Do you assume others who have more money, success, or possessions are happier than you?

3. Do you find no matter how much you achieve, you're constantly striving for more?

4. Are you basing your definition of success on someone else's criteria?

5. Are you constantly looking toward a point in time when you believe you will be happy?

6. Are you spending all of your time chasing success instead of enjoying your life?

7. Are you missing out on the joys of today because you're so focused on preparing for where you are headed?

8. Are you trying to prove yourself to your parents, teachers, or other influential people in your life?

9. Are you so competitive that you aren't happy unless you win?

10. Are you constantly comparing yourself to friends, colleagues, or neighbors?

Breaking the Spell

1. Focus on yourself and all you have to be grateful for.

2. Understand that "the grass is always greener" is often an illusion. Before you assume someone else has it better than you, find out if that's really the case.

3. Learn to be happy where you are and with what have. You can still strive for more, just don't put your happiness on hold in the meantime.

4. Choose your own criteria for success. If you're happy, that's all that matters.

5. Choose to be happy now. If you're not, change your circumstances or your attitude.

6. Be present and live in the moment.

7. Start a daily gratitude or appreciation journal.

8. Recognize you have nothing to prove to anyone.

9. Enjoy the competition of sports and realize you can't always win. Look for ways you or your team did win even if you didn't come out on top of the contest.

10. Break out of the comparison trap. Remember, the Joneses don't really exist. Learn what makes *you* happy, and build your life around that.

CHAPTER 3

THE CULT OF SUCCESS

"In order to properly understand the big picture, everyone should fear becoming mentally clouded and obsessed with one small section of truth."

~Xun Zi, philosopher

Referring to success as a cult may seem a bit extreme. However, as I shared in the introduction, my own pursuit of success did become somewhat cult-like. It definitely had a hold on me. My preoccupation with success negatively affected other areas of my life. In many ways, I was obsessed. And I can tell you, in all the years I spent attending success conferences and rubbing elbows with other success-seekers, I was not alone. I saw many of the same people at conference after conference. They too seemed to be hooked.

In his book *SHAM: How the Self-Help Movement Made America Helpless*, Steve Salerno writes about people's addiction to self-help despite no evidence that it actually works. In my case, while I admit I learned a lot, I never achieved that ultimate level of success I was searching for, probably because it was a moving target. Yet I persisted for years, investing hundreds of thousands of dollars. I know people who lost their homes and went bankrupt in search of success. So while it may sound a bit outrageous to some, calling it a cult really seems accurate to me.

According to Steven Hassan, cult expert, founder of Freedom of the Mind, and author of *Releasing the Bonds* and *Combating Mind Control*, cults are not only religious. He identifies five kinds of cults: religious, psychotherapy, political, commercial, and personality. The cult of success falls under the description of commercial cult. It's not a cult in the traditional sense, run by one individual. It's more of a collective cult. The International Cultic Studies Association's website, HowCultsWork.com, provides the following descriptions of commercial and self-help cults, which eerily mirror what I experienced and witnessed in my seduction by the success industry [punctuation modified]:

Commercial Cults

Cults that use commercial gain as their base are called "cults of greed." They will promise you that if you join them and follow their special program for success, then you will become very rich. Often they will hold up their leader as an example and explain that if you do what he or she says, then you will be successful too. Commercial cults use mind control to get you working for them for free and to make you pay for an endless stream of motivational tapes, videos, books, and seminars, all of which are supposedly designed to help you succeed, but in reality are designed to enhance the cult's mind control environment and keep you believing in their almost impossible dream of success. Of course they never mention that the primary way the leaders make money [is] by selling these motivation materials to their group!

Self Help & Counseling

Cults that use "self help" or counseling or self-improvement as their base often target business people and corporations. By doing their courses and seminars, they claim you and your staff will become more successful. Business people locked away in hotel rooms are subjected to quasi-religious indoctrination as they play strange games, join group activities, and share their innermost thoughts with the group. Once you have completed one course, you are told you need to do the more advanced course, which naturally costs more than the last. These cults will sometimes request that you do volunteer work and that you help recruit your friends, family, and work mates. These groups specialize in creating powerful emotional experiences [that] are then used to validate your involvement in the cult. The religious overtones are couched in terms [that] don't sound religious. They usually come to the surface as you near the end of a seminar. Many people have been bankrupted by involvement with these cults.

Dr. Janja Lalich is a researcher, author, and educator specializing in cults and extremist groups. She is also a professor of sociology at California State University, Chico, and the founder and director of the Center for Research on Influence and Control. Dr. Lalich defines a cult as "either a sharply-bounded social group or a diffusely-bounded social movement held together through shared commitment to a charismatic leader. It upholds a transcendent belief system (often but not always religious in nature) that includes a call for a personal transformation."

The similarities between these definitions and the self-improvement industry are too many for me to ignore. And, while the individual experts and success gurus may not be cult leaders, knowingly implementing mind control, I do believe the self-improvement movement has taken on a cult-like status. I am absolutely a proponent of learning and self-growth. However, when you become so focused on trying to improve that you can no longer be happy or satisfied with the way things are, it's not healthy. When you begin spending all of your time, energy, and money on self-improvement, it's dangerous and can be very destructive. My preoccupation with success did not result in my life improving. It resulted in me losing myself, almost losing my business, and ending up in debt. Thankfully, I woke up before it was too late. I realized what was happening and got out. I was able to turn things around without completely losing my business, my home, or my family. Others haven't been so lucky.

Buying Happiness

"I bought a Corvette hoping it would make me look rich.
I thought I was 'rich,' but I really wasn't."

~MJ DeMarco, *author of* The Millionaire Fastlane

At the top of MJ DeMarco's website is the phrase "Life, Liberty, and the Pursuit of Fastlane Financial Freedom," along with a picture of DeMarco leaning over a Lamborghini. I expected DeMarco, as the author of *The Millionaire Fastlane,* to be all about the money. I was pleasantly surprised when we spoke. The first thing he said was, "I think a lot of people misattribute that success will make them happy, but actually it's the other way around—happiness creates success." He cautions against the "I'll be happy when . . . " mentality and, when asked why he believes so many people get caught up in it, replies, "That's what we're being indoctrinated to believe. Every single day we are inundated with advertising messages. This car is what's going to make you happy. This house will make you the envy of your friends and neighbors." He's quick to point out that anyone who has been down that path will tell you that happiness comes from inside, not from things you buy. He then talks about the Corvette he purchased with the big check he received when he sold his company the first time. (He sold the company for $1.2 million and later bought it back for $250,000 after it was mismanaged and nearly run into the ground.) After a few weeks he realized the car didn't make him happy, it was the process of getting to the point where he could buy the car that made him happy.

While DeMarco hopes his book will teach people how to retire young and rich, his real message is about enjoying life. He argues that the path we're conditioned to follow in life—go to school, get a job, work for forty years, and one day retire and live your dreams—robs people of time. "It makes people bankrupt in time, and when you're bankrupt in time, the things that truly make you happy ultimately suffer."

He's says what makes him feel wealthy and rich is his freedom. He admits money is a big part of the freedom equation. But he says most people use the money they do have to further entrap themselves by buying things they can't afford. They are in effect financing their own misery. While he acknowledges some people may be trying to buy happiness, he believes it's really about a lack of financial discipline: spending more than they earn, racking up credit card debt, having no financial plan. "It doesn't matter what these people make. This is why normal people file for bankruptcy and why seemingly rich people file for bankruptcy." He says too many people are spending money they don't have trying to maintain an image.

Seduced by Success

> *"I know how easy it is for some minds to glide along with the current of popular opinion, where influence, respectability, and all those motives which tend to seduce the human heart are brought to bear."*
>
> *~Benjamin F. Wade, politician*

Every person I interviewed for this book said being successful was important. In my survey on money, success, and happiness, 88 percent of respondents said their level of happiness is at
least somewhat related to their level of success. There are more
than 125,000 success books available on Amazon. According to
Marketdata Enterprises, the self-development market is an $11 bil-
lion-a-year industry. To quote Marketdata research director John
LaRosa, "There is no shortage of demand for products and programs that cater to Americans' desire to make more money, lose
weight, improve their relationships and business skills, cope with
stress, or obtain a quick dose of motivation."

In chapter 2 we looked at some of the reasons we may be so
focused on success and achievement. This chapter includes some
more. While there may not be scientific evidence linking these
factors to a preoccupation with success and achievement, I encourage you to have an open mind. My goal with this book is to expand
your awareness; get you to think about money, success, and happiness in a new light; and ultimately help you live your life in a way
that provides all three, without giving up anything in the process.
All I ask is that you consider how the following cultural phenomena may be impacting the way we live our lives and how we view
and pursue money, success, and happiness.

Reality TV

*"In 1992, reality TV was a novelty. In 2000, it was a fad. In
2010, it's a way of life."*

~Time magazine

One of the first reality TV shows I remember watching
was *Lifestyles of The Rich and Famous*. It aired from 1984 to 1995
and, as the name implies, featured the extravagant lifestyles of

entertainment celebrities, athletes, and other wealthy individuals. We no longer had to imagine how the other half lived; we could see for ourselves every week on television. *Lifestyles of the Rich and Famous* was followed by *MTV Cribs,* which ran from 2000 to 2010 and once again featured exclusive tours of the grandiose homes and lifestyles of celebrities.

These shows paved the way for reality TV hits such as *The Real Housewives,* which, as of this writing, has seven franchises featuring housewives in cities across the country. Shows like *Million Dollar Listing* and *Million Dollar Decorators* invite us into high-priced homes most of us will never be able to afford. Reality TV has turned our televisions into virtual windows to an often-glamorized "real" world. We see "real" people living what seem like surreal lives. Yet, in an odd way, seeing them on TV—witnessing it—makes them feel a bit more real. After all, if they can achieve that level of wealth and success, we know it is possible.

Like it or not, watch it or not, reality TV has become a part of our culture. According to Nielsen Media Research, the company that measures television viewership, five of the top ten shows for the 2010–2011 season were reality shows.

In a look back at ten years of reality TV, *Time* magazine identified two types of reality shows: competitions and naked voyeurism. *Lifestyle of the Rich and Famous* and *MTV Cribs* fall into the naked voyeurism category. In the competition subgenre, *Survivor* was the first to reach phenomenon status. It spawned some of reality TV's biggest hits, including *American Idol, The Bachelor, The Amazing Race, The Biggest Loser,* and *Project Runway.* In chapter 2 we talked about the focus in our society on competition and winning, and these shows are just more examples of that preoccupation. While shows like *American Idol* require talent and offer a way for people to be discovered, *Survivor* simply asks a person to do whatever it takes to win a million dollars, including lying, cheating, and stealing.

But reality TV isn't only for adults. There are plenty of shows depicting the real lives and competition among children and teens too. TLC's *Toddlers & Tiaras* features tiny tots prancing around in makeup, false eyelashes, fake hair, and thousand-dollar dresses, competing to win money, prizes, and the chance to be crowned "Ultimate Grand Supreme."

While it's easy to watch these shows and laugh them off as ridiculous, one has to wonder how they might be shaping our culture, what we expect life to be like, and what we might be willing to do for money and fame. One day, while I was listening to a discussion about reality TV on the radio, a concerned father called in to say his five-year-old daughter had seen *Toddlers & Tiaras* and decided she wanted to compete in beauty pageants. While the father wanted to support his daughter, he was having a hard time with the idea of her donning full makeup and dressing up like a grown woman. The little girl saw nothing wrong with it, probably because she saw lots of little girls doing it on television. Interestingly, her mother saw nothing wrong with it either.

Shows such as *16 and Pregnant* and *Teen Mom* chronicle the lives of single teenage moms. In reference to the teen stars of these shows, a 2011 *Time* magazine article stated, "Though MTV recruited them to be the subjects of cautionary tales, the network has turned them into success stories: television stars and cover girls, gainfully employed just for being themselves." These young mothers are featured on magazine covers and sought out by paparazzi. One *Teen Mom* star recently disclosed MTV paid her $140,000 for a six-month contract.

My twenty-two-year-old daughter, who used to enjoy watching *Teen Mom*, recently shared with me how disgusted she has become with the show. She is angered by the attitudes of entitlement the young mothers display and commented that one actually talked about having another baby just because she was bored. Also, my daughter said she's heard via social media about young women asking how they can get pregnant and get on one of these shows.

When we have television shows willing to turn teenagers into celebrities and pay them six figures just because they've had babies out of wedlock, the impact on society is certain. TV is creating a career opportunity out of a situation that could damage many lives, not the least of which are the lives of the innocent babies these women are giving birth to.

Another type of reality TV show that glamorizes life is the wedding show. Programs such as *Four Weddings* and *Say Yes to the Dress* make getting married seem like it's all about the perfect wedding or dress. And we can't forget about the diamonds. In her book *Living Large: From SUVs to Double Ds, Why Going Big Isn't Going Better,* Sarah Z. Wexler writes that the size of the engagement ring has increased over the years. One-carat rings are the new standard, and sales of them jumped 80 percent between 1996 and 2006. The average cost of a wedding has gone up too. In 1945 the average wedding set the bride and groom back just $2,000. In 2007 that cost skyrocketed to nearly $29,000. And in the first two quarters of 2011, while significantly lower than just a few years ago, costs were still hovering around $19,000.

Granted, you have to take inflation into account, yet I think you'd be hard-pressed to find someone who doesn't agree weddings continue to get more extravagant as the years go by. An extreme display of this was the August 2011 wedding of reality TV star Kim Kardashian. The price tag of her widely publicized nuptials? A rumored $10 million! The marriage lasted a mere seventy-two days, and there were rumors the entire spectacle was a publicity stunt.

With so much focus on the event of getting married instead of the commitment of marriage, is it any wonder the divorce rate is so high? Brides often seem more concerned with throwing an incredible party than with the marriage itself. My husband and I have been married thirty years. When we got married it was about us, not the party or the dress. I believe that attitude is one of the reasons we are still together and happy.

📷 Blog Snapshot

Thirty Years Ago This Weekend, I Said "I Do"

My husband, Louie, and I are celebrating our thirtieth wedding anniversary this weekend. Thirty years is a long time. We've been through a lot together. Some tough times and some truly wonderful times. There was a time I didn't think we were going to make it. I'm guessing anyone in a relationship that's stood the test of time has experienced the same thing.

As I reflect on why we have made it, a few things come to mind. When we got married, it was about being together. It wasn't about the wedding. My daughter and I sometimes watch *Four Weddings* and *Say Yes to the Dress* on TLC. These reality shows are about getting married. But so often, when I hear the comments by the women who are featured, they're about the wedding. It's all about the dress, the venue, and the reception. I've got news for you: that's all just stuff. It's not what the day is about.

I was only nineteen years old when I said "I do." Most people thought I was too young. How could I make such a big commitment? I didn't look at it that way. If I had, the enormity of it probably would have scared me away. I'm not saying it wasn't about forever. It absolutely was. But when it came down to it, it was about being together. Creating and building a life. Being best friends. Spending our time—initially days and ultimately years—with each other. It was about us, not the wedding, not the dress, not the venue, not the flowers, not the reception. Sure, those things were nice, but they were definitely not the focus.

As I look back, it's hard to believe it's been thirty years. A lot has changed. Sure, we've both grown . . . grown up really! But one thing hasn't changed. We are still best friends. Each of us is still the first person the other turns to when something wonderful or terrible happens. We fight. We get angry. But we work it out. Because we know we're in it for the long haul and we don't expect it to be perfect. Yet in many ways, it is.

Source: www.FollowingInspiration.com

Cultivation Theory

"There are two sayings that are familiar in every news room across the country: 1) sex sells; 2) if it bleeds it leads."

~Armstrong Williams, journalist

In discussing the impact of television on how we see the world, *Time* magazine references media psychologist George Gerbner and his cultivation theory: ". . . exposure to cultural imagery can shape a viewer's concept of reality. Simply put, the more TV a person watches, the more that person believes in the world of TV. Using his 'cultivation theory,' Gerbner showed that heavy news viewers believed they resided in a 'meaner' world."

Watching the news and deducing the world is mean is one thing. The news is real, although the way the news media sensationalize stories, it's often not an accurate representation of the truth. I vividly remember the earthquake and resulting fires in the Marina District in San Francisco in 1989. On the TV news, it appeared the entire city was on fire. I visited San Francisco a short while later and saw the area that had burned, and it was actually quite small. I don't mean to diminish the impact of the fires. However, what the news portrayed made it seem much worse than it actually was.

A few years ago we had a similar occurrence in our hometown. There was a large fire burning, yet, as was the case in San Francisco, it was contained to one area of San Diego. My daughter, who was away at college and watching the coverage online, called and was extremely upset. Based on what she saw on the news she thought our home was in danger. I assured her we were far enough away from the blaze and told her there was nothing to worry about. Once again I was reminded how "big" a story can get when it's reported on the news.

As someone who worked in the advertising industry as a media buyer for years, I know the primary goal of television is ratings. Big stories and sensational headlines get people to watch, resulting in higher ratings, which in turn result in higher advertising revenue. Simply put, networks want you to watch their programs so you will watch their commercials. The game is changing with the advent of digital video recording (DVR) services such as TiVo, but make no mistake, television is still a ratings game. Watch it with your eyes wide open!

While the realness of TV news may be questionable, it's clear the goal of reality TV is *not* to inform. Its goal is to entertain. Yet with the name "reality television," clearly the line is blurred. According to an article published by the Association for Psychological Science, shows such as *Survivor* turn 1,000 hours of film into fifteen hours of programming. Heavy editing determines what viewers see and how characters are portrayed. Editing creates storylines and an entertaining show. I'm guessing following every move of reality TV stars might prove a bit boring, or at least a lot more ordinary than what we see on TV. When you can showcase the big moments of life and edit out the mundane, it's not an accurate portrayal. Yet when these shows are marketed under the guise of reality TV, one wonders what expectations this may be creating for what life *should* be like.

For this reason, it also invites comparison. When we watch these people living lives overflowing with money and apparent success, our lives may pale in comparison. It elevates "keeping up with the Joneses" to a whole new level. Seeing the nice homes, luxury cars, designer clothes, extravagant parties, and exotic vacations, it's not hard to come away believing those things make life better. It quite possibly feeds the quest for material possessions, even if at a subconscious level. Yet it's not real, apparently even for some reality stars themselves. In 2011, Russell Armstrong, husband of *Real Housewives of Beverly Hills* star Taylor Armstrong, committed suicide, supposedly due to the pressures of keeping up with the lifestyle portrayed on the show. Armstrong's attorney told ABC News, "These couples join these shows, and then they keep trying to outdo each other, and they end up spending all their money trying to sustain a lifestyle that's unrealistic and wasn't there prior to the show." What does it say when reality stars themselves are trying to keep up with the way they are portrayed on TV?

It's clear reality TV is here to stay. And I'm not necessarily saying that's a bad thing. There are a few reality TV shows I enjoy watching. However, I believe it's important to reconsider how we label these shows. By acknowledging that, while they may not feature actors (an arguable point) or written scripts (another gray area, as reality shows do employ writers to create stories), they are just a form of entertainment. In this light, they are no different from sitcoms, dramas, or soap operas. And while, according to the cultivation theory, they still influence our view of the world, perhaps the impact is lessened. At least we are looking at reality TV for what it really is—entertainment and not real life.

Madison Avenue

"Advertising reflects the mores of society, but it does not influence them."

~David Ogilvy, advertising executive

As I leaf through an issue of *Allure* magazine, I am greeted by advertisements for skin care products that promise to make me look younger, cars to help me look stylish and successful, and makeup to bring out my individuality. These ads all include images of beautiful people. Models. Airbrushed models, to be exact. I have to step back and remind myself that if I choose to purchase these products, it doesn't mean I will look like the people in the advertisements. After all, I can't retouch myself before I step out the front door.

I recall an ad I saw a few months ago that purported to be the first unretouched makeup ad. The headline literally read, "You're Looking At The First Unretouched Makeup Ad.*" The asterisk refers to small-print copy running down the side of the ad that reads, "Make Up For Ever's first campaign with no retouching—certified by a notary public." I'm guessing they didn't think readers would believe the ad wasn't retouched, thus the need for the asterisk and the notary. Looking at the ad, it *is* a bit hard to believe. The model is young and beautiful. Her face looks flawless. She may look like that *without* makeup. I believe they call that genetics, and that's not for sale in a bottle.

Most of us are not model-beautiful. The reality is, we will not look like the models in the ads even if we buy and use the products being promoted. Once again, I feel the sting of an empty promise. I decide to look up the "unretouched" ad on the Internet to see if I'm the only person disappointed by this attempt at truth in advertising. I find the ad featured on HuffingtonPost.com. With the ad is a poll asking readers to cast their votes for whether they believe the ad is a step in the right direction or looks like all other makeup ads. I take the poll, casting my vote for "It looks like all the other ads," and I'm surprised to see I'm in the minority. More than 78 percent of voters believe the ad is a step in the right direction. Only 21 percent are in my camp.

I'm not sure what to make of this. Perhaps it's the *intention* people approve of. The *idea* that the ad is real is encouraging. It does feel like a step in the right direction. Still, I don't expect the entire advertising industry to join this movement. After all, their job is to make products and services look as alluring as possible. If that means firing up Photoshop, my guess is, they're going to do it.

While advertising may not influence the values of society, it certainly influences people (and I'm not certain there's a big difference). Influence is advertising's purpose. The goal is to sell. To do that, you must convince people the product or service will benefit them. You must have them believe it will make them happier or make their lives better. I speak from personal experience. Marketing has been my profession for twenty-seven years. I studied it in college. I worked in advertising agencies for thirteen years. And I've taught people how to market their own businesses for fourteen years. While I spent many years toeing the traditional advertising line, these days I approach marketing from a different perspective. The idea of persuading and influencing doesn't sit well with me. I believe if a product or service is good, people will recognize that and want to buy it. In my view, marketing's job is to generate awareness. Let people know what's available. Honestly present what a product or service can do for them. After all, if you have to work that hard to sell something, perhaps it's time to create a more inherently valuable product.

📷 Blog Snapshot

It's Time to Change the Conversation around Marketing

When it comes to being marketed and sold to, how do you feel about being . . .

- persuaded?
- influenced?
- seduced?
- manipulated?

Probably not too good, huh?

No one wants to feel controlled by a marketer, and that's exactly what those words imply. No one wants to be led down a slippery slope of marketing copy into making a purchase, yet that's often how business owners and marketers are taught to write.

Why, as business owners, do we succumb to creating marketing that does those things? After all, if you look at marketing and much of the traditional wisdom about how to do it, those are the words used. You're taught how to do these things to your prospects and clients, even if we don't want these things done to us.

Whatever happened to the golden rule? It got sacrificed on the way to the bank.

There's a popular book titled *Influence: The Psychology of Persuasion*, by Robert Cialdini. Many experts in the marketing industry view it as the marketer's bible. As a marketer myself, I bought into that idea and purchased the book, but I never could get through it. It still sits on my shelf with the bookmark on page forty-seven. Even though I've been a marketer for over twenty-five years, I'm uncomfortable with the idea of persuading people to buy.

But, of course, marketing was invented to make people want to buy. I have a degree in advertising and marketing and spent the first part of my career working in advertising agencies, and the root of the conversation was always what will get them to buy. Heck, really good marketing can get you to buy something you didn't even know you wanted!

Why? Because it uses psychology and manipulation tactics to create desire. It often makes us feel as though we're not good enough if we don't have whatever they're selling. I know I've fallen victim to this, and you may have too. After all, it's at the root of the materialistic society we live in and the "keeping up with the Joneses" mentality I believe is at least partly responsible for the mortgage industry crisis and maybe even the economic crisis.

Is anyone else seeing a problem here?

I believe the role marketing plays in society is changing. At least I'm on a mission to change it, and I hope you'll join me. I believe marketing today, especially for service professionals, is about creating connection and resonance. As a business owner or marketer, if you make that your goal, people will not be tricked into buying your products and services. They will not be led down a slippery slope. They will be getting the information they need to make informed decisions.

How do you create connection and resonance? By being in touch with your purpose and the message you're here to share. By truly understanding how your product or service fits into someone's life and makes it better. By understanding your ideal clients and what their struggles are so you can create products and services that address those struggles. By respecting people, truly caring and wanting to help, and speaking and marketing from your heart.

Do you see it's not about selling stuff? It's about SERVICE.

Look, I'm not against making money or making a living. I teach people how to do both. I just do it from a little bit of a different perspective. Because I've found that when you come from three places—connection, resonance, and service—it not only works better, it feels better.

Source: www.DebbieLaChusa.com/blog

What You See Is What You Get . . . or Is It?

"Reality is merely an illusion, albeit a very persistent one."

~Albert Einstein, physicist

As someone who pays a lot of attention to advertising, I see a direct correlation between the messages we are exposed to daily and our obsession with self-improvement. I see a connection between the dissatisfaction with the realities of life and an attachment to fantasies. Every day the fantasy is right there—on television, on the Internet, in magazines—beckoning us. Making us believe it can be our reality. I'm not saying these products and services can't make our lives better; in some cases they can. The problem is when we expect to measure up to the retouched fantasy that is being marketed. In most cases that simply is not possible because it's not real.

My daughter loves to watch the reality TV show *America's Next Top Model*. Nowhere else is it more apparent how much lighting, professional styling, hair, makeup, and retouching alter reality. Some of these young women are not all that attractive without all of these enhancements. I was watching one episode with my daughter and commented to her about one contestant who was quite lanky and awkward looking. My daughter's response was, "Yeah, but you should see her photos. They're beautiful." The challenge is, young girls see these beautiful photos in magazines and want to look like them. Yet in real life the model herself doesn't even look like the photos.

In his book, *SHAM*, Salerno refers to a book written by former *Ladies Home Journal* editor Myrna Blyth entitled *Spin Sisters: How the Women of the Media Sell Unhappiness—and Liberalism—to the Women of America*. Blyth was editor-in-chief and publishing director of *Ladies Home Journal* for more than twenty years. Salerno writes that Blyth "repents for her own role in an industry that was supposed to help women grow but instead wreaked incalculable harm on the psyches of its devoted followers. What women's magazines mostly have done, argues Blyth, is create and implant worry, guilt, insecurity, inadequacy, and narcissism that did not exist before the magazines came along."

I don't think we can ignore the impact of advertising on our obsession with self-improvement. Advertising promotes products—from toothpaste and makeup to laundry detergent and luxury cars—and paints a picture of how our lives will be better with them. It can make us want things we didn't know we wanted. Ever been watching TV and see a commercial for a Dairy Queen Blizzard and suddenly want one? Or find yourself hankering for a Subway sandwich after seeing them advertised on TV all week? That's the purpose of advertising, to entice you to buy. Where reality TV may indirectly influence our behavior and how we view the world, advertising seeks to directly influence us. In both cases, we are most certainly being influenced.

Hollywood

"Celebrities are nowhere as rich as some people think they are."

~Robin Leach, host of Lifestyles of the Rich and Famous

I'm standing in line at the grocery store, waiting to check out. Beautiful faces stare back at me from the magazine rack. The faces of Hollywood celebrities next to sensational headlines announcing the details of their love lives, diets, exotic vacations, weddings, infidelities, divorces, children . . . it seems nothing is off-limits. Tune in to TV shows like *Entertainment Tonight, The Insider,* or *TMZ* and you get a sneak peek into the personal lives of celebrities. You can even follow your favorite star's every move on Twitter. And millions of people do. Some of the most popular Twitter celebrities (as of this writing) include Lady Gaga (17.4 million followers),

Justin Bieber (15.8 million), and Ashton Kutcher (8.9 million). Reality star Kim Kardashian has been paid as much as $10,000 to tweet about products she loves to her 12.1 million followers.

As a society, we are enamored with celebrities. Their glamorous lifestyles are on display in magazines such as *People, OK!*, and *Us Weekly*. Unlike publications such as *Entertainment Weekly* that focus on the business of Hollywood, these magazines shine a spotlight on the personal lives of Hollywood celebrities—where they live, who they hang out with, what they do in their free time, the clothes they wear. Hollywood celebrities appear to "have it all" and live "the sweet life." It's hard not to feel a bit jealous or want a little bit of what they have. But is it all it appears to be? Is it real? I would argue that celebrities, and their highly paid publicists, are the ultimate spin-doctors. We see what they want us to see, to ensure their continued fame and fortune. It's a business. Yet one has to wonder how this infatuation with celebrity life affects our lives.

Plastic Surgery

> "I wish I had a twin, so I could know what I'd look like
> without plastic surgery."
>
> ~Joan Rivers, comedienne

I see photos of Demi Moore, who is exactly one year younger than I am—to the day—and I'm amazed at how young and beautiful she looks. While the years have been kind to me and I think I look pretty good for my age, it's still hard not to compare and feel a little twinge of envy. I quickly remind myself she's probably had a little help. Demi admits she's had work done, although she says none of it has been to her face. Plastic surgery experts speculate that, while she may not have had any surgical procedures performed, she has likely indulged in nonsurgical remedies such as Botox, fillers such as Restylane and Juvederm, and laser skin resurfacing. While we may never know the truth, there is no denying that Moore looks years younger than her age.

I suppose when people make their living on television and in movies, in a society obsessed with youth and good looks, it's hard to blame them for wanting to look young and beautiful. It's their livelihood. But what impact does this have on us "regular folk" who don't make our living in front of a camera? According to the American Society of Aesthetic Plastic Surgery, since 1997 there has been a 155% increase in the total number of cosmetic procedures. In 2010 Americans spent nearly $10.7 billion on cosmetic procedures. Do we believe looking younger or more beautiful will make us happier?

Consider Heidi Montag, the infamous reality TV star who in 2009 underwent ten cosmetic procedures in one day. In a 2011 interview for *The Daily Beast*, Montag said, "I would go back and not have any surgery. It doesn't help. I got too caught up in Hollywood, being so into myself and my image. I don't regret anything, but if I could go back, I wouldn't do it."

One gets the impression she too was chasing an idealized version of success—in her case, in the form of beauty. Perhaps Montag believed if she achieved it, she would be more successful and happy. It clearly did not turn out that way. Instead she suffers daily pain and her career appears to have long since peaked. As with every point I have made so far in this book, I'm not saying plastic surgery is good or bad. My goal is merely to encourage us all to step back and think about what we are doing and why. And to ensure we do not expect all of these external things to bring us happiness. If we are not happy with ourselves, plastic surgery may provide a temporary lift (pun intended), but my guess is, long-term, it's not going to change much. At least be willing to ask yourself the tough questions before you start mortgaging your future happiness.

Fall from Grace

"Just like real stars, there is an expiration date for every celebrity out there."

~*Popcrunch.com*

While we admire the success of celebrities, we all too often also witness their falls from grace. It's further evidence their lives may not be as happy as they look. From alcoholism, drug addiction, and mental breakdowns to jail sentences, rehab, and suicide, they struggle with the same challenges many of us face—perhaps more. Yet for celebrities, these challenges often are magnified under the microscope of publicity. We need to be careful about putting celebrities on pedestals, worshipping them, and assuming their lives are perfect. No one's life is perfect, whether they have millions of dollars or not.

As I was doing research for this chapter, singer-songwriter Amy Winehouse was discovered dead in her London apartment. Just twenty-seven years old when she died, Winehouse struggled with substance abuse for years despite considerable talent, critical acclaim, a successful career, and millions of fans. Winehouse suffered from depression and admitted using alcohol heavily. Sadly, Winehouse's death is not an isolated incident.

The 27 Club represents all of the musicians who have died at the age of twenty-seven. According to some sources it has fifty members, including such well-known music icons as Jimi Hendrix, Janis Joplin, Jim Morrison, Kurt Cobain, and now Amy Winehouse. While some may chalk up these early deaths to the "rock and roll lifestyle," which often includes drugs and alcohol, I think it's important to recognize that many of these artists allegedly had it all. They had fame. They had fortune. They were what many of us would define as truly successful. Yet one has to wonder how happy they were if they chose to escape reality through drugs, alcohol, and, in some cases, suicide.

Olympic Suicide

"Suicide is a permanent solution to a temporary problem."

~Phil Donahue, former talk show host

In July 2011 at age twenty-nine, freestyle aerialist and 2010 Olympic silver medalist Jeret Peterson shot and killed himself. He was facing drunk driving charges and actually called 911 to report he was about to commit suicide. According to *People* magazine, Peterson ". . . had long fought depression, gambling and alcoholism, and once told *Men's Journal,* 'Things have been going wrong for me since the day I was born.'"

According to Yahoo Sports, Peterson is not the first Olympic athlete to commit suicide. Yahoo cites three others: twenty-nine-year-old 2004 silver medalist in Judo, Claudia Heill; forty-two-year-old runner and 2000 gold medalist, Antonio Pettigrew; and twenty-seven-year-old marathon runner and 1964 bronze medalist, Kokichi Tsuburaya. A fourth, twenty-four-year-old Kenyan runner and 2008 gold medalist, Samuel Wanjiru, may or may not have committed suicide; the details surrounding his death are still a bit of a mystery. Then there are the highly publicized falls from grace of other Olympic athletes. Most notable were Michael Phelps, who was caught smoking marijuana in 2009 (in addition to his previous DUI arrest after the 2004 Olympics), and 1994 gold medalist Oksana Baiul, who suffered a drunk driving accident and entered an alcohol rehabilitation program in 1997.

Are the pressures of being an Olympian too much for these athletes to deal with? According to ABC News, "psychological experts say the common thread to these examples may be a reaction to the stress of victory on the international stage—and the new pressures of dealing with their extraordinary achievements." Dr. David Spiegel, associate chair of psychiatry and behavioral sciences at Stanford University, says this behavior among athletes who have reached the pinnacle of success is not unusual: "The stress of this publicity can be overwhelming. It's an extreme amount of attention and press."

Whether the stress brought on the problems or merely magnified what was already there is somewhat irrelevant for this book. The story here is, despite reaching the epitome of success and achieving fame and fortune, the behavior of many celebrities does not indicate happiness. We ought to pay attention to this if we believe money and success are going to pave our road to happiness.

Success Redefined

"My definition of success is to live your life in a way that causes you to feel a ton of pleasure and very little pain."

~Tony Robbins, author and motivational speaker

I do believe the cult of success exists. As a society, we have a preoccupation with success that I believe is at least partly driven by the media, advertising, and Hollywood. But we can "just say no." I don't mean to say no to success in general. Rather, I believe we can put it into a healthier perspective. We can be happy where we are and still seek to learn, grow, and improve. We can stop comparing ourselves to other people, whether they are people we know, experts or gurus we admire, or people we see in the media. We can stop trying to be like others, assuming they are happier when we don't know if that's actually true.

I believed ever-increasing levels of success would translate into ever-increasing levels of happiness. I was wrong. I was so preoccupied with achieving success that it ultimately brought me pain and frustration.

Times Are Changing

"Change brings opportunity."

~Nido Qubein, author, speaker, educator

The good news is, while my research shows most of us are still pre-occupied with success, how we define that success appears to be changing. It appears that many people have spent a lot of time and energy to acquire material possessions and levels of achievement they thought would make them successful, only to realize they still weren't happy. Something was still missing. As a result, I believe many people are stepping back and re-evaluating their definitions of success. In my research for this book, I discovered that, while most people at one time admit they defined success by money, achievement, and material possessions, today their definitions of success are quite personal and varied. There appears to be a trend away from defining success materialistically and toward defining it more holistically.

Terry, a forty-eight-year-old information marketer from Arizona, has realized that having a bunch of money isn't success. "I know enough people that have a lot of money that don't really have a lot of friends," he says. "And I know people that have enough money to get by that seem happier." Terry believes what it really comes down to is financial security. "It's not having a lot of money. It's having enough money to do what you need to get done." He also believes that success is learned. "It means that you've learned how to be happy with who you are."

Here are some of the other responses I received when I asked people, "How do you define success?"

"Having more disposable income."

❦

"Never having to say, 'I can't afford it.'"

❦

"Reaching my full potential intellectually and doing work that makes a difference."

❦

"Being good at something and being known for it and probably creating an income from it."

❦

"Doing good for myself and other people."

❦

"Achieving goals and setting a standard."

❦

"Being able to reach into my pocket and not have to worry where the next dollar is coming from."

❦

"Not working for anyone else but myself."

❦

"Having an abundance of what's important to me."

❦

"Living my life to the fullest."

❦

"Using the skills and experiences and the gifts I have for the benefit of others and being able to make a positive impact."

❧

"Doing what I want to do when I want to do it."

❧

"Being at a point in your life where you are happy with how things are, not worrying too much about what could have been, should have been, and knowing that the time you have is spent wisely with the people you love."

❧

"Having time and money."

❧

"Climbing the corporate ladder . . . working to the best of your abilities."

❧

"Feeling good about myself and what I'm doing. Having more freedom to actually do the things I want to do."

"Taking that next step in your career, even if it's scary."

"Satisfaction you have accomplished what you set out to do."

"Being able to respond rather than react."

"Seizing every moment of every day to the best of my potential."

Perhaps one of my favorite definitions of success comes from Michael Angier, who runs a company called SuccessNet.org and has been working in the success industry for thirty-five years. Michael wrote the following definition of success more than twenty years ago: "A successful day: to learn something new; to laugh at least ten times; to lift someone up; to make progress on a worthy goal; to practice peace and patience; to do something nice for yourself and another; to appreciate and be grateful for all your blessings." Perhaps we can all adopt this definition of success. I know it would change my life. How might it change yours?

Spellbound

1. Is your constant pursuit of success or happiness negatively affecting your financial status?

2. Do you find yourself consistently attending success conferences, looking for "the one thing" that will finally enable you to be successful?

3. Are you addicted to the energy of live events, continually going back to get motivated and re-energized?

4. Do you put the gurus and experts you seek advice from on a pedestal?

5. Do you find yourself looking at celebrities or reality TV stars' lives and wishing you were as rich or famous as they are?

6. Do you find you're never quite satisfied with your home, your clothing, your looks, your car, or other aspects of yourself or your life?

7. Do you view life as a competition you're always seeking to win?

8. Are you easily influenced by marketing and advertising, often buying things you don't really need or spending money you don't have?

9. Do you spend a lot of time watching reality TV shows or entertainment news shows or reading beauty magazines and feeling like you or your life don't measure up to what you see represented?

10. Do you find yourself secretly wishing your life could be more like the rich and famous people you see on television?

Breaking the Spell

1. If you're going to invest in self-improvement, live within your means and use money you already have. Resist going into debt to finance more success or happiness.

2. Stop attending success conferences until you implement what you have already learned. Choose conferences strategically based on your life or business plan.

3. Recognize that the energy you experience at success conferences is purposely simulated by the conference promoters. The events are designed to keep you coming back to "fill up." Instead, find ways to get energized by real life.

4. Recognize those gurus and experts are people just like you. Instead of putting them on a pedestal, appreciate their strengths and know they have weaknesses, too.

5. Recognize that reality TV does not reflect the life of the average person. Its storylines and characters are created. Embrace your life; it's the only life that truly counts anyway.

6. Be happy and grateful for all you have. Appreciation is the quickest way to shift your attitude.

7. Recognize in most cases there can only be one winner, and that means others have to lose. Find ways to celebrate the daily wins in your life, especially those that don't make someone else a loser.

8. Recognize marketing and advertising are designed to influence you. Have realistic expectations. Do your research. Think before you buy.

9. Unplug from all the reality TV and entertainment news if it's making you feel "less than." Tune in to media that make you feel good about yourself and your life. There are plenty of choices out there!

10. Recognize the rich and famous may not always have the perfect, happy lives that are portrayed in the media. Stop focusing on them and what they have. Instead, focus on yourself and do something every day that makes you feel good.

CHAPTER 4

YOU CAN BE, DO, OR HAVE ANYTHING

"The will to win, the desire to succeed, the urge to reach your full potential . . . these are the keys that will unlock the door to personal excellence."

~Confucius, philosopher

"Double your income, double your time off." Those were the words that hooked me. The year was 2003, and I was sitting in one of my first success seminars. I had already spent an entire day learning how changing my mindset would change my life. I had learned about something called a money thermostat and how it was responsible for holding me to a set level of income, just like a thermostat regulates the temperature in a room. Who knew *I* had a thermostat? I'd even been taught I needed to make sure my cup was big enough to hold the ever-expanding me (success-wise not waistline-wise).

I was fascinated. I had never heard anything like this before. And, while I was already running a successful six-figure business, the idea of doubling it and working half as much was too enticing to resist. After all, my business was a full-time job. Who wouldn't want to work less and earn more? It was an irresistible offer, one of many that would follow in the years to come. It should have been a giant red flag, because ultimately it failed to produce the promised results. But it wasn't. Instead, I became a raving fan.

Raving Fans

"Just having satisfied customers isn't good enough anymore. If you really want a booming business, you have to create Raving Fans."

~Ken Blanchard, in his book Raving Fans

How does a business create satisfied customers or go one step further, as Ken Blanchard advocates, and create raving fans? It's been years since I read *Raving Fans*, and it's no longer on my bookshelf, but I'm going to imagine it involves things like providing great customer service and exceeding client expectations. How then is it possible that a smart, successful, college-educated person can invest thousands of dollars, not experience the promised results, and still become a raving fan? That's exactly what I wanted to know.

It's not that I didn't accomplish a lot through the "double your income, double your time off" coaching program. Quite the contrary. I started a new business, created a new income stream, learned about Internet marketing, and became aware of—and broke through—some of my limiting beliefs. I was very happy with all of these outcomes. At the end of the program, I had definitely made progress toward my goals, but I did not come anywhere close to doubling my income or doubling my time off. In fact, I was working more hours, because I now had two businesses to run. While I hadn't achieved the promised results, I felt good about where I was, or perhaps it's more accurate to say I felt good about where I was *heading*.

While in that coaching program, I also attended seminars nearly every month that introduced me to a variety of business- and wealth-building strategies. It turns out there was an entire world of ways to make money I didn't even know existed. I learned about business opportunities such as owning vending machines and self-storage lots (these were promoted as great passive income businesses); real estate investing, including flipping, lease-options, and buy-and-hold; investing in tax liens and trust deeds; online FOREX trading (foreign currency exchange); and even investing in oil wells. I did not invest in most of them (thankfully!), but I did test the waters in a few. After all, those who were selling these opportunities made them sound simple—like something anyone could do. And I had learned if I wanted to achieve financial freedom, I needed to find ways for my money to work for me, instead of the other way around.

I was also introduced to the world of asset protection. While I appreciate the importance of protecting what you have, it's not an inexpensive proposition. It meant purchasing additional insurance policies and establishing various legal entity structures, as well as hiring an attorney and CPA who understood the ins and outs of my business dealings and investments. This was a whole new world to me. It was complicated and expensive. Even though I wasn't rich (at least in my eyes at the time), in many ways all of this made me *feel* rich. I thought to myself, "So this is how the rich get richer! They know about all these things us regular folk don't." In fact, at the seminars, we were told these opportunities simply were not available to the average person. We were lucky, because the seminar leaders were providing us access to these wealth-building secrets of the rich and famous. Oh yeah, my mindset was shifting all right!

I saw the same people at seminar after seminar. I became friends with many of them. It began to feel like a family, a family of like-minded people who shared my values. They understood my new anything-is-possible mindset and my wealth-building goals. My seminar friends and I wanted to make the most of our lives. We weren't willing to settle for the status quo. These weren't pie-in-the-sky dreamers, either. Most of the people I became friends with were smart, hard working, and already successful in their careers or businesses. Like me, they saw room for improvement. They wanted more out of life. They were willing to invest time and money and do whatever it took to become financially free.

It wasn't long until I realized that doing whatever it took was often easier said than done. In the rah-rah seminar environment, it was easy to dream big. Taking action on those dreams in the real world was another story.

While I actually did take action on much of what I was learning, I realized many people did not. They showed up at seminar after seminar, admitting their lives hadn't really changed. They still hadn't started the businesses they were dreaming of or made the life changes they had vowed to make. I didn't understand this. Why would people pay to learn how to become more successful and not implement what they had learned?

Since then I have spent seven years mentoring and coaching people myself, and I think I now understand the answer. Number one, fear. More often than not, dramatically changing your life the way most seminars and experts promise requires doing things you've never done before. You have to take risks. It's scary. While you may not be happy with your current life, it is comfortable.

Second, it's hard work. It's never as simple or easy as it sounds. Changing your lifelong habits, starting a new business, or making a million dollars aren't easy things to do. It's one thing to sit in a seminar room with five hundred to a thousand people and get caught up in the positive energy. It's another to go out into the real world and make it happen. The seminar environment is very different from the real world. Seminars are carefully designed to make you feel good. The seminar hosts play music that makes you want to get up and dance. There's a constant focus on "anything is possible." It's empowering. And, it can easily become addicting. So, instead of going back to your life and taking action, you just keep going back to more seminars to fill yourself up with motivation and feel-good mojo. But every time you leave the event bubble and go back to your life, the energy dissipates. The fears, and loss of the anything-is-possible seminar energy, can make it challenging to carry through with the actions required to change your life.

Oversimplification

"Your wish is my command."

~from the movie, The Secret

The 2006 movie *The Secret* introduced millions of people to something called the Law of Attraction. The Law of Attraction says that if we want to attract things (e.g., money and success) into our lives, we need only to change our thoughts and focus on those things, and the universe will respond by bringing them to us. In the movie, self-help guru James Arthur Ray compares the Law of Attraction to the story of Aladdin's lamp. When Aladdin rubs his lamp, out pops a genie who says, "Your wish is my command." Ray contends that the genie represents the universe. If we want something, we simply need to ask for it—as Aladdin did with his three wishes—and the universe will bring it to us. Ray adds that, in reality, we are not limited to three wishes—we can have whatever we want.

I'm not going to debate the message in *The Secret* or the validity of the Law of Attraction. I think both have their merits. But I think the movie oversimplified the concept and set up a lot of people for disappointment. It takes a lot more than just thinking about something to make it happen. While Ray's analogy made for an entertaining story (and quite a powerful story as well, based on the popularity of *The Secret* and the Law of Attraction), we can't overlook the fact that the story of Aladdin is just a fairytale.

The self-improvement industry promises us we can be, do, or have anything, very often oversimplifying what it takes to do so. It offers an ever-growing library of books, videos, audios, information products, training programs, mentors, coaches, and experts that promise to show us the way. We're taught the path to happiness and success is through the pursuit of personal growth, financial freedom, and spiritual enlightenment. We're led to believe when we *have* these things we will *be* happy. So we seek out advice and experts who will tell us exactly what we need to do to achieve these goals. Collectively we spend millions of dollars a year in this pursuit. Is it delivering us to the place we dream of? Is it resulting in success, financial freedom, spiritual enlightenment, and happiness?

As I have shared, in my case, despite spending hundreds of thousands of dollars, it was an elusive quest. No matter what I achieved, it was never enough to make me happy or make me feel as though I had finally gotten "there." Instead, I just kept wanting more. This begs the questions: Is the self-help industry helping people improve their lives, or is it setting them up for disappointment? Does self-help really work? Can we really be, do, or have anything? Let's take a closer look and find out.

How It All Began

> *"Until the advent of modern self-help . . . writers usually saw themselves as mere conduits of information, not experts in their own right."*
>
> ~*Steven Salerno, in his book* SHAM

The self-help industry was born some two or three hundred years ago. Some consider Benjamin Franklin's *Poor Richard's Almanac*, written in 1732, to be the first self-help book, because it included proverbs such as "Would you live with ease, do what you ought, and not what you please" and "What one relishes, nourishes." In 1859 Samuel Smiles published what others consider the first true self-improvement book, aptly titled *Self-Help*. In the twentieth century came the publication of several self-help books that are still considered mainstays in the industry today, including *How to Win Friends and Influence People*, written by Dale Carnegie in 1936; Napoleon Hill's 1937 classic, *Think and Grow Rich*; and *The Power of Positive Thinking*, written by Norman Vincent Peale in 1952. According to Salerno in his book, *SHAM: How the Self-Help Movement Made America Helpless*, these books set the tone for the industry until 1967, when the book *I'm OK—You're OK* was published. This book marked a shift in the industry that saw writers going from being conduits of information to taking on guru status. Salerno describes this shift as "the rise of the guru, the transformation from simple advice giver to cultural and motivational soothsayer."

He also suggests *I'm OK—You're OK* transformed self-help in three ways: (1) it validated the viability of self-help publishing as a genre, (2) it took the psychological focus off the individual and placed it on how individuals are shaped by relationships, and (3) it introduced the idea that most people are not OK. According to Salerno, this opened up a world of victimization that dominated the self-help industry for the next quarter century. The victimization movement eventually gave way to the empowerment movement that is the cornerstone of the self-help industry and the "be more, do more, have more" world we live in today.

Salerno, an investigative journalist by trade, represents an extreme opinion in the self-help industry—he describes it as a sham. In the introduction to his book, he writes, "Never have I covered a phenomenon where American consumers invested so much capital in every sense of the word—financial, intellectual, spiritual, temporal—based on so little proof of efficacy. And where they got such spotty, if not nonexistent, returns." In the rest of the book he makes the case that the industry has caused more harm than good. It's a compelling argument. Yet as someone who has both benefited from and been disappointed by the self-help industry, I think it's unfair to define the entire industry as good or bad—it's simply not that black and white. It's a complex industry, and its many facets warrant a closer look.

The Evolution of Self-Help

"All change is not growth, as all movement is not forward."

~*Ellen Glasgow, novelist*

The self-help industry started quite humbly, with a few books sharing words of wisdom. In the last few hundred years it has grown way beyond books. The industry now includes motivational speakers, seminars, training programs, coaching, and infomercials. Along with the advent of all these methods of delivering help we have seen the growth of bigger and bigger promises and the introduction of the expert and self-help guru.

We also have seen the growth of one aspect of the industry that I believe has contributed the most to the "be more, do more, have more" epidemic: information marketing. Information marketing is the packaging and selling of information, most often how-to information. It gained popularity in the mid 2000s as a way for service professionals to grow their business revenue by leveraging their time. In the book *Start Your Own Information Marketing Business*, Robert Skrob, president of the Information Marketing Association, describes the concept behind information marketing as "do the work once and get paid many times." For self-employed consultants and coaches who felt they had maximized their business revenue within the hours they had available to work, or who simply wanted to make more money while working fewer hours, information marketing was a dream come true.

I don't have a problem with the idea of information marketing. Books are a form of information marketing, and I love books. However, I believe the focus on making big money by selling what you know—or what you can compile—has led to an explosion of self-proclaimed experts who often are sharing advice and information they may not be qualified to share, or that's simply bad advice. I suppose it's one thing if it's being marketed as information designed to educate. But that's usually not the case. Many information products are sold as "proven systems" and "success blueprints." They promise big outcomes, such as making six or seven figures while working from home in your pajamas. I'm not saying the outcomes promised aren't possible. They may be. But as we very often see in the information marketing industry, the process is almost always oversimplified. The amount of work is almost always underrepresented. Marketers know people are less likely to buy something that sounds hard or complicated. So they make it sound simple and easy—like something anyone can do. And, because we want to believe it, we buy.

Personal Coaching

"It is indeed an exciting time to be a coach!"

~International Coach Academy

The coaching industry has seen tremendous growth in the last decade. Today we have coaches in every discipline imaginable, including life coaches, business coaches, sales coaches, health coaches, fitness coaches, wellness coaches, relationship coaches, spiritual coaches, executive coaches, creativity coaches, and career coaches. According to Marketdata Enterprises, a research firm that tracks growth of the self-improvement market, from 2000 to 2004 the market grew by 50 percent, and within that, personal coaching soared. In 2005 the personal coaching market was estimated to be worth $2.4 million and was projected to grow 17.5 percent per year until 2010. While the recession took its toll on the personal coaching industry, it still leveled out at a healthy $1.3 million in 2008 and 2009.

According to the International Coaching Federation (ICF), full- and part-time coaches earn an average of $50,000 per year. In a $1.3 million industry, that roughly translates into twenty-six thousand coaches. ICF alone boasts seventeen thousand members. And, because the coaching industry is unregulated and anyone can call himself or herself a coach, those figures are likely under-represented. The International Coach Academy states that, according to the U.S. Bureau of Labor Statistics, the area of consultancy and human development, of which coaching is a part, is expected to grow heavily through 2016.

In all my years as a marketing and business consultant, the majority of my clients have been coaches. It's common for people who have been laid off or downsized—something we see frequently in a recession—to turn to coaching as a new career. Coaching has also become a popular second career choice, because it's a profession that promises freedom, flexibility, and the opportunity to make a difference in the lives of others (something many people appear to be seeking in their second careers). And, because the barriers to entry are low—there's no industry regulation and little startup capital required—it's no wonder coaching has become such a popular vocation. There is no doubt in my mind that we will continue to see more and more people stepping into the coaching profession. The question is, will they all be qualified?

There's certainly no shortage of coach training programs. A Google search on coach training organizations yields 6.4 million

results and advertisements such as "Life Coach Training $397—
Become a Certified Coach in 16 hrs." Now that's a scary thought.
For an investment of $400 and two days, a person can be certified
to advise others on vitally important life decisions. While organizations such as ICF are working to establish professional standards in
the industry, the fact remains no form of certification or licensure
is currently required. Nor are there any standards that certification or licensing programs need to meet.

The coaching industry has the potential to help many people.
But unqualified coaches also have the potential to harm people.
Bad advice can be expensive in more ways than just monetarily.
It can impact your business, your relationships, your health, and
your self-esteem. As consumers, we need to be careful that the
coaches we're considering hiring are indeed qualified to be doing
the work they're doing. Just as we might when hiring an employee,
plumber, or any other person we're paying to do a job, we need to
check qualifications and ask for references (and not just rely on
the testimonials we see in a coach's marketing).

Explosion of Experts

"Who's to say who's an expert?"

~Paul Newman, actor

There's a phrase I've heard repeatedly over the years: to become
an expert in something, you simply need to proclaim yourself one.
I even shared this advice several years ago, writing the following
in an article: "Remember, all it takes to become an expert is to
appoint yourself THE expert." I shudder to think I once wrote
that, because I fear too many people without established expertise have taken it literally. I know my expectation when I wrote
it was that most people have expertise in something; they're just

shy about claiming it. I would never want someone to proclaim himself or herself an expert in something he or she did not have vast knowledge and deep experience in. I consider these things obvious prerequisites.

Yet there are people who believe that as long as you know just a little bit more than the people you're promising to help—as long as you're at least one step ahead of them on their journey—then you're an expert in their eyes. I disagree. Knowing just a little bit more than someone else does not make you an expert. It makes you someone who knows just a little bit more. The dictionary defines an expert as a person who has special skill or knowledge in some particular field, a specialist, or an authority. Knowing just a little bit more than someone else about something hardly makes you an authority on the topic. There's nothing wrong with wanting to help people from a place of knowing just a little bit more, as long as that's how you're positioning yourself. Unfortunately, that's often not the case in today's self-help industry. Too many people who are eager to build coaching practices and million-dollar information-marketing businesses are presenting themselves as experts when they are not.

📷 **Blog Snapshot**

Faux Experts

A few days ago I became aware of someone offering a program very similar to one I recently launched. Their sales page included some of the same copy and stock photos I had used to promote my program. The program outline was very similar, and the language used to describe the program was the same language I use.

In looking further, I discovered this program appears to be outside this person's core expertise (based on reading about their experience and looking at their websites and other services).

Obviously, it didn't sit well with me. I suppose it could be a coincidence. After all, there is the notion that there are no new ideas. Although, when I posted a description of this situation on my Facebook page along with the question "Copy or coincidence?" the consensus was overwhelming: copy!

I've been copied before. A few years ago a program and sales page of mine were copied almost verbatim. So, while I want to give people the benefit of the doubt, this latest experience prompted me to step back and consider what may be going on.

Tough times often bring out the worst in people. Good people in bad situations may not always make the best decisions. The economy has been tough on a lot of people in the past few years, and many are reaching to find a way to support themselves or sustain a business they started that may have fallen off. They may be looking for the magic formula or a product or service to resurrect their business. Perhaps they see someone else doing something that looks promising, so they decide to model it. Because it's outside their primary area of expertise, they model a little too closely and end up copying.

While I feel for anyone who is struggling in business, this is not the way out of struggles and into success.

Following Blanket Advice

Something else that may be contributing to this . . . over the past few years there's been some fairly common advice given out by mentors and coaches that says to be an expert you just have to proclaim yourself one. As long as you know just a little bit more than the people you're advising, you're fine; you don't have to know everything.

While I agree with the last part, because it's impossible for anyone to know everything (and as long as you admit what you don't know, that's fair), I think this blanket advice can be dangerous. It has the potential to give license to unqualified people and have them believing it's OK to portray themselves as experts, even when they're not.

In fact, a friend told me of a well-known mentor who was teaching his clients to claim expertise they clearly didn't have. While, for the most part, I want to believe this kind of outright lack of integrity is not the norm, even the most well-intentioned advice given a bit too carelessly can lead to problems.

Combining blanket advice promoting that *anyone* can be an expert, along with the idea that *anyone* can start a business as a coach or mentor, has created a problem in the personal development industry. There are too many people selling services outside their true areas of expertise.

That may sound harsh, but I believe it needs to be said. I believe it's time to clean house. It's time for a shakeout in the industry. Just as the bubble burst in the real estate industry after everyone and anyone was led to believe they could make a mint as real estate investors, and speculation over-inflated the market to a point that was not sustainable, I believe the same point has been reached in the personal development industry.

When the economy is strong and people are spending money freely, it's easy for an industry to get inflated. It's easy for anyone to think, "Hey I can jump in and make money doing this!" And when they're being encouraged to do exactly that by mentors making a small fortune by training people to sell their expertise, it can get out of control.

I believe that's where we are. A personal development industry bloated with too many experts who are not, information products without substance, and systems and blueprints based on unproven processes. It's been far too easy to proclaim yourself an expert and whip out an information product based on a system you've done once and sell it to people hungry for shortcuts to success.

Time for the Bubble to Burst

There are many qualified experts who are doing a great job, and we need these people to help us grow and learn. Unfortunately, there also are many people who are not qualified to be selling the advice they're selling.

I spoke to a woman one day on a free consultation. She was seeking my help for her struggling business. On the web and social media she looked to be *very* successful. Her business was based on teaching people how to create success, joy, and abundance in their lives. To my surprise, her business was anything but successful or abundant. She was barely making a few hundred dollars a month and was struggling to get clients. I felt for her. Her heart was in the right place. She wanted to help people, but *she* needed help. In my opinion, she had no right offering to teach others how to be successful when she couldn't even do it for herself. And there are others like her out there.

What's the cliché? Those who can't do, teach? Maybe that's what this is about. If you can't make a living doing it, maybe you can make a living teaching others how to do it. But if you can't do it yourself, how does that qualify you to teach others? You may have studied something or taken a how-to course or created a system, but if you haven't proved that what you're teaching works consistently and repeatedly, you have no business teaching it.

Claim Your Expertise Carefully

Before you think I'm poo-pooing the entire personal development industry and all experts, I'm not. However, I think self-help experts need to claim their expertise carefully. While I view myself as an expert (and I don't really like the term "expert") in marketing and branding (I have twenty-plus years of experience in both), I would never claim to be an expert in social media or Internet marketing. Do I know a few things about both? Yes, but I'm no expert, and I'll be the first to tell you that.

If we all took this approach, what a difference it would make. It certainly takes the pressure off. You don't have to be good at everything. It's also the best way to carve out a niche and build a brand.

If you're a coach or other self-help expert, I encourage you to look at your unique collection of life and professional experience, training, education, and talents. What does it uniquely qualify you to do? What do you have a solid track record in? What can you promise and deliver on? There *is* something. And that is what you should be packaging, branding, and putting out into the world.

It's not about copying what someone else is doing. It's not about going to one course and deciding to make that your area of expertise. It's not about letting a coach or mentor talk you into building your business around something just because it worked for him or her. (If it doesn't *fit* you, it won't work for you.) It's about honestly owning *your* expertise.

Buyer Beware

Because it's an unregulated industry, it's up to us as the buyers of self-help and coaching to investigate those we're looking to for advice and make sure they're actually qualified to help us.

I've done a lot of things in my life, admittedly some quite successfully. I think I've raised two pretty good kids. I've completed several marathons. But I would *never* pretend to be an expert in those areas just because I've done it myself. I don't have training, education, or experience helping others be successful in those endeavors.

My business is based on what I studied in college, what I had a successful thirteen-year corporate career doing, and what I have done successfully on my own for another fourteen years. I also have invested consistently in continuing my education to stay current, and I have practical experience doing what I do, over and over, in my business and for many clients. I would never even think of trying to build a business around anything less.

Yes, I had to start somewhere. But even when I started my first business, it was in an area I had expertise in and had practiced in the real world for thirteen years prior.

What if you're starting a new career? Build it based around your expertise, education, career and life experience, and what you can truly serve people with. Make sure you're practicing what you preach. Start small or in an area you know. After your expertise and experience expand, expand your business. But only *after.*

There are two ways we can weed out the faux experts. First, by only claiming expertise we deserve to claim and building our businesses, products, and services around that. Second, by making sure the people we're thinking of buying from, or the people we're considering hiring as mentors or coaches, are truly qualified.

Source: www.DebbieLaChusa.com/blog

Welcome to Gurudom

"One does not become a guru by accident."

~James Fenton, poet

The explosion of experts has led to another phenomenon in the self-help industry: the birth of the guru. Once a title reserved for religious teachers and spiritual guides, we now see the term "guru" liberally applied to experts in just about every field. Gurus are like experts on steroids. We tend to view and treat them like celebrities. We are willing to hand over thousands of dollars for the privilege of being in their presence and learning their secrets to success. Gurus have gone from being mere teachers to being larger than life. Case in point: a few years ago I attended a seminar, and the host actually had bodyguards escorting him to and from the stage. Yes, bodyguards! Mind you, this was a seminar, not a rock concert, and he was a teacher, not a rock star.

I once heard a speaker say, "I don't want to be a sage on the stage, I want to be a guide by your side." I believe that should be the premise the self-help industry is built on. I don't think we should turn our teachers into celebrities or place them on pedestals. As soon as we do, it clouds our judgment.

In October 2009 three people died and eighteen others were injured in connection with a sweat lodge ceremony at James Arthur Ray's Spiritual Warrior seminar in Sedona, Arizona. Just three years earlier Ray had risen to guru status after being featured in the movie *The Secret*. He had become known as the "Rock Star of Personal Transformation," a title he apparently also used himself. By 2009 attendees were paying as much as $10,000 each to participate in Ray's five-day Spiritual Warrior program—a program designed to push them beyond their physical and emotional limits. According to CBS News:

Ray used the sweat lodge as a way for participants to break through whatever was holding them back in life. He warned participants in a recording of the event played during the trial that the sweat lodge would be "hellacious" and that participants were guaranteed to feel like they were dying but would do so only metaphorically. "The true spiritual warrior has conquered death and therefore has no fear or enemies in this lifetime or the next, because the greatest fear you'll ever experience is the fear of what? Death," Ray said in the recording. "You will have to get to a point to where you surrender and it's OK to die."

Three people actually did die, and in 2011 Ray was convicted of negligent homicide and sentenced to two years in prison. A cousin and spokesman for one of the sweat lodge victims said he feared "Ray exhibited a 'godlike complex' during the event that might have kept people from opting out of activities that Ray acknowledged could cause 'physical, emotional, financial, or other injuries.'"

In her book *Tragedy in Sedona: My Life in James Arthur Ray's Inner Circle,* Connie Joy, a former Ray follower, shares the changes she saw in Ray after he appeared in *The Secret* and on *Oprah* and *Larry King Live.* She referred to Ray prior to this fame as "the old James" and described him as friendly, very approachable, and interested in how people were doing. She said the "new James" became more and more distant and hired bodyguards to keep people away. His tough love approach turned into "more tough than love."

Joy describes Ray as having a god-like complex, sharing that in one exercise he even wore a white robe and ordered people to die—fall on the floor and stay there until he told them they could get up. She said in an interview that some people lay on the concrete floor for hours, even missing meals. In the same interview, Joy said the people attending the seminars were not cult followers. They were smart, successful people just trying to improve their lives. While she says she learned much from Ray's teachings, she cautions people not to mix up the messenger with the message. Joy also claims Ray used techniques such as neurolinguistic programming and stage hypnosis at his events—which attendees were not aware of—to get people to buy more products.

Joy shares the following words of warning to those following self-help gurus: "You have to be your own guru. Just because they say they're spiritual or religious you can't let your guard down. If you're giving them money, you're a consumer. They're selling something and you have to be a conscious consumer."

Gurus can be very influential. Guru worship can result in people following advice that goes against their own better judgment. I speak from personal experience. I have participated in a sweat lodge (mine was actually run by Native Americans, an important distinction in my opinion) and other experiential events in my pursuit of success and happiness. While I experienced profound benefits from some of these activities, I admit I did feel pressure to comply. I never considered any of the events could result in death. One has to wonder where the line is between pushing people past their limiting beliefs and pushing them too far. Ray's case may be an extreme, however I don't believe it's isolated. It's time to step back and re-evaluate the god-like status to which we have elevated many self-help teachers. Their teachings are not gospel. We must not lose ourselves in their power. They are not gurus; they are teachers. We are not followers; we are students.

Things Are Not Always What They Seem

"Appearances often are deceiving."

~Aesop, Greek writer

In the digital age, it's easier than ever to *look* like an expert. It used to be that getting a book published required a publisher. That meant if you didn't have a well-written book that shared worth-while content, your book didn't get published. Today anyone can publish a book, sell it on Amazon, and enjoy the credibility that comes with being a published author. Similarly, anyone can write and post articles online or publish a blog sharing his or her thoughts with the world. As a result, the proliferation of self-pro-claimed experts and self-published information has turned the self-help industry into a virtual free-for-all. It's becoming more and more difficult to separate the quality information and real experts from the questionable information and self-appointed experts.

In my personal quest for success I've bought more than my share of programs that didn't deliver what they promised. When you invest in a program and it doesn't work, it often leaves you looking for something else that will. And, more often than not, the experts make it clear that if the program didn't work, it's not the fault of the program, it's *you* who is flawed. Salerno writes in *SHAM*:

> Invariably, in fact, they project the blame back *on* the individual . . . . If SHAM [the self-help and actualization movement] doesn't transform your life, it's not because the program is ineffective. It's because *you're unworthy* . . . . And so you go away thinking, *well maybe the next book or seminar will do the trick. Or the next after that . . .*

Is it any wonder so many people keep investing more and more time and money, looking for answers? The *experts* keep telling us they're right around the corner!

Million-Dollar Promises

> *"My religion? Well, my dear, I am a Millionaire. That is my religion."*
>
> *~George Bernard Shaw, playwright*

While the self-help industry began innocently enough, with books promising us *How to Win Friends and Influence People* and learn *The Power of Positive Thinking*, today the promises are much loftier. We can look back at some of the classics sold by Nightingale Conant, a leader in the personal development industry since 1960, and see a marked difference from today's programs. The classics include programs from industry mavericks such as Jim Rohn, Zig Ziglar, Brian Tracy, Denis Waitley, and Napoleon Hill, with titles such as:

Cultivating an Unshakable Character
How to Have Your Best Year Ever
Seeds of Greatness
Take Charge of Your Life
The Art of Exceptional Living
The New Dynamics of Goal Setting
The Psychology of Achievement
The Psychology of Winning
The Psychology of Selling

Fast-forward to 2011 and the current programs have a very different flavor. They clearly reflect a shift from personal excellence toward success, money, and the sharing of secrets. Today's programs also make bigger promises and have more sensational titles:

Secrets of the Millionaire Mind in Turbulent Times
More Money, More Life
Channels of Profit: 12 Easy Ways to Make Millions for Yourself and Your Business
The Missing Secret
The Secret to Attracting Money
New Rules to Get Rich
Million Dollar Sales Secrets from the Masters
The Power of Passive Income: Don't Work for Money, Make Money Work for You

When the collective tone of an industry shifts from teaching people how to maximize their personal potential to selling the secrets to success and making millions, it's bound to have an effect on our culture. Especially in a society where we have been conditioned to believe fame and fortune is the way to happiness (as we discussed in chapter 3).

While it's easy to spot this change in the industry simply by looking at the programs that have been offered over the years, I have personally witnessed this shift as well. As I recently wrote in an article, I want to know the exact day and time God came down and proclaimed that unless you're making six or seven figures you're not successful. Everywhere I turn on the Internet these days is another coach or mentor promising to teach people how to make six or seven figures. They make it sound easy—just follow their three, five, or seven simple steps and anyone can do it. The problem is, it's not that easy for most people. But once the expectation is set, it's hard to let it go. Especially when we see the people peddling these six- and seven-figure systems appearing to live the good life, and especially when we want the good life too.

I've also seen a shift in the language used to market self-help programs, particularly those targeted at people seeking financial success through entrepreneurship. Before the recession hit in 2007, when the economy was booming and people were freely investing in self-help, marketing copy for these business-building programs was relatively tame. For the most part, the marketers of these programs promised to help business owners learn how to attract more clients and make more money. After the recession hit, the marketing promises got bigger. They began promising people how to do things such as . . .

"Attract more clients than you can handle"
"Keep your bank accounts full"
"Get clients to chase you"
"Make millions by making a difference"

"Imagine a full pipeline of clients who can't wait to invest with you"

This is all actual copy pulled from websites selling business-building programs and coaching. And while it may be compelling marketing copy, I have to wonder how many of the people making these promises actually have clients "chasing" them or clients who "can't wait to invest with them" (i.e., give them money). It sounds nice, but in most cases, it's not reality, it's just marketing. We need to remember that.

Having worked in the industry as a marketing and business consultant for seven years and seeing the impact of the recession on many businesses, including my own, my guess is that many marketers are making bigger promises because that's what it takes to keep making sales. If consumers are being more cautious about spending money, sales can be harder to come by. Business owners who are eager—or in some cases frantic—to continue attracting clients may feel pressure to make their programs sound irresistible or to promise to solve all of their clients' financial woes.

I don't know if that kind of marketing actually works, but there sure are a lot of marketers using it. It appears that it's no longer enough to promise someone you can help make his or her life better or business more successful, especially when others are promising the secrets to making millions. It's tough to compete with that unless your promise matches its loftiness. As a culture we have become more and more focused on money and success, and the self-help industry has kept pace, with plenty of programs that promise to deliver us both.

So, did the industry lead us to wanting more or did we lead the industry to promising more? I'm not sure. But clearly there has been a shift. A shift that has led many people—me included—on a never-ending quest that, unfortunately, far too often does not result in happiness and wealth, but in frustration and debt.

Falling for the Million-Dollar Promise

Kirsty, a thirty-six-year-old wellness coach from Australia, admits she and her husband James fell for the big promises of wealth and success. They bought into the idea that being successful meant making a million dollars and traveling the world—a picture that was painted for them by gurus selling success. Kirsty says she believed what she was told, that she needed to be rich to be successful and happy. "People try to sell you get-rich-quick schemes and tell you that you can have this and you can do anything," she says. "Anything is possible if you just put your mind to it. You're really sold a huge story, and we bought the story."

Until Kirsty and James realized that was not actually what they wanted. They looked around and realized they already had everything they wanted. They began questioning why they needed to try and get rich quick. Not that they didn't try. They did. It just didn't work out. Instead of getting rich they ended up nearly broke. At one point they had no money in the bank and didn't know how they were going to pay the rent. Still, Kirsty says getting involved in personal development has had a positive influence in their lives. But she acknowledges there is a dark side to the industry too. She cautions people to be wary. She knows how easy it is to get caught up in other people's ideas of what success should look like.

While money struggles are notorious for putting a strain on relationships, that's not the case for Kirsty and James. Their financial challenges have actually brought them closer together. As she sits outside her home in Queensland, watching the sun rise on a beautiful day, Kirsty sounds close to tears as she shares how happy she is today. She defines success very differently now. It's about having a happy family, something she is grateful she and James have. It's about enjoying what she's doing, and it's about making a difference. Kirsty and James have realized they have everything they want. They've realized they're already rich, and it doesn't have a lot to do with money.

Truth is, there are many factors that go into building a six- or seven-figure income or business (any level of business for that matter). To promise people they can accomplish it simply by reading a book or taking a course is to promise something unrealistic. I believe most people know it's not that easy. After all, if it were, we'd all already be millionaires. Yet, people continue to buy into these promises because they can be very seductive.

I also find it disturbing that some experts promising to teach people how to make six and seven figures did not make their fortunes doing what they're teaching. They made their money as information marketers. Real estate investor turned information marketer Robert Allen even boasts on his website, "It's No Secret That I Made My First Million As A Nothing Down Real Estate Investor But, I've Generated Well Over 100 Million Dollars Marketing How-To Information!"

So, while someone may be promising to help people become seven-figure coaches (in effect saying, "I'll teach you how to do what I have done so you too can become a seven-figure coach"), the reality is they may not have made seven figures from a coaching practice. They may have made their millions selling how-to information products or services such as seminars, training programs, and mastermind programs. That makes them seven-figure information marketers, not seven-figure coaches. As consumers we need to pay attention to this important distinction.

Self-made multi-millionaire and author of the book *The Millionaire Fastlane,* MJ Demarco, agrees. He suggests that much of what's being marketed as the way to make millions is false. He says the advice that's being sold by those promising secrets to financial freedom simply doesn't work. Instead he points out most of them have become rich selling their ideas, not because they practice what they preach. "The guy that tells you to stop drinking expensive coffee is worth millions. Why do you think he's worth millions? Because he stopped drinking expensive coffee? No, because he's sold ten different books ten million times. That's why he's rich, because he's impacted the lives of millions."

As DeMarco talks about the financial experts who advocate advice from clipping coupons to investing in the stock market, he says, "They're living the high life, but not because of what they're teaching." He is quick to point out the reason he wrote his book was to expose this hypocrisy. He didn't write it to make money. "I don't need the money. If I sell one book or ten thousand, it's not going to make a difference in my life."

Michael Angier has been involved in the success industry for thirty-five years and currently runs a company called SuccessNet. org. He's seen the industry grow and evolve over the years and is the first to admit he really dislikes the hype, the selling of secrets, and the idea there is just one thing people need to do to become successful. He believes that, unfortunately, there are a lot of people out there, particularly in the Internet marketing field, who will gladly take your money for information that does not work.

"Instead of utilizing the same set of skills and knowledge and strategies and tactics themselves to build their business, they're saying, 'Oh, I can teach other people how to do it,'" he says. Angier believes people buy into these promises because they're looking for a shortcut to success. They want to believe all they need is that one missing piece and that when they put that piece into place they're going to go from $50,000 a year to a million dollars a year. As Angier told me, "You and I both know that's pretty unlikely, but people still do it."

Angier believes the promise of millions alone—even if it can't be delivered on—is enough to intrigue people to invest money in these systems. He says it makes it hard for people who are teaching the basics and don't overpromise. When I ask if he thinks the charlatans (as he calls them) will eventually be shaken out of the industry, he responds, "I think some of it probably has already happened. There are a lot fewer people in the game than there used to be. And that's a good thing, because the ones who have the better track record, the ones who are operating businesses with integrity, they're the ones for the most part who have stayed in business, and they have a real dedication to it. They didn't get into it just for the money. They got into it because they really wanted to make a difference."

In my opinion, overpromising and under-delivering are far too common in the self-help industry, particularly when it comes to teaching people how to make money. The fact is, big promises sell. But, when the promises are not delivered on, it can lead to people chasing system after system, trying to find "the one" that will work. It's important to understand there is no such "one" system. I hope that at some point enough people will wake up to the fact that many of these promises aren't realistic and they'll stop buying into them. As consumers we need to demand accountability from the success experts. We need to demand that their programs live up to their promises. I believe only then will the promises come back down to earth.

JOBs Are Bad

"I have nothing against having a job, but for most people, the acronym of J.O.B., 'Just Over Broke,' is accurate."

~T. Harv Eker, author and motivational speaker

JOB = just over broke. It's a common principle taught at success seminars. After all, the success experts aren't selling jobs (there's no money in that for them), they're selling entrepreneurship and investing—independent avenues to financial freedom.

It's important to know that while some people do become very wealthy through entrepreneurship, most people don't. In fact, the real numbers are quite sobering. I recently saw research stating that 65 percent of solo professionals make less than $25,000 a year. According to the 2009 US census, the median income of self-employed workers is $47,000. According to 2008 IRS tax data, the average annual revenue per sole-proprietor non-farm business was $58,000. Just 12 percent of tax filers had an adjusted gross income of $100,000 or more (keep in mind 80 percent of households earning $100,000 or more are dual-income households). A minuscule 0.2 percent of tax filers had an adjusted gross income of $1 million or more.

It's not that it isn't possible to make six or seven figures, but unfortunately, most people don't. To lead people to believe that quitting their jobs and starting their own businesses or making risky investments will quickly turn them from cash-strapped employees to financially free millionaires is irresponsible. There's nothing wrong with entrepreneurship, investing, or striving for financial freedom, but you owe it to yourself to get the facts and know what you're getting into. Too many times the success sellers glamorize and simplify things. It can be very misleading. Yet, because they are viewed as experts people take their word at face value and shell out thousands of dollars to be shown the way. The gurus are certainly getting richer, but how many of the clients are?

To be totally transparent, I don't have a job; I am an entrepreneur. I didn't choose to become one to make millions (although I've certainly tried), but rather to give myself more control over my time. Running my own business is the right choice for me. It suits my personality, and I'm very willing to accept the risks and challenges it involves. In fact, in many ways I thrive on them.

Conversely, I believe having a job is the right choice for many others. Not everyone is cut out to be an entrepreneur. It concerns me that people are being told if they have jobs all they can expect is to be "just over broke." That advice could adversely affect the very people it is supposed to be helping—I've seen it happen. There were many people at the seminars I attended who were still employed. My husband was one of them, and he very quickly began feeling as though it wasn't OK to have a job. For a long time he felt like a failure because he didn't have his own business, yet he didn't even know what kind of business he might start. The seminars that were supposed to empower him ended up making him feel unworthy. He didn't have a pressing reason to start a business, nor did he have an area of expertise he was passionate enough about to turn into a business. Yet he felt constant pressure to start a business so he could leave his job and be financially free.

One step we did take was opening a real estate investing business together, although I took the lead in running that business. After a few years I encouraged him to take over the business, because I no longer had the time to devote to it. He tried running it, but that didn't work out very well. There were too many aspects of business management he was unfamiliar with or just not very good at. And, maybe more important, he didn't enjoy it. It caused a lot of friction in our relationship. Eventually, we sold our investment properties and closed the business.

My husband later started a small side business that he is passionate about and continues to run part-time today. It gives him a creative outlet he enjoys. It may never be a full-time endeavor, and he's OK with that. He has come to realize having a job suits him well. There are many aspects of it he enjoys, and it provides him with a reliable income, paid vacation, and great benefits.

In the afore-mentioned book *The Happiness Advantage*, psychologist and author Achor shares research conducted by Yale psychologist Amy Wrzesniewski that indicates how we view our jobs actually affects our performance. After interviewing hundreds of people from various professions, Wrzesniewski discovered three work orientations, or mindsets about work. We view work as: (1) a job, (2) a career, or (3) a calling.

As one might expect, those who view their work as a calling find it more rewarding and are more likely to be successful. The interesting point is that the orientation was not tied to the *type* of work. In summarizing Wrzesniewski's findings, Achor writes, "She found that there are doctors who see their work only as a job, and janitors who see their work as a calling. In fact, in one study of 24 administrative assistants, each orientation was represented in nearly equal thirds, even though their objective situations (job descriptions, salary, and level of education) were nearly identical."

This research clearly shows that if we want to be happy, and in turn successful, it's not necessarily about the type of job we have or whether we own our own business. Rather, it is more about our attitude toward the work we're doing.

Perhaps jobs don't lead to financial freedom. But as the research shows, self-employment and entrepreneurship don't necessarily lead to financial freedom either. Maybe what we need to reconsider is making financial freedom our number-one goal. As discussed in chapter 2, money is a necessary part of life. Up to a certain point it can make us happier—the research says that point is $75,000 per year—but beyond that it doesn't really make that much of a difference. We have also learned that happiness leads to success and not the other way around. And, according to Wrzesniewski's research, attitude plays a large role in the outcomes we experience. Maybe, instead of focusing on financial freedom, we ought to be more focused on doing what makes us happy. That shift alone may actually lead to more of us finding greater success, and perhaps even financial freedom. Even if it doesn't, at least we're enjoying life in the meantime.

Parroting

"To repeat or imitate without thought or understanding."

~dictionary definition of "parroting"

Parroting in the self-help industry is the adoption and repackaging of popular ideas and theories. It's another common occurrence that has contributed to the proliferation of quasi-experts and questionable information. Rather than sharing expertise they have personally gained through experience or training, some experts adopt what they hear other experts saying (or what they've read) and repackage it into their own advice, books, and programs. In his book *Help! Debunking the Outrageous Claims of Self-Help Gurus,* business school professor Paul Damian calls this the explosion of instant knowledge, a typical formula within the self-help industry: "(1) rephrase others' ideas; (2) mix with complete *non*-ideas; (3) claim everything fits into your paradigm; and (4) market all of it with the aid of two or three buzzwords."

The Law of Attraction is an example of a frequently parroted theory. Popularized by *The Secret,* the Law of Attraction has been liberally applied by self-help experts to everything from material possessions and money to business and relationships. I'm not suggesting it can't be applied, but in many cases some experts are running a little fast and loose with the information.

A business mentor once advised me that the more money I invested in my business, the more successful that business would become. She suggested my investment was a signal to the universe I was serious about the business and I would therefore be rewarded in kind. In other words, if I focused on my business, with money in this case, the business would expand. Unfortunately, because I wanted the business to succeed so badly, I'm embarrassed to admit I took this advice. I invested tens of thousands of dollars in a matter of months, more than I had invested in any business in the past in such a short period of time (and at this time I had already built two successful businesses). Yet, the business did not expand. In fact, it was a total flop.

The universe is not a bank. It does not keep score. That's not what the Law of Attraction states. I knew that, yet I still followed the advice. All I can say is, the promise of quick success from a guru with strong convictions can easily blind even those of us who know better.

📷 Blog Snapshot

Too Many Parrots

My goal on this blog is to stay positive. After all, one can't really follow inspiration from an angry place. But I'm human. And sometimes things make me angry and I feel compelled to share. There are times I want to shake things up, rattle a few cages, get you to stop and think, yank you off autopilot, and prevent you from blindly following the masses. Because you must do these things if you truly want to follow inspiration. So I hope you'll forgive me for a few rants. Here's one:

How many times have you heard a phrase repeated over and over, passed along from one person to the next? There's nothing wrong with repeating mantras or phrases you believe in. However, in my experience, too many times these phrases are passed along more because they sound good and less because the passer really grasps their meaning.

Case in point: The other night, my husband and I were having a fairly deep conversation over dinner. I'd just had the epiphany that I'd been following the money path and chasing success and that it wasn't working for me. I was expressing guilt over how much money I'd spent and was thinking about what I could have done for my family with that money.

After telling me not to feel guilty and being very supportive, Louie said, "Money is just energy."

While I appreciate his support and his helping me see I can't change the past, I couldn't resist responding with, "Do you really believe that? Do you really understand what you're saying when you say 'Money is just energy' or is it just something you've heard so many times—and it sounds good—so you're repeating it now?"

Nothing against my husband, but he too still gets caught in the grip of money. We're both working on reframing the role we let money play in our lives. By restating that plati-tude, he was being a parrot. And there are a lot of parrots out there, repeating phrases they've heard that sound good, that they want to believe, but that they really don't have a full comprehension of. And it bugs the heck out of me.

Words have an impact. Choose the words you choose to share carefully. Don't say (or do) something just because everyone else is saying (or doing) it.

Source: www.FollowingInspiration.com

The Verdict

"Each man must reach his own verdict, by weighing all the relevant evidence."

~Leonard Peikoff, philosopher

I encourage you to consider your personal experience in the self-help industry, along with what I have shared, and draw your own conclusions about whether you believe it helps or hurts people. There are certainly plenty of opinions on both sides of the subject. On the Internet it's easy to find glowing testimonials as well as scathing complaints about self-help experts and their programs. It's definitely an industry with no shortage of fans or critics.

After spending years working and participating in the self-help industry myself, and doing considerable research for this book, I definitely believe the industry—or at least some of the gurus within it—have gotten out of control. While I believe we can learn from people who have experience and expertise that we don't possess, there are simply too many big and unrealistic promises being made. The mentality that "it's all the client's fault" if a program doesn't work is far too prevalent. Guru worship has the potential to result in people being harmed mentally, spiritually, financially, and even physically, as we saw in the case of James Arthur Ray.

Yet, I am not willing to close the door on self-help. I'd like to believe the majority of people working in the industry have integrity and would never knowingly mislead or hurt people just to make a quick buck. I'd like to believe that maybe they too have gotten caught up in the web of gurudom and the exaggerated promises, perhaps feeling they need to act or market that way to get clients. After all, it's difficult to compete with the big gurus and big promises if you aren't promising something even better. I know. As someone selling programs and services to help people grow their businesses, I found myself getting caught up in the marketing hype as well.

Despite all of its shortcomings, I do believe the self-help industry has a place in today's world. I have reaped many benefits from it. However, I do believe we need to be very careful about the promises we buy into. We need to recognize we may not be able to be, do, or have anything and that's OK. It's not necessarily about being, doing, or having it all—it's about being the best we can be. It's about striving for personal excellence, and that means something different for everyone. It's not about being like someone else or feeling as though we must live up to other people's goals and standards. It's about setting our own goals and standards.

We need to recognize that becoming successful—however we choose to define it—takes work. It can't be bought. And it most certainly involves more than three, five, or seven simple steps. We need to view self-improvement as a learning opportunity and not the fast track to wealth and success. We need to acknowledge that no one guru has all the answers. We need to carefully scrutinize the experts we choose to follow and what we choose to believe.

As Connie Joy advocates, we need to separate the message from the messenger. Messenger worship is not healthy. We need to test theories before we accept them as gospel. We need to take the gurus off their pedestals and see them for who they are: people who make a living selling information. Yes, they may talk about helping and serving people—and they may genuinely mean it and do it—but we must never forget they're in business and that the purpose of business is to make money. We need to hold experts accountable for their advice. That's the only way we can weed out the faux experts from the qualified teachers and the quality information from the questionable.

Spellbound

1. Are you so focused on the journey that you're ignoring or justifying the lack of results for the individual programs you've invested in?

2. Have you gotten caught up in the wealth industry, acting and spending as if you're wealthy when you're actually not? (If you're racking up debt trying to create or buy wealth, this is a good indicator you're under this spell.)

3. Are you taking action on what you're learning, or are you instead spending your time going from one program or event to another?

4. Do you miss the seminar energy and find yourself constantly attending seminars trying to recapture it?

5. Are you easily persuaded by marketing copy that promises big results, even if you secretly doubt those results are possible for you? (Or if you have repeatedly not gotten the promised results in the past?)

6. Are the experts you're learning from proven experts in what they're teaching, or did they make their fortunes as information marketers?

7. Do you feel bad because you have a job and not a business of your own?

8. Do you feel inadequate because other people have been able to achieve a level of success that has eluded you, even though you may have followed their proven system or steps?

9. Are you an expert or coach hopper? Do you jump from expert to expert or coach to coach, trying to find the one person or system that will finally make you successful or rich?

10. Do you tend to put experts on a pedestal and view them as celebrities?

Breaking the Spell

1. Individually evaluate each program you invest in. If a program doesn't live up to the promised results (as long as you took the required action), hold the expert accountable. He or she may not give you a refund, but at least you've made your dissatisfaction known.

2. Do not invest beyond your ability to pay back. For some people, that may mean paying cash for self-help programs. For others, credit may be acceptable if they're already generating income to pay back the investment. Do not count on the program you're investing in to earn you the money to pay off your investment.

3. Implement what you've learned before you invest in learning something new. Or, at least make the decision not to implement before moving on. Avoid building up a backlog of "things to take action on."

4. Recognize that seminars are carefully designed to create environments of positive energy that are highly conducive to getting you to buy and keep coming back. Don't expect this artificial energy to measure up to real life. That's like expecting every day to be like your wedding day or some other significant event. Instead, find ways in your daily life to energize yourself and feel good.

5. Think before you press the "Buy Now" button. Make sure you're investing in something that is strategically aligned with your business or life goals and the specific areas you have identified you need to learn more about to move your business or yourself forward.

6. Research the experts you're seeking advice from. Make sure they actually made their money doing what they're teaching and not just by selling how-to information (unless they're promising to teach you how to make money selling how-to information).

7. Do not feel bad about having a job. If it's supporting you and you enjoy it, there's nothing wrong with having a job. If you aspire to more, aspire away. But leave the job only when you know you can support yourself financially through your next endeavor or when you have adequate savings. And remember, starting a business takes money!

8. Stop comparing yourself to other people. Recognize there are many factors that contributed to their success and that, even if you follow their exact steps, you may still get different results.

9. If you choose to invest with multiple experts or coaches, make sure you implement what you learn from each one before moving on to the next.

10. Take the experts and gurus off the pedestals. Recognize they're just people. They have strengths and weaknesses. They're teachers, not celebrities. Don't worship them; it can cloud your judgment.

CHAPTER 5

THE WONDERFUL
WORLD OF WEB 2.0

*"But don't be fooled by the radio, the TV, or the magazines.
They show you photographs of how your life should be, but
they're just someone else's fantasy."*

~from the song "The Grand Illusion" by Styx

The year was 1977. I was a sophomore in high school. The
popular band Styx had released its seventh album, *The Grand
Illusion,* which rose to number six on the Billboard music charts.
I listened to the title track a lot that year—and even sang along—
yet I don't think I ever really *heard* the lyrics. Today those words
ring like a haunting premonition. Who knew that I—and so many
other people—would get so caught up in those fantasies?

With the introduction of the Internet and Web 2.0 (web applications that facilitate participation and sharing, such as blogging,
chatting, and social media), we're no longer limited to receiving
messages from the radio, TV, and magazines. Anyone can contribute to the conversation—or the propaganda, depending on how
you view it. The Internet has multiplied the advertising noise that's
constantly urging us to seek more. It has also moved us from an

era of living our lives fairly privately to living them out loud for the world to see.

The question is, how much are we as individuals contributing to this grand illusion that has led to our "be more, do more, have more" society? How much are we perpetuating the pressure to succeed while at the same time criticizing marketers for subjecting us to it? Are we living out loud honestly, or are we painting the picture we want the world to see?

The truth is, on the Internet we can portray ourselves in any light we choose. We can be whoever we want to be. We can shape other people's perceptions of us by what we opt to post on our social networking profiles. Just as reality TV leaves out the mundane details of everyday life, we too can choose to post the good and exclude the bad and the ugly. One must wonder how this edited portrayal of life is contributing to the constant quest for more and the idea that more success and more money will make us happier.

Are we chasing reality, or are we chasing perceptions? Are we trying to be like other people and accomplish what they have, when in reality they may only be portraying a life or image they want us to see? Are we chasing a mirage? Are we setting ourselves up for disappointment by modeling lives portrayed by real people, in effect turned actors, on the social media stage? Are these online "friendships" we're creating real? How are this new technology and the era of living out loud via social media affecting our quest for money, success, and happiness? To answer these questions we first need to step back in time.

The Way We Were

"Can it be that it was all so simple then?"

~from the song "The Way We Were"

As a child growing up in the 1960s and 1970s, my primary experience with the outside world coming into our home was the little bit of television my parents allowed us to watch. On Friday nights we looked forward to watching *The Brady Bunch*. On Sunday evenings it was *The Wonderful World of Disney*. One was an innocent sitcom—family life as it was portrayed on TV in the 1970s. The other was a weekly excursion into the world of fantasy with Disney's movie of the week. Would I say I led a sheltered childhood? I don't think so. At least no more so than most kids growing up during that time.

Back then, if we needed to do research for a school report, we didn't power up our laptops and search the Internet. We hit the library. We couldn't send e-mails or text messages to our friends. If we wanted to communicate in writing, we wrote letters or postcards and dropped them in the mail, and it took *days* for them to be delivered. We didn't have twenty-four-hour news stations or CNN.com to provide us with the latest news on demand. If we wanted to know what was going on in the world, we read the newspaper, turned on the radio, or watched the evening news. We didn't have VCRs or DVRs to record our favorite shows. If we wanted to watch a TV show, we had to be home when it aired or hope to catch it in reruns. We didn't have cell phones. If we wanted to call someone, we had to wait until we got home to use the landline or fork out ten cents to use a pay phone. Most of us didn't have answering machines, and voicemail didn't exist. If we called someone and that person wasn't home, we called back later.

All of this began to change in the 1990s when cell phones and personal computers started becoming mainstream. I still remember getting my first cell phone in the early '90s—it was a perk from the advertising agency I worked for at the time. Suddenly I didn't have to be in the office to reach a client; I could call anyone from anywhere. At the same time it meant I was reachable 24/7, and the concepts of privacy and work hours immediately began to change. My first personal computer enabled me to work from home part-time, something that was previously unheard of in my line of work. Ultimately, these events would significantly blur the line between work life and personal life, for me and for millions of other people.

The 1990s marked the debut of a brave new, wired world. A world that would change the way we live, in so many more ways than we could imagine. All of this connectivity was quietly ushering in a "live out loud" culture. It was the dawn of an age that would enable us to instantly connect and share whatever we were thinking or doing with people around the globe. People, news, entertainment, information, friends, shopping—just about everything was now at our fingertips. And, it was all available on our timetables. Today I can use my smart phone to send and receive information almost instantly. When I want details about the latest news story, I no longer have to wait for the evening news. I can look it up online or tune in to a twenty-four-hour news station and get the scoop immediately. I can even turn to my friends on social media—I learned about Michael Jackson's death on Facebook.

While technology has definitely improved many aspects of our lives, it also has fueled a growing preoccupation with instant gratification. And, in many ways it has created an environment in which it's easy to feel as though the world revolves around us. Technology has changed how we communicate and has influenced how we live our lives. Heck, we nicknamed an entire generation the "MTV generation" because of television's influence on their behavior and buying habits. These are the same people who today have cell phones perpetually attached to their hands, text instead of talk, and are multimedia multitaskers, watching TV while they surf the net, cruise Facebook, play video games, and listen to their iPods. They don't turn to the phone book to find people or places, they log on. They watch TV on their computers. They video chat with friends around the globe. Remember how futuristic video chatting seemed when we saw it on *The Jetsons*? Well, *that* future has most definitely arrived!

All of this technology has also made the world feel like a smaller place. We can access every corner of the globe in an instant. Friendships are no longer dictated by geography. We're fed streaming video of news around the world as it's happening. In fact, news reporting is no longer solely in the hands of the professional media. We're actually documenting and sharing it too. Think of how often you see a cell phone video featured in a major news story. For better or worse, technology has changed how we define news, friends, entertainment, marketing, and privacy.

The Social Media Stage

"I do suspect that privacy was a passing fad."

~Larry Niven, writer

While it may be difficult to remember what it was like before e-mail, instant messaging, blogging, and social media, it really hasn't been that long. E-mail didn't exist until 1971 and didn't become popular until personal computers became a mainstay in our homes in the 1990s. While the idea that computers could talk to each other dates back to the 1950s, commercial Internet service providers didn't arrive on the scene until the late 1980s and early 1990s. The World Wide Web wasn't even born until 1991. I remember my entry into the online world, using CompuServe, in my marketing jobs back in the 1990s. Compared to today's sophisticated and user-friendly web services it was a dinosaur. But it was a dinosaur that enabled me to connect with people via e-mail and do online research, and, as such, it changed my job immensely.

Social networking first came around in 1994 with the introduction of Geocities. In 1997 we saw the arrival of another social networking site called SixDegrees (named after the concept that we're all just six steps from, by way of introduction, any other person on earth). Yet, social media didn't hit the mainstream until the debut of MySpace in 2003. Facebook joined the party in 2004, followed by Twitter in 2006. And, as they say, life would never be the same.

I was recently reminded of how much things have changed while watching an episode of *That '70s Show*, the popular sitcom about a group of teenage friends growing up in the 1970s. In the episode, the mother, Kitty, discovers she is going through menopause. While Kitty seems quite comfortable bringing up this issue with her friends and family, no one wants to talk to her about it. Not her husband, not her teenage son and his friends, and particularly not her mother (hysterically played by Betty White). In fact, her mother is so uncomfortable with the subject that she even denies going through menopause herself. Clearly Kitty's mother's perspective was "there are some things you just don't talk about." Today a Google search on "menopause blogs" yields more than 7,000 results. That's a lot of women talking publicly about a topic that not long ago was considered taboo. My, how times have changed!

According to Facebook founder Mark Zuckerberg, privacy is no longer a social norm. In January 2010, *The Telegraph* quoted Zuckerberg:

> People have really gotten comfortable not only sharing more information and different kinds, but more openly and with more people. When I got started in my dorm room at Harvard, the question a lot of people asked was, 'Why would I want to put any information on the Internet at all? Why would I want to have a website?' Then in the last 5 or 6 years, blogging has taken off in a huge way, and just all these different services that have people sharing all this information.

In 2008, Facebook took over as the leading social networking site. As of 2012, it claimed to have more than 800 million active users who spend a collective 700 billion minutes per month on the site. Just to put that into perspective, if Facebook were a country, it would be the third most populous country in the world, behind China and India. Yes, Facebook has more residents than the United States, more than twice as many as of this writing!

According to a Pew Internet Research study released in 2011, 65 percent of adults who are online are using social networking sites. That's more than double the percentage that were using them in 2008. According to Nielsen's *State of the Media: The Social Media Report—Q3 2011*, nearly four in five active Internet users spend nearly 25 percent of their time online visiting social networks and blogs. Americans spend more time on Facebook than on any other U.S. website. That's a lot of time actively involved in a pastime that didn't even exist ten years ago. As for whom we're spending all this time with, Pew Research says our online friends are a mix of past and present and personal and business connections.

Whom we're connecting with on social media:

- 22% people from high school
- 12% extended family
- 10% coworkers
- 9% college friends
- 8% immediate family
- 7% people from voluntary groups
- 2% neighbors

However, more than 31 percent of our Facebook friends cannot be classified into any of these categories. The Pew study shows that 7 percent of our Facebook friends are people we have *never* met in person, and 3 percent are people we have met only one time. The rest are friends of friends and social ties with whom we do not currently have active relationships.

The reality is, many of the friendships we have today would not exist if it weren't for social media. It allows us to connect with people we might never meet in our day-to-day lives. When we're seeking like-minded people to engage with, it can be a good thing. However, as we'll discuss a bit later in this chapter, if we're using social media to cure loneliness or expand our sphere of influence, we may be missing the mark with these superficial friendships.

In addition to connecting with people, social websites allow us to keep track of our friends. They have opened a virtual window that enables us to peer into their lives. We can log on and instantly see what our friends did that day without ever talking to them. We can view pictures of their latest travels, family birthday parties, or business trips. We can find out how their children are doing, how their businesses are fairing, or what they thought of the movie they saw last night. In today's busy world, this certainly has its benefits. We can feel connected even when there is little time to connect. We can live vicariously through our friends. Maybe we can't afford that vacation to Bali, but by looking at our friend's photos of her vacation, we can share in the experience.

However, our relationships with social media and these virtual connections can become problematic when they begin to take the place of actually living our lives or making real, in-person connections with people. We must never forget that just because the virtual world is convenient, that does not make it better nor a replacement for personal connections. When it comes to growing and maintaining relationships, talking on the phone tops e-mail every time, and getting together in person trumps the phone. Relationships take time and energy to maintain. It is important to recognize those superficial friendships on social media will remain superficial if they never move beyond the virtual stage.

We have the opportunity to use social media to share valuable information—the equivalent of creating value in relationships. Or, we can share trivial information—the online counterpart to meaningless small talk. If we're having a good day, we can share it and invite others to join our celebration. If we're having a bad day, we can share that too, and inevitably evoke sympathy so we don't feel so alone in our misery. One of the most interesting aspects of social media is that many of us think nothing of posting information that just a few years ago we wouldn't even have shared with our neighbors. In fact, we *still* might not be sharing it with our neighbors. There seems to be something about the virtual nature of the web that provokes more transparency and openness. Maybe it's the fact that we aren't face-to-face with the people we're sharing with. We're safe behind our computer screens in a sort of virtual bubble. Additionally, while we express concern that our personal lives are being intruded by Big Brother, *we* are publicly sharing more personal information than ever before. It's an interesting irony.

What is it that prompts so many of us to share our feelings and lives so openly on the net? Perhaps we can find an answer in the following quotation from popular social media expert Trey Pennington (who, sadly, passed away in September 2011): "There are three basic human needs we all have: Everyone wants to be heard. Everyone wants to be understood. Everyone wants to know that his or her life matters."

Maybe we just want to be able to express ourselves and be heard. There's no denying that social media have provided a stage for anyone who wants to step onto it. Perhaps we just want to know that we matter—that our lives are making a difference. Maybe we want to connect with people who share our beliefs, and that may not be our current friends and family or the people we're interacting with daily in our neighborhoods or jobs. Whatever the motivation, virtual communication is the new way of life for many people. And, with digital giant Google joining the party in 2011 with Google Plus, it certainly doesn't appear to be going away any time soon.

Digital Natives

"They embrace multiple modes of self expression. Three-quarters have created a profile on a social networking site."

~*description of the Millennial Generation by the Pew Research Center*

Whereas many of us have grown into this era of living out loud, the demographic group known as the millennials has grown up with it. For those born after 1980, it's all they've ever known. In the article "Privacy, schmivacy — Gen Y will keep on sharing" published on MSN in July 2010, this group is referred to as "digital natives." They've always been connected. They share information openly online, and research shows that behavior is unlikely to change as they grow older. The MSN article goes on to point out, "There are too many benefits to living with a certain degree of openness for digital natives to 'grow out of it.' Job opportunities, new personal connections, professional collaboration, learning from others' experiences . . . are all very powerful benefits to engaging openly with others online, and this is something that Gen Y understands intuitively." And, the Pew Research Center's Internet & American Life Project says this group is "leading society into a new world of personal disclosure and information-sharing."

Not only are social media sites a way of life for generation Y, they're also very much about self-promotion and attracting attention, according to a national study conducted in 2009 by San Diego State University psychology professor Jean Twenge. Her research revealed that 57 percent of young people believe their generation uses social networking sites for self-promotion, narcissism, and attention seeking. Additionally, not only did these gen Yers view their social media behavior as narcissistic, nearly 40 percent agree that being "self-promoting, narcissistic, overconfident, and attention-seeking is helpful for succeeding in a competitive world." According to Twenge in her book *The Narcissism Epidemic: Living in the Age of Entitlement,* there has been a "relentless rise in narcissism in our culture." She points to data from 37,000 college students that indicates narcissistic personality traits have risen just as fast as obesity since the 1980s. She writes, "The narcissism epidemic has spread to the culture as a whole, affecting both narcissistic and less self-centered people."

Increasing narcissism is the byproduct of a generation raised on self-love and taught that feeling good about oneself is job one.

A separate Canadian study conducted among one hundred Facebook users aged eighteen to twenty-five by Soraya Mehdizadeh of York University found that individuals higher in narcissism and lower in self-esteem spent more time on Facebook and filled their pages with self-promotional content. Mehdizadeh writes, "The question is, are these really accurate representations of the individual or are they merely a projection of who the individual wants to be?"

A study conducted by Larry D. Rosen, a professor of psychology at California State University, Dominguez Hills, also found that young people who use Facebook more often are more likely to display narcissistic tendencies.

Apparently the same holds true for Twitter. In 2009 Rutgers University professors dissected more than three thousand tweets from more than 350 Twitter users' status updates and concluded that 80 percent of users are what they dubbed "meformers." They describe meformers as "people who use the platform to post updates about their everyday activities, social lives, feelings, thoughts, and emotions."

Meformers step onto the center of the virtual media stage and shine the spotlight directly on themselves. It appears social media and narcissism are a match made in heaven. And, it begins to explain much of the behavior we see exhibited on social networking sites and the connection between that behavior and our "be more, do more, have more culture," in which *me* is at the center of it all.

Perception vs. Reality

"Illusion is needed to disguise the emptiness within."

~Arthur Erickson, architect

In a blog snapshot in the last chapter, I shared a story about a woman who contacted me for help with her business. She was struggling to get clients and was making just a few hundred dollars a month. She was so broke and in debt she couldn't afford to invest in the help she needed to turn her business around. Yet, visitors to her website or Facebook page would have had no idea of her dire circumstances. Her business offered to help people find success, abundance, and happiness. I don't understand how someone who has not mastered all three can promise to deliver those outcomes to other people. But, as we also discussed in the last chapter, anyone can call herself a coach.

The Internet has done amazing things for the self-employed. In many ways it has leveled the playing field, enabling anyone to look professional and successful. Newbies can compete with established service providers. The "little guy" can compete with larger, more established companies. All have equal access to potential clients via the web. Because it's so easy to create the perception of success online, it begs the question, can we trust what we see?

Kimberly Englot, founder of The Center of Authentic Self Development, believes that, unfortunately, a lot of what we see online is surface stuff and hype. She points out that attention spans have shrunk to the point of 140 characters or less (a reference to Twitter's maximum word count). "I think that people have to really hype it up to get attention," Englot says. "You have to be really careful about what you believe."

Not surprisingly, research indicates that it's easier to stretch the truth and get away with it in the digital world. According to Michael Woodworth, a forensic psychologist at the University of British Columbia Okanagan who has studied deception in computer-mediated environments, lying in person can create signals that a person is trying to deceive. Lying online avoids these telltale physical cues. Woodworth says deception is "one of the most significant and pervasive social phenomena of our age. On average, people tell one to two lies a day, and these lies range from the trivial to the more serious."

Woodworth also points out that a growing number of people are falling prey to deceptive practices and information from digital sources such as the Internet. If it's easier to lie online, that shouldn't surprise anyone. And it doesn't appear to. According to a 2011 article published in *Discovery News,* many of us are more concerned than ever about the believability of what we see online. The article, "Do People Lie More Online?" shares that we really do believe people lie more online than in face-to-face interactions. But that perception may not be accurate. Research indicates that while technology may make it easier to lie, it isn't tempting us to lie any more than we normally do. It appears that it has just opened up another avenue for us to do what we're already doing.

Jeff Hancock of Cornell University and Catalina Toma of the University of Wisconsin–Madison—who have studied online deception—suspect our distrust of the online world is actually rooted in our fear of technology. Toma writes, "Every time a technology is new, it elicits great fears. Many people are fearful about what it's going to do."

As much as we may not want to believe it, it appears it is simply human nature to deceive and to portray ourselves in the most favorable light possible. Because of its virtual nature, social media are the ideal media in which to do both. And nowhere is this more apparent than among those trying to sell to us online.

Virtual Marketing Frontier

> *"Social Media, it turns out, isn't about aggregating audiences so you can yell at them about the junk you want to sell. Social Media, in fact, is a basic human need, revealed digitally online."*
>
> ~Seth Godin, author and entrepreneur

Social media sites have opened up a vast and virtual marketing arena for all the self-help experts, coaches, and information marketers we talked about in chapter 4. They are a virtual stage that can put these marketers in front of a worldwide audience, all from the comfort and convenience of their homes or offices for the cost of an Internet connection.

Not that long ago, expensive and exhausting book tours were the only way experts could gain the widespread exposure necessary to get their books on the best-seller list. Now they can reach millions virtually. It used to be necessary for self-help gurus to host expensive live events to share their teachings. Now they can conduct virtual events such as teleseminars and webinars and quickly spread the word via their social networks and Internet marketing. Because social media sites are free resources, they have created a virtual marketplace that anyone—real experts and faux experts alike—can use to market and sell their products and services.

But should social media be used for *selling*? It's clear that wasn't the original intention. After all, Facebook was started as a place for Harvard students to connect. Social networking was originally designed as just another way to *socialize*. But very quickly, business owners realized it also afforded them the opportunity to reach thousands, if not millions, of potential clients for free. This has had a huge influence on not only the content we see posted on social media, but also on the way many people approach growing their social media friends lists.

I love the quotation by Seth Godin at the beginning of this section, because I agree that social media should not be used to recruit an audience and inundate them with constant marketing messages. Unfortunately, the lion's share of what I see on social media does exactly that. Perhaps it's the circles I run in, but I have many clients and colleagues who share my sentiment. In his book *Tribes,* Godin talks about building a tribe—or a following—by inspiring others. The idea he shares, and that I wholeheartedly agree with, is that it shouldn't be about begging or bribing people to join your tribe (or "friend" you or "like" your Facebook page); it should be about doing something worth following.

As we saw in the previous chapter, the barriers to entry into the self-help/expert/coaching industry are low to nonexistent. Add to that our growing narcissism and a free marketing vehicle that promises to put you and your message in front of millions of people, and you have . . . well, you have much of what I believe is wrong with the way social media are used today. Too many people begging and screaming for attention instead of focusing on connecting with others. While social media sites can be a great place to inspire a following, too many people are spending their time essentially yelling, "Look at me!" and "Follow me!" instead. For many people, social media sites have become just another marketing vehicle for their latest program or service. And as a result, too many people are talking instead of listening and starting conversations.

Coincidentally, in the middle of writing this chapter, I opened Facebook and found the following post. Clearly I'm not the only one with these concerns!

> I really want to see more talking WITH on Facebook than talking AT. A simple question at the end of the profound quote you're posting can get a whole lot more engagement going. I opened up Facebook and scrolled the feed and felt so barked at! If we were all in person, it would be a room full of noise.

It does feel noisy. I too feel barked at. On any given day, I'd estimate 90 percent of the notifications I receive on Facebook are promotional in nature—"experts" inviting me to attend teleclasses, webinars, Internet radio shows and other events that ultimately are designed as marketing for their services. Perhaps those sending out these notifications view it as sharing. As for me, it reminds me of the barkers at the county fair, forcefully trying to sell me their wares as I stroll by. Or the salespeople in the mall kiosks yelling at me as I walk by: "Do you have a cell phone plan? Want to try this lotion? It will make your skin softer. Try our hair straightener; it won't harm your hair."

I don't know about you, but none of these invitations make me want to stop, listen, or try their products. They make me want to run the other way! I feel intruded on. I don't get the sense that they care at all about my needs. I know they just want to sell their products or services, and that's not very inviting in my book.

As I often tell my clients when teaching them how to market and sell, while people don't like to be sold to, most do love to buy. Effective and respectful marketing generates awareness and lets the buyer make the decision. It doesn't forcefully try to sell. The latter is too reminiscent of the stereotypical used car salesmen, and I'm sure we all feel pretty much the same way about them. Unfortunately, too many people using social media for marketing either forget this or don't think about it, and they end up alienating the very people they're trying to attract.

📷 Blog Snapshot

Everybody's Talking at Me

When I visit Facebook I am struck by the thousands of people talking about themselves and inviting me to like their pages or attend their events. I'm reminded of the Harry Nilsson song lyrics, "Everybody's talking at me, I don't hear a word they're saying."

I feel bombarded. I wonder if I'm the only one. When did we all become so brash and start spending our time constantly talking about ourselves and what we're doing?

Remember Sally Field at the 1985 Academy Awards exclaiming, "You like me!" after winning the Oscar for Best Actress? Everyone poked fun at her, yet there was truth in her words. People had voted for her, not because she asked them to, but because they thought she had done a good job.

Today, instead of exclaiming "You like me!" too many people are simply begging, "Like me!" And too often, it's before they've done anything to earn it. Instead of taking time to build a solid platform and do things worthy of following (like all great leaders in history have done), people are begging and bribing others to follow them. For me, this is a great big negative in the wonderful world of Web 2.0. Call me old fashioned, but I think we ought to earn our followers.

I love what Seth Godin says in his book *Tribes*: "Through your actions as a leader, you attract a tribe that wants to follow you." That has nothing to do with *asking* people to follow you. It requires doing or saying something so they are *inspired* to follow. Godin also writes about what he calls "true fans," those people who will go the extra mile to support you. He then points out that too many organizations (and I would add people when it comes to social media) care about numbers, not true fans.

I also love this quote from *Harry Potter and the Deathly Hallows Part 2*: "It's the quality of one's convictions that determines success, not the number of followers." We are not successful because we're able to get lots of people to follow us. We're successful when people support our views (or our products and services) and therefore want to share them with others. Then we've created a movement, something worth following or being a part of. And then, just maybe we've done something that will make a difference, and not just a quick buck.

If more people spent their time and energy developing strong points of view and sharing their convictions instead of trying to be popular, I would be more inspired to follow them. Instead, I ignore most of what I see on social media. On the rare occasion someone says or does something inspiring, I'm the first person to join the conversation and pass it along. Sadly, that's a rare occurrence.

Just because you can market free of charge and ask everyone to like or follow you doesn't mean you should. And, it doesn't mean it's an effective way to build a tribe, following, or business.

Source: www.FollowingInspiration.com

Race to Five Thousand

"The more the merrier."

~*proverb*

For years the primary goal of online marketers has been to build a large e-mail list. An e-mail list is considered to be their golden goose, because it's filled with potential customers (and therefore, potential income). Once a list is built it's something that can continue to support a business for years. With the primary goal of Internet marketing being list-building, it's no surprise that when social media came onto the scene the same mentality was applied.

Social media became another place to build a list. The goal was to acquire as many friends and followers as possible. The race was on to acquire five thousand friends—the maximum allowed by Facebook for a personal profile page. Once the five thousand maximum was achieved it was time to create a separate Facebook fan page (now called simply a page), where there is no limit to the number of followers. Most online marketers have both a personal profile and a page on Facebook. After all, that's what the social media experts recommend.

As a result of this preoccupation with list size, in the early days for many online marketers, social media sites weren't about connecting and sharing with people they already knew. Instead, they were about enlarging their sphere of influence. More friends meant more potential clients, and that meant more sales and more money. Additionally, in a world often measured by the size of your friends list, having lots of friends or followers and people who like your page makes you *look* successful. Just consider what you think when you hear of someone having hundreds of thousands, or even millions, of Twitter followers. It becomes a virtual popularity contest. And for many—especially the narcissistic and the self-help experts—popularity is a prized asset.

I admit that a few years ago I participated wholeheartedly in this race to five thousand. I wanted as many Facebook friends and Twitter followers as I could get. I accepted any and all friend requests. I created a separate Facebook page for my business so I wouldn't be limited to five thousand friends. Truthfully, at the time, I saw it as no different from building my e-mail list. I didn't know or screen the people joining my e-mail list. Why did I need to know or screen the people wanting to befriend me on Facebook or follow me on Twitter?

Then, one day in 2009 I saw a Facebook post from a woman complaining about how tired she was of receiving friend requests from people she didn't know. She was put off by people asking to be her friend without so much as a personal note of introduction or explanation as to why they wanted to be friends. My reaction at the time (I feel very differently now) was, how is that any different from people wanting to join your e-mail list? (She was an online marketer, and I knew she had an e-mail list.)

However, over time I began to appreciate her point of view. As my Facebook friends list grew, I found myself being inundated with marketing from all those people who had requested to be my friend. I'm guessing their goal was not so much to make new friends, but instead to grow their own audiences for marketing purposes, much like mine had been. Most of the marketing I received on social media—and still receive to this day—is not targeted to me. And in some cases it's the equivalent of spam e-mail marketing.

The most notable example was a Facebook friend who almost daily sent me promotional messages about his programs designed to help women find partners. If he had taken two seconds to look at my Facebook profile (i.e., get to know his new friend), he would have seen I have been married for thirty years and am not in the market for a partner. This is what is often referred to in the marketing world as shotgun marketing—just fire and hope it hits someone. While marketers may pick up an occasional client this way, it is not an effective or efficient way to market. And if you do it as incessantly as this man did, it not only doesn't get you clients, it makes people not even want to be associated with you; I very quickly unfriended this offender. Yet, in my experience, it's the way most folks market on social media. They have the ability to blast their promotional messages out to all their friends, and so they do. Because it's free marketing, they figure, why not?

Sadly, it reminds me of the way many people also approach in-person networking events. They show up eager to market themselves, and the focus is all on me, me, me. They shove their business cards in your hand and talk up their services, trying to sell you. There's no give and take, no conversation. They don't even bother finding out whether you might be a potential client or referral partner. Their actions say they don't care about you; all they care about is themselves. How many of us want to be friends or business partners with that type of person?

In many ways, social networking sites have become giant virtual networking rooms where everyone is talking and trying to sell their stuff. The result is a lot of noise. Everyone is talking about how they can help you be more, do more, and have more.

📷 Blog Snapshot

Everything I Need to Be Successful, Rich, Happy, Healthy, and Conscious I Can Learn on Facebook THIS WEEK

This blog post is a tongue-in-cheek look at how you can purportedly get everything you want in life or business, free, on Facebook. I hope it makes you smile and makes a point. At the end I share some foundational marketing principles you'll want to make sure you're employing. By the way, this is NOT a slam on anyone's event . . . that's not what this post is about. Read on to see WHY I wrote this.

Another week has gone by, and once again I'm amazed at the plethora of educational opportunities available to me on Facebook. Did you know everything you need to be successful, rich, happy, healthy, and conscious is available absolutely FREE on Facebook? (All of the italicized copy in this post represents the names of real events that were marketed to me.)

Following is a taste of the events I've been invited to in just the past seven days. Note to self: I will have to find at least twenty-eight hours in my schedule over the next week to partake in all of this education. Doesn't leave much time for actual work, but hey, some of the marketing copy makes it sound like I may not actually need to work to attain all of my dreams and goals. Case in point: one event promises me that *It's Not About How Hard I Work.*

This week, I can attend a telesummit and become an *Ultimate Mompreneur.* Hmmm, is that who I want to be? Better decide before I go. If my business is stuck, I can *Get a Business Breakthrough in 2011 and Beyond!* Well, OK then, to infinity and beyond I go! (Sorry, I couldn't help thinking of Buzz Lightyear when I read that event title). I can learn how to *Go from Fearful, Scattered and Strapped to Fearless, Streamlined and Flush.* Wow, didn't even know I wanted to be all those things.

If my business is suffering from lackluster sales, I just need to learn *5 Keys to Skyrocket My Sales*, and problem solved. If I'm feeling a little down in the dumps about my marketing and the number of people who know who I am, that's easy. I can *Discover My Spotlight Style for Marketing Success and Big Time Visibility*. Oh, thank goodness.

If I'm feeling a little lost or disconnected, no worries. I have *The Power of Choice and Waking Up My Truest Power*, or I can learn how to tap into my *Personal Intuitive Guidance* and *How to Celebrate My True Divine Worth*. Or, I can learn how to *Color My Life Happy* or discover *The Limitless Power of Conscious Freedom*, try a little *Sacred Sound Immersion*, or even attend a *Business Retreat to Sync Mind, Body, and Spirit for Success!* Well why didn't you just say so?

If I want to add a new income stream, Facebook events have that covered too. I can go on the *Real Estate Buying Bus Tour* or learn how to *Turn My Next Event into a Money Machine!*

If I decide I'm tired of playing small, not to worry. I can learn the *5 Mistakes that Keep Smart Women Overwhelmed and Playing Small in Business*, and I can learn *3 Simple Steps to Having it All!* Good to know this one will help me do it *Easily and Effortlessly*. What a relief—I thought it might actually take some work!

If my online presence isn't attracting all the traffic I want, that's an easy fix. I just need to learn *How to Attract More Traffic to my Website or Blog* or *How to Create a Successful Facebook Business Fan Page!* or discover *The Secret Sauce for Sizzling Website Sales*. So that's where I went wrong—it's about the sauce!

Because health and fitness is important to me, it's good to know Facebook events have me covered there too. I can learn *How to Easily Overcome Emotional Eating* and *How to Safely Detox My Body Without Pills, Drugs, or Dr. Drew!* Good to know, because I don't think Dr. Drew is a good fit for me.

And, just to ensure I keep all of this in perspective and that it's all working toward my highest good and purpose, I can learn *Big Picture Mindfulness*, how to *Live The Bigger Vision*, and how to achieve *Success for the Soul in Business*. And, I can rest assured *The Universe Has Reserved a Spot Just For Me*. SO glad that seat isn't already taken!

Lastly, to make sure all of these dreams I'm fulfilling this week via Facebook events are protected, there's the *Wealth Women Lawyers Workshop*.

Just imagine what's available NEXT week or what's possible if I branch out to Twitter and LinkedIn!

Now, let me just say I have NOTHING against any of these programs or the people offering them. Apparently, the people putting on all of these events thought I was the perfect attendee, because they took the time to send me an invitation. Not so sure I agree with that, and that actually opens up another topic, the concept of targeted marketing and something I don't see a lot of on Facebook.

All these events may very well be great programs. I'm certainly NOT going to criticize programs I'm not familiar with. THAT's not my point. My point is, the amount of training and education available to us on Facebook alone is overwhelming. Many of the events sound great, so it's easy to lose sight of our priorities and our businesses and be lured in by the promises these event names suggest.

So how do you decide what to pay attention to and what to ignore? The key is to know WHO you are, what's important to you, what you know, and what you don't know. Then, you can strategically decide what continuing education serves you best. While I could probably learn something from all of these events, it's not necessarily going to be what I need right now to reach my goals. There are only so many hours in a day, and if I'm focusing on designing a successful business that will finance the lifestyle I want, I need to be very thoughtful about how I spend my time.

My advice is to choose how you spend your time wisely. Be focused and clear about what will serve you. Otherwise, you'll end up overwhelmed, confused and unclear about who you are and what you should actually be doing to achieve your goals.

It's easy to get caught up. A few years ago I attended far too many conferences, workshops, and teleseminars because I was looking for that "missing piece." You know the one. "If I only had it, I would finally reach ALL my goals." (Note: there is no ONE missing piece—building a successful business is a process that involves many pieces!)

I ended up with so many other people's voices in my head that I couldn't hear my own. I lost my way and ran my successful six-figure business into the ground. I had to take a sabbatical at the end of 2009 just to find myself, my confidence, and my path again. Thankfully, I did and was able to quickly rebuild my business.

Yes, learning is good. It's necessary. But be choosy. And, make sure you're leaving enough time in your week to actually implement what you're learning, because all the knowledge and education in the world doesn't mean a thing if you don't DO something with it.

Lastly, think about who you are inviting to your events. A few months ago, one of my Facebook friends sent me messages and invitations almost daily about his events to help single women meet men. My Facebook page clearly stated that I was married. As you can imagine, he's no longer a Facebook friend. He may have been a nice guy with a good program, but he was spamming me with all his messages and invites. A little marketing homework would have quickly told him that.

Together we can cut down on the overwhelm. If you're going to promote your events on Facebook, please don't send messages inviting ALL of your friends. Segment your friends list. Send invites only to those for whom the event is a good fit. That's just good marketing. It's called targeting, and it's the opposite of what some marketers affectionately call "shotgun marketing." With shotgun marketing you blast your marketing out to everyone and hope it reaches someone who might be interested—NOT the way to market effectively, if you hadn't already guessed.

Another option is to post news about your event on your wall and let your friends see in it their feeds. Or, create a Facebook page and send relevant event invitations only to people who have liked your page. This is called permission-based marketing, and it means you send e-mails only to people who have raised their hands and said they want to receive your news. It's a bit of a stretch with a Facebook page, because it really applies to e-mail marketing. However, it can be loosely applied, because your fans have essentially "joined your tribe" on Facebook, thereby expressing interest in your business (or the content of your page). Just don't abuse this by sending them too many messages.

If we all follow these basic marketing principles with our social media marketing, just think how much clutter we can eliminate. Who knows? If that happened I might actually start paying attention to the event invitations I receive.

I also encourage you to consider other, more targeted ways to market your services. A free teleclass marketed on Facebook might be a good tactic, but something else might get you better results.

Source: www.DebbieLaChusa.com/blog

More "Friends" Doesn't Mean More Friends

"Wishing to be friends is quick work, but friendship is a slow ripening fruit."

~Aristotle, philosopher

The date was September 4, 2011. It was the middle of Labor Day weekend, and word was spreading like wildfire across Facebook. A popular social media personality had taken his life earlier that day in a church parking lot. The deceased's Facebook page quickly filled with condolences from many of his nearly five thousand friends who wondered how this could have happened. Why hadn't he turned to them for help?

While a few friends hinted of his struggles, his posts from the previous days and weeks yielded no clues that he was so close to the edge. His final Twitter message to his more than one hundred thousand followers read, "Sure am thankful for online friends who are real friends offline, too. Love you." A day after the suicide one of his friends wrote a blog tribute saying, "I've been asking myself for the past 24 hours how someone with a 100,000+ acquaintances could have felt so lost and dark that they would take their life?"

How indeed? Coincidentally, the next day my horoscope said the following (I'm not into astrology, but I read my horoscope on my smart phone every morning just for kicks):

Many people spend a lot of their time on social media web-sites. They might use up a lot of time conversing with people they haven't seen in years, developing pseudo-relationships that seem like old friendships. They might play games where they can create their own towns and create the perfect inhabit-ants. They might watch videos posted by people they've never met. None of it is genuine, but that's okay, because these things provide a faux sense of belonging that satisfies some people.

I don't know whether social media interactions are genuine. Perhaps they do provide people with a faux sense of belonging. After all, how can someone with thousands of friends still feel so alone and be so unhappy that he decides to end his life? While we don't know what else was going on that contributed to his decision, it's a clear indication that virtual friendships are very different from real friendships.

📷 Blog Snapshot

True Friends

On Saturday I attended a celebration of life for my neighbor's mother. Even though we both get busy with our lives and don't spend a lot of time together, I consider this neighbor a friend. We've lived next door to each other for seventeen years.

At the services for her mother, one of my other neighbors commented on all of the great friends our mutual neighbor had there to support her and help organize the services. We agreed she is one lucky woman to be surrounded by so many true friends: friends from work, friends from the neighborhood, friends who live nearby.

I realized my local circle of friends is considerably smaller. It wasn't always. But, because I run my own business out of my home, I no longer have work friends who I see every day. The work friends I do have aren't local—we met at conferences or online and live in different parts of the country or world. Yes, a few of those virtual friends are close friends, but the miles between us mean we don't see each other often. While we enjoy connecting by phone or e-mail, it's not the same as being there live. And I may have thousands of friends on social media, but let's be honest, Facebook friends are not the same as in-person friends.

After spending so many years attending personal development and business growth conferences, I've realized two things have happened in terms of my friendships. As I've grown, I've drifted apart from many people. First, while we may live close geographically, we are in different places mentally and emotionally. Second, I think I spent so much time focusing on growing myself and my business, in some ways

I forgot how to just relax and enjoy life with friends. As a result, many relationships simply fell away. It's sad.

I'm definitely making changes in my life. I hope to one day be surrounded by as many caring people as my neighbor. Not that it's a competition; I just believe that relationships are the cornerstone of life. Being successful means nothing if you have no one to share it with. At the end of the day, the success or the business probably aren't going to mean a lot when what you really need is a shoulder to lean on.

Source: *www.FollowingInspiration.com*

In a 2009 article in *Scientific American* titled "Are Social Networks Messing With Your Head?" David DiSalvo wrote, "Logic would have it that abundant social contacts would be a cure for the blues: the greater number of contacts, the greater chance of finding rewarding relationships. The truth of the matter is less straightforward." Early studies suggested that people using social networking sites were actually lonelier than those who didn't. However, later studies failed to show this correlation. But, when researchers studied loneliness as a precursor to membership in social networks, they did find a different connection. Apparently lonely people are more likely to experience a heightened state of alertness for social threats. This means they are more sensitive to what their interactions—or lack thereof—may mean. So, they may interpret an online response or nonresponse, such as a long silence between replies during an online chat, as being "locked out of the conversation" by others.

DiSalvo also references the size of one's friends list as another problematic area for those prone to loneliness. Social media popularity is often measured by the number of contacts one has. He writes, "Having a mere handful of contacts when others could fill a stadium with their roster can leave lonely individuals feeling that their desires are moving farther out of reach." He goes on to say that the social networkers who fare the best tend to be those who use the web to support their existing friendships.

This highlights the primary difference I have seen in the use of social media among young adults using it to stay in touch with their friends and those using it to grow their spheres of influence. My twenty-two-year-old daughter and her friends use Facebook as a way to communicate with one another. Most wouldn't dream of accepting a friend request from someone they don't know. As my daughter says, "It's creepy to think someone you don't know is looking at your pictures and watching what you're doing." For them, social media sites are simply another way to talk, just as texting has in many ways replaced phone conversations. That's a very different perspective from those using social media for marketing purposes. I'm sure both can be valid uses of social media. However, it's quite clear that social media marketing etiquette is still evolving.

📷 Blog Snapshot

Quality vs. Quantity

We've all heard the advice of focusing on quality over quantity. It's a critical concept if you want to be happy and successful in business. Unfortunately, I see too many people focused on quantity, and that's not the way to design a happy, healthy, wealthy business. Well, at least wealthy in the way I define it, which is about more than just money. Being wealthy is about being rich in every aspect of your life.

Here are a few questions you can ask yourself to determine whether you're focusing on quality or quantity:

- Are you focused on building a big list of Facebook friends (quantity) or building relationships (quality)?
- Are you focused on how much money you can make (quantity) or designing a business that provides a lifestyle that makes you happy (quality)?
- Are you focused on the number of clients you have (quantity) or the impact you're making with each one (quality)?
- Are you choosing to work with mentors or coaches who flaunt their success and money (quantity) or those who exhibit the lifestyle and qualities you admire and want for yourself (quality)?
- Are you trying to keep up with all the latest marketing techniques (quantity) or committed to marketing in a few ways that consistently fill your business with clients (quality)?
- Are you focused on selling as much as you can (quantity) or serving people in the best way possible (quality)?

It's so easy to get caught up in the quantity game. It's modeled all over the place. It's the basis for "keeping up with the Jones." It's how so many mentors and coaches market (i.e., "Look how successful I am, and I can make you successful too").

I'm embarrassed to say I fell into this trap a few years ago. But when I realized I was going down this path and it didn't feel good, I did an about-face. Now my goal is to focus on service, teaching, and, yes, maybe even inspiring, but certainly not by flaunting all I've done and telling you I can help you do the same (you're not me, so your journey will never look like mine). Instead, my mission is to help others find their own paths.

Seeking quantity is a surefire way to become frustrated and burned out, because someone will ALWAYS have more. You spend all your time trying to keep up and measure up. You're never good enough where you are. And here's the real kicker: in case you haven't figured it out yet, MORE does not always mean better. You also never really know what's going on behind the scenes for those you're modeling. What looks like more on the outside may not really be the case.

I encourage you to take a look at your life, your business, and your marketing and ask yourself if you're focusing on quality or quantity. If you need to make some adjustments to get your focus back in line with what's really important, make them. I promise you won't be disappointed.

Source: www.DebbieLaChusa.com/blog

Virtual Water Cooler

> *"Half the time men think they are talking business, they are wasting time."*
>
> *~Edgar Watson Howe, editor*

When I opened my own business, one of the first things I noticed was how much work I was able to accomplish in a day. In those early years, I did a lot of contract work with other businesses, and it required me to go into the corporate environment regularly for meetings. As a self-employed contractor, my goal was to get in, get my work done, and get out so I could get on to other things. I was very efficient. I began to notice how much time nine-to-five employees waste on the job shooting the breeze—talking about what they watched on TV the night before, what their weekend plans were. It's what's often referred to as "water cooler talk."

In many ways, social media sites have become a virtual water cooler for those who are self-employed and work from home, spending their days isolated and alone. Social networking sites are a place where these people can connect, and it's often for water cooler talk. With as much time as I see some people spending on social media, I've often wondered how they get any work done or whether their businesses are even profitable. While they might view their time spent on social media as marketing, I wonder how much this "marketing" is actually contributing to their businesses' bottom lines. Or, is it perhaps just taking away billable hours the same way it does for employees?

As it turns out, even if it isn't marketing, socializing may actually improve productivity and increase our chances of being successful. In *The Happiness Advantage,* Achor writes about the importance of social investment, claiming social support is our greatest asset when it comes to being happy and successful. Achor suggests that happiness precedes success, not the other way around. He cites the Harvard Men study, which is tracking 268 men from their entrance into college in the late 1930s all the way to the present day. The study identified "the life circumstances and personal characteristics that distinguished the happiest, fullest lives from the least successful ones." He quotes the psychologist who directed the study for more than forty years regarding the conclusions: "70 years of evidence that our relationships with other people matter, and matter more than anything else in the world."

Achor cites another study, in which researchers sought to identify the characteristics of the happiest 10 percent of people and discovered strength of social relationships topped the list. He also shares results from his own research among 1,600 Harvard undergraduates, which showed "social support was a far greater predictor of happiness than any other factor—more than GPA, family income, SAT scores, age, gender, or race."

All of the research Achor shares supports the idea that spending time socializing is good for us, our careers, and our businesses. The time we spend shooting the breeze around the water cooler—whether it's an actual water cooler or the virtual social media version—is likely to make us happier, which in turn can make us more successful.

Friend Trimming

"Friend Trimming is the act of deleting the friends you do not know on any social network."

~urbandictionary.com

Recently I have started to notice a shift on Facebook. People who just a few years ago were focused on amassing huge lists of friends are effectively starting over. They're pruning their lists of virtual friends by unfriending anyone they don't know personally. In some ways, they're retreating to using social media much the same way younger generations do, to stay in touch with the people they already know in the offline world. Perhaps they're realizing they don't really want to share all that private information with a bunch of strangers. Perhaps they don't want to live quite so out loud anymore, or at least in front of people they don't know. Like me, maybe they started out accepting any and all friend requests and are now rethinking that strategy. They too may be wondering whether having all those friends is really benefiting them or their businesses, for those who have businesses. They too may be tired of being inundated with marketing pitches from people who friended them for precisely that purpose.

While I haven't yet done any significant friend trimming, I have strongly considered purging my friends list down to just family and people I know. However, I admit I feel a slight twinge of fear when I think about deleting so many people. There is something about being surrounded by five thousand people who *want* to be your friend that makes you feel important, popular, and, yes, successful. I realize this too is part of my addiction to success that I must deal with. I've never been one to let go of things quickly or easily. There's a sense of comfort in the status quo, even if it's not serving you (and my frustration with all the marketing and posturing by friends who really are not friends is definitely *not* serving me). Intellectually, I get that my self-worth is not connected to how many friends I have on Facebook, how much money I make, or how successful my business is. But it's become so ingrained—such a way of life—that it's not easy to let go of. There is definitely a fear of not having an audience for the message I feel so compelled to share.

But I suppose the question we all must ask ourselves is, how many of the people in our audience are actually listening? How many are too busy talking and promoting themselves to hear what anyone else is saying? Clearly I'm still trying to find my own way in the wonderful world of Web 2.0. I don't think I'm alone.

Finding Our Way

> "'Would you tell me, please, which way I ought to go from here?'
> 'That depends a good deal on where you want to get to,' said the Cat."
>
> ~Lewis Carroll, Alice in Wonderland

I think most of us are still trying to find the best way to integrate these new media into our lives. We're still experimenting. We're modeling what others are doing. We're following experts who, in many ways, are still finding their own way. After all, these experts are subjected to the constant evolution of social media and are trying to figure it all out just like the rest of us. That's because it's all unfolding as it happens, in real time. We're all trying to navigate this brave, new, wired world. And I fear many of us are so busy following what others are doing or what they're telling us to do that we haven't really considered how we want to use these new media to enhance our lives. It's like one big experiment, and we're all the guinea pigs!

Unfortunately, it's easy to become spellbound when you feel lost or haven't established your own bearings. Additionally, for some people, this virtual world may feel like the one place they *can* be, do, or have anything—or at least look like it. It begs the question, is this new era of living out loud a good thing or a bad thing? Once again, I don't think there's a simple black-and-white answer. As with the self-help industry, I believe it's important we approach social media with our eyes wide open, acknowledging there are both positive and negative aspects. It's important that we understand true friendships take time, energy, and attention to cultivate, both offline and online. We need to remember that all that glitters is not gold: people can portray themselves online any way they want, and it's human nature to paint the most attractive picture possible.

How then do we proceed in this live-out-loud world? How can we use social media to cultivate true friendships or enhance existing ones in a way that enriches our lives instead of just as another measure of success? Ultimately, I think it's about identifying our reasons for using social media and then using them intentionally toward those goals. That requires thinking about the information we're sharing, with whom we're sharing it, and for what purpose.

I also believe we have an obligation to be truthful. The virtual world we create will be only as real as we make it. While I don't believe it's necessary to air all of our dirty laundry, a balanced perspective is healthy and will ultimately serve all of us more effectively. The other day I was reading a blog post written by a friend—the mother of a college sophomore. She was sharing how difficult the first year of college had been for her and her daughter. She felt maybe they both would have felt more prepared for the challenges and not felt so alone if others were more forthcoming about their own experiences. She wrote, "If more people were open about their feelings, their insecurities, their failures, their true life experiences rather than what we call in our family the 'holiday card version of life,' we wouldn't all feel so alone in our struggles."

I agree. I believe we can connect more deeply and serve others more fully if we share the truth and, as my friend Amy wrote, not simply share the "holiday card version of life." I believe self-help experts and coaches have a moral obligation to paint a realistic picture, not just a rosy one. People need to be aware of the challenges they may face when embarking on any journey and know that, when they meet with struggle, they're not alone. They need to understand that while it may be possible to make six or seven figures in a business, it might not be easy or comfortable. If given a more realistic view of what to expect, they will be in a better position to make informed decisions and not be so easily spellbound by the enticing promises of fame and fortune.

Sharing the details of our lives opens up a world of possibilities if we are willing to share openly and honestly. We can help pave the way for someone else facing similar struggles. We can support each other. We can become true friends. To accomplish this we need to be willing to show our vulnerability as well as our strengths. After all, isn't it our imperfections that make us human?

In wrapping up this chapter, I thought I'd share a bit of encouraging research about the generation that cut its teeth on social media. The millennials don't appear to be buying into the "be more, do more, have more" trap. According to the Pew Millennial Research Study, their top priorities are more grounded. According Pew, gen Yers value the following:

- 52%: being a good parent
- 30%: having a successful marriage
- 21%: helping others in need
- 20%: owning a home
- 15%: living a very religious life
- 15%: having a high-paying career
- 9%: having lots of free time
- 1%: becoming famous

This is promising news. Perhaps this generation will break the spell!

Spellbound

1. Is the time you spend on social media having a negative impact on your offline life, e.g., your relationships, family, business, school work, health? (Hint: if your friends and family are constantly asking you to get your face out of your smart phone and pay attention to them, that's a clue you may have a problem.)

2. Are you spending all your time on social media talking, instead of starting and participating in conversations? Take a look at your wall or feed; are you the only one talking?

3. Are you being authentic on social media or painting a picture of the person you want people to see?

4. Do you spend most of your time on social media promoting yourself or your business?

5. Are you more concerned with the quantity of friends and followers you have on social media than you are with the quality of the relationships you're creating?

6. Are you *asking* people to follow you, friend you, or like you instead of doing or saying something inspiring that will make them *want* to follow you, or sending them a personal message telling them why you'd like to be friends?

7. Are you more focused on expanding your sphere of influence than on cultivating relationships?

8. Are you using online friendships to fill a void or combat loneliness?

9. Are you using your social media friend and follower lists primarily as e-mail marketing lists and constantly sending out marketing messages and event invitations?

10. Do you find yourself constantly logging on to social media sites just to see if someone has sent you a message or posted on your wall?

Breaking the Spell

1. Place your in-person relationships above your social media ones. Yes, some of your real friends might be people you met on social media, but the key is to differentiate between acquaintances or followers and true friends (the latter being people you can talk to and engage with).

2. Focus on stimulating conversations on social media instead of just sharing or talking about yourself. Add a question to your posts. Share your perspective and ask others to contribute theirs.

3. Show your true colors on social media. Let people see the real you. Don't be afraid to share your fears and your vulnerable side. It may actually inspire and resonate with more people.

4. Stop viewing social media purely as a marketing tool. Instead view social media as a tool of engagement. You may find that actually serves your marketing purposes better anyway.

5. Stop focusing on the number of friends and followers you have (or comparing the size of your following to that of others). Focus instead on engaging and creating quality connections and relationships. In the end, it will serve you and your business (if you have one) better.

6. Stop begging and bribing people to follow, friend, and like you. Be inspiring. Give people a reason to follow

you. It will help you build a higher quality and more meaningful social network.

7. Focus on creating relationships and adding value to those relationships. Give, don't just take. Remember, in any relationship, those who are focused only on themselves and taking what they can get don't build solid, long-lasting relationships. They're merely viewed as selfish.

8. If you're lonely or craving connections, reach out to people in person. Look for ways to connect with people in the offline world. And, in the online world, make sure you're cultivating relationships and not just placating yourself with big numbers of followers.

9. If you're using social media to market, target that marketing. Segment your lists and send marketing only to those who are ideal clients for what you're offering. Balance your marketing with conversations and other sharing.

10. Recognize whether you're addicted to social media. (Checking it constantly is a pretty good indication.) If you are, set time limits or rules. For example, you may decide you're going to visit your social networking sites only two times a day, once in the morning and once in the evening. Resist the temptation to constantly check in. Acknowledge this neediness is a probably a symptom of a bigger issue in your life and choose to address it directly.

CHAPTER 6

THE BUBBLE BURST

"What goes up must come down."

~*proverb*

My husband and I have always tried to be financially responsible. We're not big spenders. Other than incurring some credit card debt while putting me through college, we have always lived within our means and maintained a healthy savings account. While it may not appear to be the case after reading about how much money I invested in my business and personal development, the truth is, we're financially conservative. I suppose that's one more reason I'm amazed we allowed ourselves to get so caught up trying to achieve financial freedom. But it happened slowly over time.

Once we were established in our careers, had purchased a home, and had two children, we figured it was time to start planning for retirement. We hired a financial planner and, following his advice, purchased a universal life insurance policy. The monthly payments were hefty, but the policy would retain a cash value and therefore would serve as a financial investment as well. Unlike term life insurance, we would someday see the money we were paying into the policy. Not only would we be protecting our family, we would be building a retirement nest egg. It seemed like the perfect plan for our young family.

We made our monthly payments religiously for years. Unfortunately, the value of our investment didn't grow anywhere close to what we had been promised, and we began losing principal. I think the only person who profited was our financial advisor, who we learned was earning a recurring commission on our policy. Perhaps we were just naïve. We assumed he was looking out for our best interests. While we were making sacrifices to make the monthly payments and losing principal, he had a plush office and lived in an upscale neighborhood.

After years of paying into the policy, the writing on the wall was clear—it was costing us more than it was benefiting us. Putting that same money toward a less expensive term life insurance policy and investing the difference into something else would make a lot more sense. We cashed out the policy and paid the penalty. This was the first of our expensive retirement planning lessons. And, now we needed a new plan.

I was self-employed, so I had already opened a SEP IRA. I had also rolled money from a 401K from a previous employer into another IRA. My husband contributed faithfully to his company-sponsored retirement account. The problem was, *all* of these remaining investments were tied to the stock market, just as the insurance policy had been. They were volatile. We didn't feel as though we could count on them alone. We decided we needed to do more to ensure the long-term financial stability of our family.

High Times

"Remember that credit is money."

~Benjamin Franklin

The year was 2003. We had owned our home for eight years and had built up considerable equity. The real estate market was strong and had been for quite some time. Because I had done real estate marketing for years and was very knowledgeable about the industry, and we'd attended a few seminars on real estate investing, we decided real estate might be a good way to round out our retirement portfolio.

The challenge was that we live in San Diego—an expensive real estate market—and we didn't have the hefty down payment required to purchase an investment property. So we did what many people were doing at the time—we refinanced our home and took out cash. Our plan was to take only as much money as we needed to make a down payment on one rental property. Our mortgage broker encouraged us to take out the maximum amount we could qualify for. He said if we were incurring the cost to refinance, why not take out as much cash as we could? Then we'd have it if we ever needed it. It made sense at the time, so we followed his advice. Mortgage brokers often are paid a percentage of the loan amount in the form of points. Could that have been why he wanted us to take out a bigger loan? We'll probably never know for sure.

Between the cash we withdrew and all the fees, the balance of our mortgage jumped by nearly $100,000 overnight. It made us a bit nervous, but we were also excited. Maybe we could buy more than one property. It wasn't like we were going to blow the money on depreciating assets; we were investing in real estate, which would go up in value. Plus, because of the low interest rates at the time, our monthly mortgage payment actually went down after the refinance. It was the ideal solution . . . or so we thought.

We invested in a fixer-upper not too far from where we lived. We knew the neighborhood and knew it was a good deal. We enjoyed rehabbing the property and felt good when we rented it to a nice family. A year later we had an opportunity to purchase another property at a deep discount. While it required major rehab work, we negotiated with the seller to pay the rehab costs, and once again we enjoyed turning an eyesore into one of the nicest homes on the block. It felt great when we rented it to a young family. The next few years were good. All of our homes were increasing in value, and the two rental properties were nearly breaking even each month. We expected to be able to increase the rents in the future and begin enjoying positive cash flow.

Our financial future was looking bright. We were starting to embrace the risks of investing—it's easy to do when the market is going up. We also began to understand what it meant when people said it takes money to make money. Yes, we had borrowed money from our home, but it was increasing in value to a greater degree than it could have had we left it in our home. Investors call this leverage, and it's often how the rich get richer. It can be a very solid investment strategy. It can also be quite risky, especially for investors who, as they say, know just enough to be dangerous. I don't think we realized it at the time, but our risk tolerance was shifting and we were quickly turning from fiscal conservatives to fiscal liberals.

In 2005 we had an opportunity to purchase another property, and we jumped in quickly. This time it was out of state. But we had a real estate agent we trusted—he was part of the real estate investing team of one of the financial freedom experts we had been learning from. Also, we had a family member who lived near the property and was investing in the same development, so we'd have a presence in the market even if we couldn't be there. Unlike our first two investment properties, which were resale homes in established neighborhoods, this would be new construction in an up-and-coming market. We were excited about branching out and expanding our real estate portfolio. By this time we had incorporated the business and felt like legitimate real estate investors. One day these homes would be paid off, and the rental income would provide steady retirement revenue. We felt we were finally on track to financial freedom.

📷 Blog Snapshot

What You Focus on Expands

Call it the Law of Attraction or whatever you want. It's true that whatever you place your focus on, you naturally attract more of into your life. Or, at least you become aware of more things that are in line with that focus. Truth is, they were already there. It's just that you often didn't see them, because you were too focused on other things. (Ever bought a new car and suddenly see that make and model *everywhere?* This is a perfect example of this phenomenon.)

I recently realized this actually led to my becoming spellbound. I've been following inspiration (taking action on what shows up in my life) pretty consistently since 2008. Yet, I've often wondered how I got so off track in 2009.

My focus was on becoming more successful and making more money. So naturally I encountered opportunities to do both at every turn. That's where my attention was, so that's what I saw. Believing the opportunities were divinely inspired, I chased them all. And, if you've read my manifesto, "Spellbound" [also recounted in the introduction to this book], you know what happened . . . it wasn't pretty.

I get it now. My focus was in the *wrong* place. I suppose the lesson here is to be careful what you focus on. My focus has definitely changed this year, especially as I am writing *Breaking the Spell.* I'm also attracting very different people and opportunities into my life. Once again the Law of Attraction is at work. It always is.

From now on, I will maintain my focus on staying grounded and doing what's important to me. I will take it off the bright shiny objects, the shoulds, and the goals that I now see were too strongly influenced by other people.

Lesson learned.

Source: www.FollowingInspiration.com

The Writing on the Wall

"All good things must come to an end."

~Geoffrey Chaucer, poet

At a real estate seminar my husband attended in 2006, the host predicted doom and gloom, an impending real estate bubble burst that would see home values crashing. Louie came home and suggested we sell two of our investment properties (the third, out-of-state property was still under construction). At the time both properties were worth double what we had paid for them. We could have sold them and paid off our home in full and still had money left over.

Just a few years into our quest for financial freedom and our real estate investment career and we already had a net worth of more than a million dollars (at least on paper). Why on earth would we stop now? We were just getting started. I thought he was crazy to suggest we sell. After all, we had gotten into the real estate business for the long term. Our strategy was buy and hold. Plus, this was our future, the way we were going to finance our retirement. With ever-increasing home prices, these were also homes our children could live in one day if they couldn't afford to buy. Even if home values dropped, we'd just sit tight and ride out the storm. They'd surely come back even stronger, and our plans for retirement would remain intact.

The prediction at the real estate seminar came true, and 2006 marked the beginning of a downward spiral in home values. Our out-of-state property turned out to be a horrible investment. We were eating $1,200 each month on that property alone (i.e., our monthly expenses were $1,200 more than the monthly income it was generating). We "fed" the property for about a year, until our savings ran out. At the same time, the value of the property had dropped to about half of what we had paid for it. We tried to negotiate with the mortgage holder, but they wouldn't even talk to us as long as we were current with our mortgage payments. We were advised to stop making payments if we wanted to get their attention—by their customer service representatives!

We had worked hard for more than twenty years to establish good credit. We had *never* not fulfilled a debt. But we were out of money. We had been trying for months to sell the property. We had even attempted a short sale, but the mortgage company chose not to accept the offer we received. Ultimately, we had no choice but to stop making payments. At that point the mortgage company was willing to talk to us, but their process was slow and incredibly inefficient. In the end the home was foreclosed on. We lost the home and $50,000, and we decimated our credit in the process.

In the meantime we had been struggling with tenant turnover in our other two rental properties. We were appalled at how much people abused properties they didn't own. As renters we had always treated our places as if they were our own. Why couldn't we find renters like that? Every time our tenants turned over, it cost us hundreds or thousands of dollars in repairs and maintenance. The homes were declining in value. We hadn't increased the rents since purchasing the properties—the rental market didn't support any increase.

Our savings account was running on fumes. By this time we were also in debt from my 2009 personal development binge. We made the decision in 2010 to sell the properties and get out of the real estate business. Thankfully, the properties sold quickly and for more than we owed—enough to pay off our other debts and start anew.

After investing seven years of our lives and more than $150,000 in our real estate business, all we had left was a mortgage on our own home that was greater than what we had paid for it. (Thankfully, our home was still worth more than we owed.) Add this $150,000 to the $200,000 invested in personal and business development, and the quest for success and financial freedom was getting very expensive. And, we were no closer to financial independence than we had been seven years earlier. We were fifty years old with two college-age children and no savings. We were essentially starting over. We were grateful for our IRAs and my husband's retirement account, even though they were not enough to retire on. But, at least we had something left. Many people were not so lucky.

Sara's Story

Thirty-three-year-old life coach Sara is in a good place in her life now. She's been through a lot to get there. After receiving her master's degree, she landed a good job with a great salary and benefits and settled into her life. She considered herself successful. But a few years in, she knew she wasn't where she wanted to be. While it was a great job, she felt smothered, and it was taking a toll on the rest of her life. She realized the only reason she was staying in the job was the financial pressure; she had a mortgage to pay. She knew if she stayed it meant continuing to climb the corporate ladder. She also knew this was not the path she wanted to take in her life. It would not make her happy.

She decided to do a personal evaluation and ask herself why she wasn't satisfied. After all, she had all the things she thought should make her happy: a husband, a good job, a nice house. But when she asked herself what she was really passionate about, the answer wasn't her job. It was life coaching. Sara spent a year soul-searching and doing research on a possible new career in life coaching. In year four of her corporate job she began spending her lunch hours and weekends building a life coaching business. Eventually she made the decision to leave the job and become a full-time coach.

She describes this move as a huge personal growth experience. She was leaving behind a steady paycheck, benefits, and job security. At the same time she was doing something she knew in her heart would make her happier and more fulfilled. It was a huge turning point in her life and in how she views success. But this decision to follow her heart would have serious ramifications.

About this time, Sara and her husband found themselves facing a harsh reality. They were about to lose their home. After working hard in their twenties and, as Sara puts it, "doing all the right things," they were facing the realities of the deflated real estate market. They could no longer afford their home, and they couldn't refinance. They had to let it go. Sara admits they were devastated. She felt like they had done everything they were supposed to do, and yet this was still happening.

In the end, Sara says losing her home was actually a relief. It released a huge burden. The house and the job were costing her more than money, they were costing her her sanity. Sara now finds herself in a better place, a place she believes she wouldn't have come to had she not weathered this difficult storm.

This also caused Sara to step back and redefine success for herself. She learned that success isn't about what other people think. She began living her life in a way that reflects who she is. She has a sense of peace she didn't have with the job, even though she is making less money. She is no longer doing what she thought she was "supposed" to be doing; she's doing what makes her happy. She says for years the expected norm was "go to college, get a degree, go to grad school or get a job, work, and move up." With the shift in the economy and advances in technology, she sees that changing. Sara says after she left the corporate world, she had a big aha. "It seems so simple, but I realized we have a choice. We can choose to be in that corporate employee box or we can choose to do something else. It's amazingly empowering."

At this point in her life, even after all she's been through, Sara feels blessed. She's happy with her life. She would have said she was happy back in the corporate days, but she feels her general level of happiness is greater now. She's grateful to have the life lessons. She's grateful she no longer feels trapped. Her work is rewarding and fulfilling. She feels she's making a difference in people's lives. Although her income is not as high as when she had the corporate job, she is doing work she loves. She now realizes the mental, physical, and emotional sacrifices that came with the corporate job were too great. Today she feels more empowered to make her own decisions. And, that makes it all worth it.

Victimized

> *"A person who is deceived or cheated, as by his or her own emotions or ignorance, by the dishonesty of others, or by some impersonal agency."*
>
> *~dictionary definition of "victim"*

I don't really like the word "victim." It implies powerlessness, and that's rarely the case. Yet, when I look at people such as Sara, my husband, myself, and other people I know who trusted the real estate and mortgage experts, in some ways it's the only word that fits. Perhaps we had blinders on. Maybe we chose to see what we wanted to see or believe what we wanted to believe.

We certainly were not alone. Had I not experienced it myself and known other responsible people who also found themselves losing their homes, my attitude toward the millions of people who lost their homes to foreclosure between 2007 and 2010 would likely be very different. I probably would have accused those people of being irresponsible or greedy. But I didn't view myself or the people I knew as those things. We were, for the most part, smart and responsible people who were just trying to take care of our families and get ahead. People who were trying to finance their retirement, because for us, lifelong employment and pensions are extinct, and Social Security benefits are expected to dry up before we reach retirement. Financing our golden years is on *our* shoulders, and we were just doing what we thought we needed to do to secure our financial future.

I do, however, also realize that some people bought homes they clearly couldn't afford or refinanced their existing mortgages to live above their means, without really considering the potential consequences. I think it's safe to say many people got caught up in a euphoria that felt like it would never end. I also know in my situation, and for other budding real estate investors I knew at the time, we trusted the professionals who were advising us. I encountered a few red flags along the way, and when I questioned them, the professionals assured me that everything was fine. We weren't real estate experts, so we trusted the experts we had hired. I found out after we purchased our out-of-state investment property that the real estate agent and the mortgage broker had both committed fraud in our transaction, on the exact accounts I had questioned.

I should have listened to that little voice inside me that said something wasn't right. I didn't. Perhaps I was blinded by the promise of big bucks. Maybe by this time I just believed this was what it took to become financially independent. That's what you *have* to do. That's how investors play the game. In hindsight, I think I wanted so desperately to be playing at this higher level that I turned a blind eye to things that normally would have stopped me in my tracks.

Our real estate agent and mortgage broker both pocketed big commissions on the out-of-state deal. We weren't the only ones they took advantage of—many of the homeowners in the development were in the same situation. We reached out to them and began sharing stories. The misrepresentation ran deep. Nearly every investor in the neighborhood was from out of state, and we had all been misled. Along with several other homeowners, we considered legal action. However, in retracing the paper trail, we found the agent and broker had covered their tracks well. In the end, we decided to let it go. It would have likely been a long and expensive fight, and our prospects of winning were slim. We chose instead to chalk it up to experience and move on.

While it hurt to lose the home, our credit, all that money, and our pride, thankfully, we still had a home to live in. Many people, like Sara, were not so lucky. For them, the real estate market crash didn't result in merely losing investment properties. They lost their homes, along with everything they had worked for years to achieve.

We learned many valuable lessons, and, as difficult as this situation was for us, I actually remember laughing about it while sitting in our accountant's office at the end of that year. He quipped that the net result was that we had earned a Ph.D. in real estate investing. A $50,000 Ph.D.! I had to agree we had learned more in the trenches as real estate investors than we probably ever would have learned sitting in seminars or studying it. Still, it stung.

Generation Debt

"A man in debt is so far a slave."

~*Ralph Waldo Emerson, poet*

When we decided to invest in real estate and suddenly had four mortgages, I remember feeling like my parents must have thought we were crazy. Why would anyone take on four mortgages? Wasn't the goal to pay off your mortgage? Fifty years ago, you purchased a home, took out a thirty-year mortgage, and, by the time you were ready to retire, the home was paid off. Of course that was a lot easier to accomplish when homes cost tens of thousands of dollars, not hundreds of thousands, as they do in most major U.S. cities today. It was also a lot easier when people weren't constantly spending money upgrading their homes or doing cash-out refinances and living beyond their means.

For the most part, members of what's known as the greatest generation (those born between 1900 and 1924, sometimes called the G.I. generation) and the silent generation (those born between 1925 and 1945) possessed a very different money mentality from that of later generations. The baby boom generation (those born between 1946 and 1964), generation X (1965–1979), the millennials (1980–2000), and generation Z (after 2000) have grown up with credit and instant gratification as a part of their lives. They truly are generation debt.

Until The Great Recession in 2007, most boomers had not experienced economic hard times like previous generations. Boomers and subsequent generations have, in many ways, been encouraged to live beyond their means. Debt is a part of life. Credit cards. Student loans. Mortgages. Second mortgages. Auto loans, and if the car is too expensive, auto leases. At the same time, they've grown up in a booming economy. Everything kept going up: real estate, the stock market, salaries.

At the same time, the self-help industry was burgeoning, the Law of Attraction had gained mainstream exposure in 2006 because of *The Secret*, and many self-help gurus were advising that if you want to be wealthy you have to live as if you are wealthy, in order to attract that wealth. For many people, this meant spending money they didn't have and living as if they were earning six or seven figures when they weren't, in the hopes that adopting that mindset would deliver them into six- or seven-figure lifestyles.

While I understand the value of mindset and thinking "as if," unfortunately, spending "as if" proved to be the downfall of many people I know, myself included. That approach assumed the money would keep rolling in and would be there to pay off all the debt being incurred. It didn't consider that what goes up must come down. It defied historical trends in the real estate industry. It didn't take into account that this time around the real estate market had been extremely overinflated due to a rush of investors and simply couldn't maintain itself. It didn't take into account what would happen in our financial markets as a result of all the creative mortgage financing. It didn't count on The Great Recession of 2007. As a result, many boomers are now facing the harsh reality of their financial over-exuberance and lack of frugality and long-term planning.

There also appeared to be a correlation between savings rates and the booming economy. Personal savings rates in the United States averaged about 7 percent of GDP through the 1960s, 1970s, and 1980s. In the 1990s, savings rates decreased to an average of about 4.5 percent of GDP. By 2005, the personal savings rate hit an all-time low of 1.1 percent.

Savings Rates as % of GDP

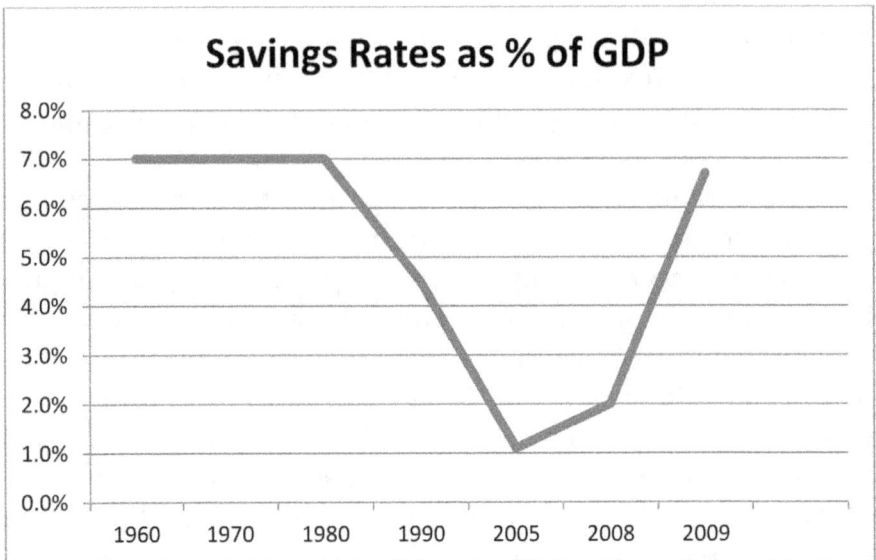

Savings Rates in the United States, published by the Congressional Research Service in 2010, said the following:

It is likely that the evaporation of household saving over the past two decades was in large measure a consequence of the sizable increase in household net worth associated with increased house and stock prices occurring at that time. Substantial increases in household wealth made it less urgent to divert current income to saving.

With home prices and stock values suddenly taking a nose dive, and no money in the bank to fall back on, many people had no way to right their failing financial ships.

There is a silver lining to all of this gloom and doom. As the economy declined in the late 2000s, personal savings rates actually began increasing again, climbing to 2.0 percent in 2008 and 6.7 percent in 2009. It appears people were actually starting to realize they couldn't keep spending all they had—and then some—and expect everything to be OK.

However, it may be too little too late for some. According to a poll of 1,160 baby boomers, 44 percent don't believe they will have enough money when their careers end. One fourth say they will never retire. Many people have done poor jobs of financial planning (24 percent say they have no retirement savings) or have seen what retirement savings they do have dwindle away. Only one in ten boomers surveyed has saved at least $500,000 for retirement. More typically, boomers have put away an average of $100,000. As a result, the reality is, most boomers will have to downgrade their standard of living in retirement. So much for dreams of sailing off into the sunset financially free!

Withdrawing from the Bank of Home

"Borrowing and spending is not the way to prosperity."

~Paul Ryan, chairman of the House Budget Committee

As home prices increased in the mid 2000s, many homeowners began tapping into all that rising equity to obtain cash to finance home improvements, business ventures, and investments. Others used this "free money" to buy cars and vacations and finance a standard of living beyond their means. A July 2006 *New York Times* article profiled a homeowner who was taking out his third adjustable-rate mortgage and $200,000 of his home's equity to invest in his four-year-old business. He rationalized this move by saying, "I could have sold my house and made my family move. But I didn't do that. I said, 'Look, I want to start a new business' and this product allowed me to do that." One has to wonder how that story turned out, considering what happened to home values *after* 2006.

According to Freddie Mac (The Federal Home Loan Mortgage Corporation), a public, government-sponsored enterprise that buys mortgages on the secondary market to repackage and sell as investments, cash-out refinances peaked in the mid 2000s. In 2004, 47 percent of total refinances resulted in a loan amount that was at least 5 percent higher than the original loan balance. In 2005, that percentage jumped to 72 percent, and in 2006 it peaked at 86 percent. That means 86 percent of people refinancing their homes in 2006 were using their homes as banks and withdrawing money. The problem is, it wasn't really money. It was a loan. But that's not what it felt like. It felt like wealth.

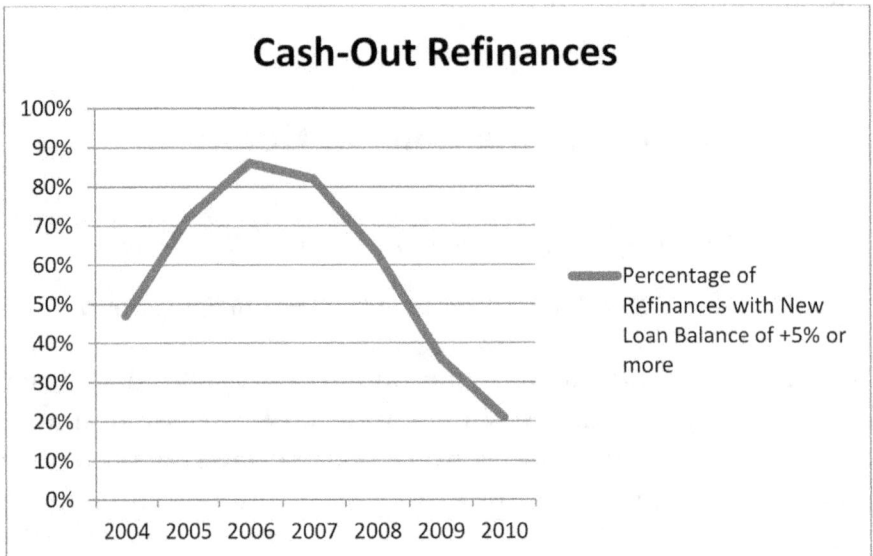

Cash-Out Refinances

Percentage of Refinances with New Loan Balance of +5% or more

The decline of real estate values closed the "bank of home" for most people after 2006. Since then the percentage of home refinances that increased the loan balance has decreased annually. In 2010 cash-out refinances accounted for just 21 percent of all mortgage refinances. According to a quote by housing analyst Michael Larson of Weiss Research in Florida, published on Bloomberg. com in July 2010, "Five years ago you had people liquidating equity to finance debt-fueled consumption. Now, refinancing gives them breathing room."

Unfortunately, that may have just been a sign of the tough times. In October 2011 I received a newsletter from a mortgage broker, and the headline on the front page read, "Refi's Have INCREASED By 63% in the Last Month!" The article quoted the Mortgage Bankers Association and stated that applications for jumbo loans had increased by almost 75% and lenders were reporting a very high percentage of cash-out refinances again. I wonder what it's going to take for some people to get the message?

Homeowners in California have been among the worst offenders of cash-out refinances. According to Equifax and www.doctorhousingbubble.com, as of 2011 California still has more than $600 billion in home equity line of credit (HELOC) debt outstanding. The average HELOC balance in California is three times the national average. Many of those homeowners are now living in homes that are financially upside-down.

As a result, what was once a situation most people would be embarrassed to talk about publicly became quite commonplace. It seemed as if everyone knew someone who was losing a home. With so many people facing foreclosure, much of the stigma has gone away. I was at the beach a few months ago and overheard a young couple talking with friends about being completely upside-down in the home they had purchased just a few years earlier. Without any overt signs of remorse or emotion they shared very matter-of-factly that they had stopped making mortgage payments months ago and would be walking away from the home. My, how times have changed!

Living Large

*"But we'd also been living large in the sense of our
conspicuous consumption, spending and acquiring so far
beyond our means in the '90s and early '00s that, following
in the way of any parable, it inevitably led to a massive
emotional and financial crisis."*

~Sarah Z. Wexler, *in her book* Living Large

In the book *Living Large: From SUVs to Double Ds, Why Going Bigger
Isn't Going Better,* Sarah Z. Wexler explores our infatuation with
more. She talks about our preoccupation with accumulation that
began in the 1990s and continued into the 2000s—our pursuit of
bigger homes, cars, businesses, and food portions. For example,
in the 1970s the average U.S. home was about 1,400 square feet.
By 2007 the average new house built in America had jumped to
2,302 square feet. Wexler talks about our infatuation with "The
McMansion," described as "a modern house built on a large and
imposing scale, but regarded as ostentatious and lacking architec-
tural integrity." Wexler defines the mentality that drove so many
people during this time: "Buying a bigger home is an unparalleled
form of expression—a tangible way to show yourself and everyone
else—that you're movin' on up." Instead of buying homes, people
were buying status symbols and believing they were investments
that could only go up in value.

I managed the marketing for a new home community from
the mid 1990s to the mid 2000s and had a front row seat for this
trend. With homes consistently increasing in value and mortgage rates at record lows, it was easy to trade up to a bigger, nicer
home. People were no longer just buying a place to live. They were
buying starter homes, first-time buyer homes, move-up homes,
and executive homes. As home prices escalated, the mortgage
industry began finding creative ways to help consumers finance
their dreams of home ownership and moving up: no-money-down

loans, 100 percent financing, low introductory (teaser) rates, option ARMs (adjustable-rate mortgages), interest-only loans, stated income loans (which required no proof of employment or income), and subprime mortgages extended to high-risk borrowers. Many people assumed they would use these creative loans as a short-term strategy to get into the home of their dreams, and in a few years—before the payments adjusted upward—they would refinance into a more stable thirty-year fixed-rate loan. After all, they'd watched the market appreciate—in some markets home values had doubled within just a few years—and expected the trend to continue.

Creative financing also fueled a refinancing boom. As homeowners saw monthly payments on adjustable-rate mortgages increasing, many chose to avoid these higher payments by refinancing. Unfortunately, the housing market peaked in 2006, home values began a steady decline, and The Great Recession arrived in 2007, which affected employment, mortgages, and salaries. As home prices tumbled and consumer debt rose, refinancing became impossible for many homeowners.

More Than Home Sweet Home

"Real estate is stable. In my opinion real estate is the perfect investment."

~Robert G. Allen, author of Nothing Down Real Estate

Another factor that contributed to the real estate bubble and subsequent burst was the sudden increase of real estate investors. I believe this was driven by two main factors: the news media's constant reporting on rising home prices and increasing equity (I believe this also fueled the cash-out refinance craze), and second, many in the self-help industry peddled real estate investing as an excellent way to generate passive income and achieve financial freedom. Every seminar or conference I attended that was promoting wealth-building systems included at least one expert pushing real estate investing as the fast path to cash. This marked a wholesale mindset shift on the part of the typical homeowner.

Prior to this, most people viewed their homes as places to live, not as bank accounts or paths to financial freedom. This focus on home equity was new. Despite owning a home since 1988 and working in the real estate industry for years, I hadn't seen or heard this heavy focus on home equity previously. By 2005 you couldn't turn on the TV news or open a newspaper without seeing a story about how much home prices had gone up. The media put the concept of home equity on center stage. They reported on it incessantly. As a result, homeowners began to feel "rich." Their homes were no longer just places to live; now they were investments. And, as we've discussed, millions of homeowners began cashing in on those investments to finance other investments; remodel; buy cars, boats, and other toys; and go on fancy vacations.

The Party's Over

"Credit buying is much like being drunk. The buzz happens immediately and gives you a lift . . . . The hangover comes the day after."

~Joyce Brothers, psychologist

The tide turned quickly once home values began decreasing in 2007 and all those adjustable-rate mortgage payments started increasing. Suddenly millions of homeowners found themselves with properties that were worth less than they owed. They were faced with rising monthly payments they could no longer afford, and they couldn't refinance. Thus began the beginning of the end.

In 2005 there were less than one million foreclosure filings in the United States. That number more than doubled in 2007 to more than 2.2 million filings. In 2008 filings topped three million, and in 2009 they reached nearly four million.

Bankruptcy filings followed suit. In 2006 there were just less than 600,000 nonbusiness bankruptcy filings in the United States. That number has risen annually, and by 2010 it had swelled to more than 1.5 million. It was time to pay the piper. Millions of people had spent credit they now could not afford to repay. The "bank of home" had failed.

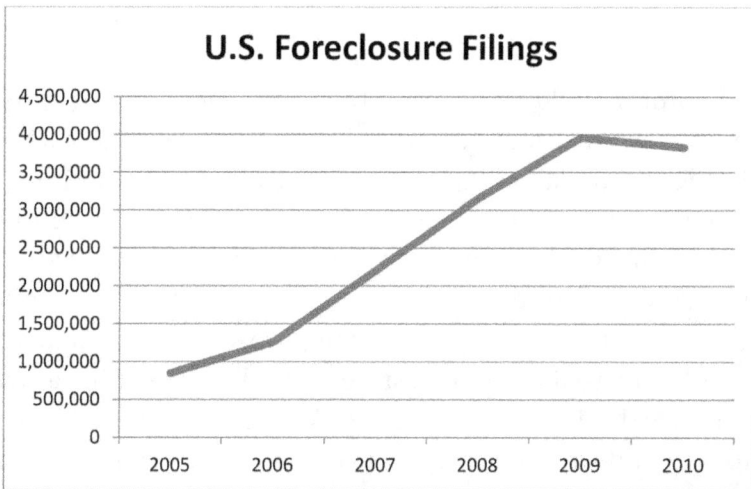

U.S. Foreclosure Filings

James, the business owner and high school student mentor we met in chapter 2, found himself explaining the realities of this to his teenage son. When the economy started its decline, his son asked how neighbors could afford the boats, cars, SUVs, motor homes, and motorcycles that he saw in their garages. James responded to his son with the question, "Do they outright own them?" When a friend's father lost his job, James and his son saw the house foreclosed on and the boat and motorcycle disappear. James explained to his son that while they may have looked like a happy family with the means to afford all of these toys, in reality they didn't own any of it. It was a perception of wealth. And, as a result, they lost it all.

The Walls Come Tumbling Down

"Humpty Dumpty sat on a wall,
Humpty Dumpty had a great fall.
All the king's horses and all the king's men
Couldn't put Humpty together again."

~*children's nursery rhyme*

It was September 2008, and my husband and I were riding in a taxi in Sydney, Australia, when we heard the news that rocked the world: the financial collapse of American-based multinational insurance company AIG. I remember everyone we talked to that day expressing great concern. We were Americans; what did we make of this? To be honest, the recession hadn't really impacted us yet. My husband had a good-paying job. My business was doing well. While our real estate investments had dropped in value, they were still worth more than we owed. We hadn't yet made the decision to sell, and we wouldn't for two more years. That day we experienced firsthand how concerned people in the rest of the world were with the financial situation in the States. It was an interesting observation, but we really weren't concerned. After all, *we* were fine.

We returned home to our lives and business as usual. Perhaps contributing to what some may call our "head in the sand" view of things was the fact that all of our business and personal development mentors kept saying the recession didn't have to exist for us. We didn't have to participate in it if we chose not to (this was one of those parroted theories referenced in chapter 4). We were taught that abundance is a state of mind. Choose not to buy into the news reports of the financial world collapsing around you, and you'll be fine.

For the most part this rang true for us. My business was still doing well, earning recurring revenue from annual consulting programs I had sold in late 2008 and early 2009. (I later realized I wasn't paying enough attention to generating new revenue to continue supporting my business beyond 2009.) Additionally, we viewed our real estate as a long-term investment and planned to wait out the downturn. I kept investing in growing my business and myself. In fact, I had stepped it up big-time. After a breast cancer scare in December 2008 I had vowed not to waste any more time on the slow road to success. I had to make my mark on the world, and I had to do it now. Looking back, it seems odd that this was my response to a wake-up call to my mortality. Instead of causing me to focus more on friends, family, and enjoying every moment of my life, it threw my quest for success into overdrive.

Unfortunately, by the end of 2009 my husband and I *were* feeling the impact of the recession along with the rest of the world. We were out of savings. We had a foreclosure on our credit report. Our American Express account had been cancelled. We were in more debt than we'd ever been in. The income in my six-figure business had dried up. Perhaps our decision not to participate in the recession had postponed the effects, but I believe it actually drove us into our dire financial circumstances. By denying that the recession existed we continued to spend and incur debt. I invested *more* money in my business and personal development that year than I made, because I mistakenly believed my actions would be rewarded in kind and the universe would begin flowing money my way. Instead, we were financially upside-down like millions of other people. That's when we made the decision to sell our real estate investments, pay off our debt, and essentially start over.

Picking Up the Pieces

"Fall seven times, stand up eight."

~Japanese proverb

As previously mentioned, for most of our married lives my husband and I were financially conservative people. After finding ourselves with $6,000 in credit card debt after I graduated from college, we vowed to pay it off and never carry credit card debt again. We held to that promise for twenty-five years. Until the mid 2000s we always lived within our means and maintained a healthy savings account. The only debt we carried was our mortgage and auto loans. And, unlike many people, we didn't buy a new car every couple of years. We paid off our car loans and continued to drive the cars until they wore out.

All of that changed when we started down the personal development path. The seeds of financial freedom were planted, and we were taught to "live as if." We were excellent students and did as we were taught. As a result, at fifty years of age, when we should be looking forward to retirement, we wonder if we'll ever be able to retire. We've returned to our financially conservative roots. We're living more simply. We're spending less. We're living within our means. And we're trying to build our savings back up. We rarely attend seminars anymore. Quite frankly, we're a bit jaded and I still harbor a fear that I could get caught up again. Most of my personal growth these days comes from buying and reading used books and e-books.

While we miss getting together with all of our like-minded seminar friends, we maintain the friendships that matter. Our marriage is stronger. We no longer fight about money the way we used to—ironic, as we have less of it. And, we are sharing our lessons learned with our adult children. While I used to preach about the importance of owning your own business and pursuing financial freedom, I now encourage my kids to do what makes them happy and be financially responsible. I just hope it's not too late.

I also appreciate the little things in life more now that I'm not running so fast—not constantly chasing success. I no longer define my self-worth by what I do for a living, how many properties or businesses I own, my net worth, my bank account balance, or how much money I'm making. Sometimes it's a little unsettling. Old habits die hard. At the same time, there's a childlike curiosity about what the future will bring that I find exciting. I no longer feel like I'm driving so hard all the time and forcing things to happen. I'm open to what will be. It's been quite a shift. And, while I'm certainly not at all where I expected to be business-wise or finance-wise eight years after beginning my quest for success and financial freedom, I'm more content than I can remember being in years.

As I continue to hear news reports about our nation's trillion-dollar deficit and states' budget crises, I know it will be some time before our world fully recovers from the overconsumption and greed that led us to this place, if it ever recovers. At the same time, I feel there is a global shift taking place. Everywhere I turn I hear people talking about simplifying their lives and getting back to what's really important. People are shifting their focus from materialism to meaning. Perhaps out of necessity, but regardless of what prompted it, it's refreshing. And, while we can never go back, maybe someday we will find ourselves and our world in a better place. As the saying goes, "It's always darkest before the dawn."

Spellbound

1. Have you consistently spent more money than you make, using credit cards to finance a standard of living beyond your means?

2. Have you incurred debt you don't have the means to repay, on the hope your investments will grow and enable you to repay it?

3. Have you used your home like a bank, withdrawing money to finance things you otherwise could not afford, either through a cash-out refinance or a home equity loan?

4. Have you refinanced your home multiple times, trying to put off the inevitability of higher monthly payments?

5. Are you paying only the interest on your mortgage and increasing the principal you owe on your home?

6. Have you gotten into investment opportunities without doing your due diligence, instead relying on other people's expertise or advice?

7. Do you carry a monthly balance on your credit cards instead of paying off your balance in full?

8. Have you heard what you wanted to hear from the experts instead of thoroughly researching the pros and cons of investment opportunities?

9. Have you neglected your savings account, assuming your investments will grow and be there to take care of you and your family?

10. Did a decision to believe you didn't have to participate in the recession cause you to spend irresponsibly?

Breaking the Spell

1. Start living and spending within your means. Simplify your life if necessary. If you feel like you can't have all the things you want, recognize that if you live in the United States you're already wealthier than most people in the rest of the world. Be grateful.

2. Find a way to pay off any credit card debt, and in the future use credit cards for convenience only, paying off your balance in full each month.

3. If you owe more on your home than it's worth because you took cash out, assess your situation honestly and make a plan to get back on track. View your home as a home, not an investment or bank account. Additionally, know the value of your home only matters when it comes time to sell or refinance.

4. Recognize you can't keep refinancing your home forever. If you want to own it and have it truly be an asset, you need to begin paying off what you owe. Make a plan to do so and stick with it.

5. If you're paying only interest on your mortgage, find a way to begin paying down the principal. Cut expenses in other areas if necessary. By paying only interest, you're

adding to your mortgage balance and living on value that is not guaranteed to be there in the future.

6. Fully research any investment opportunity you're considering. Talk to others who have invested and find out what their experience has been. Make a list of the pros and cons. Consider the worst-case scenario and invest only if you're prepared to accept that. If it happens, as much as it may hurt, at least you'll know you can afford to get through it.

7. Don't allow yourself to be blinded by slick investment salespeople. Remember they're likely making money on your decision to invest. Make sure it makes financial sense for you. Do your homework before you commit!

8. Make sure you have money in a savings account. How much is up to you. Just make sure you have a nest egg to fall back on.

9. Realize you can maintain a positive financial mindset and still accept that our country has experienced a debilitating recession. Denial is not the answer. You don't have to stop spending or investing, but be smart and make sure you have the ability to repay any debt you incur.

10. Honestly evaluate your financial situation, budget, and investments. It may make more financial sense in some cases to cut your losses and move on versus continuing to invest good money after bad.

CHAPTER 7

DEFINING SUCCESS

"There is not one big cosmic meaning for all, there is only the meaning we each give to our life, an individual meaning, an individual plot, like an individual novel, a book for each person."

~Anais Nin, author

We've talked a lot about success and how easy it is to get caught up chasing it. We've talked about the negative effects this pursuit has had on millions of people's lives and our world. The bottom line is, we've created a great big problem, and I believe it's time to remedy it. To do so, it's important to first define what we mean by success. It's a word that's thrown around a lot. But what does it really mean? As I set out to uncover the definition of success, I discovered it was not a simple task. In all the books I read, research I reviewed and conducted, and people I interviewed, I didn't find one universal definition.

In talking with people about success, I discovered that everyone defines it differently. To paint a clearer picture of what we're all chasing, I'd like to share some of the definitions that surfaced in my interviews. When I asked people how they define success and the role it has played in their lives, I found their stories enlightening and thought provoking. I'm sure you will too. I believe it's much more valuable to look at how people define success in the real world than to rely on a dictionary definition, although we'll start there. After we take a look at what success looks, feels, and tastes like to people just like you and me, we'll dive into what motivates our often insatiable quest for success. In chapter 8, we'll take a look at the psychology behind it, whether personality type affects it, and other factors that contribute to our success drive.

Struggling to Define Success

> *"The favorable or prosperous termination of attempts or endeavors."*
>
> *~dictionary definition of "success"*

The dictionary defines success as an end result, the favorable or prosperous termination of an attempt or endeavor. In other words, set a goal, pursue it, and achieve it. And if you don't achieve it, you're not successful. It really does discount the journey, and as a result it discounts much of our daily lives, because most of us are always moving toward a goal. Achieving those goals happens at a fleeting moment in time. It's no wonder we set goal after goal and often don't feel satisfied with where we are.

Additionally, when we have other people, the news media, advertising, TV, and other influencers telling us what success *should* look like, it's easy to lose sight of what's most important to us. Add to that the confusion that arises when we've bought into all these external definitions and have spent much of our lives pursuing them only to find they weren't achievable—or if they were, they didn't deliver us into the blissful state we anticipated—and it's no wonder so many of us have changed our definitions of success in recent years. And, as you'll see when you read about my discussion with Scout, a fifty-six-year-old self-employed mind-repatterning expert from Montana, all of this can make it a real struggle to define what success actually means to us.

The first question I asked Scout was, "Is being successful important to you?" She responded, "Being good at what I do is important to me. Being confident is important to me. Making a lot of money is not important to me. In the traditional sense, being viewed as successful is not important to me. I would use the word 'confident' much more than the word 'successful.'"

The introspection continues when she's faced with the question, "How do you define success?" She answers, "I've got what I think the rest of the world calls success, and I've got what I call success." Scout admits she has a major reaction—and not a good one—to what she believes the world considers success: "The big house, the fancy car, the kids in the right school, making sure you dress right, cocktail parties. There's a whole bubble that the world would call success, and I would say that in my gut I reject almost everything in that bubble."

To Scout, all of those things seem false and pretentious. It's not what matters. Instead, she says what matters are deep relationships, connection, love, and compassion. "What really matters is being authentic, and most of the things that I put in that bubble—if they come from a place of authenticity, that's great. But my perception, especially having been raised in the suburbs of the East Bay of San Francisco, is that success equals pretention. Which is why I guess it's hard for me to leave Montana and move back there." After considering what she's just shared, she adds, "This is really a pretty good look inside my own little head!"

Scout determines that, for her, success means being able to live her truth. It means being able to follow her heart. "That's success for me no matter what." She's quick to add this doesn't mean money isn't involved. It's important that she has the resources to help others.

This discussion prompts Scout to wonder, if she doesn't have money, if she doesn't have the resources to take care of business and help others, can she really call herself confident (the word she prefers over success)? In this context money is just another resource for Scout. And, in this regard—being able to share, give, and support others—money is very important to her.

As she's talking she realizes that money represents opportunity and freedom. She adds that there's a bit of a disconnect when she says this, because there's a little piece inside her that says to get money you have to give up freedom. She realizes she has just uncovered one of her own limiting beliefs, and it makes her uncomfortable. She discovers she's still exploring a lot of these concepts. What's really most important to her? Time or money? Is it even a choice she has to make? She traces this internal battle back to her childhood and what she saw modeled by her family. It's clear these questions about success are prompting an evaluation of her current beliefs.

I observed this type of introspection and in-the-moment evaluation frequently in the interviews I conducted. I witnessed people discovering their own definitions of success as we were talking. I think that, so often, we've come to accept society's definition, or even our own beliefs, without giving either too much thought. When we begin to dig deeper we start to question and re-evaluate our beliefs, and this is often driven by our assessment of what's most important to us at that particular time in our lives.

Sometimes this questioning can lead to uncertainty. We've believed something for so long that we've taken it for granted. Such introspection is a good thing. It's healthy to step back periodically and re-evaluate our beliefs and lives. It's a system of checks and balances that can help us avoid getting too far off track and waking up one day wondering why we're unhappy or how we ended up where we are.

The longer Scout and I talk, the more clearly she begins to define what success means to her. As she describes success, she paints a visual picture of a circle and a swinging pendulum. A part of the circle represents security. The opposite side of the circle represents something she values deeply: living what she calls an epic life, filled with travel and adventure. It's the complete antithesis of security. Parts of Scout's circle are also represented by two more dichotomies: poverty and wealth. She explains that success is not about being way out on the wealthy or epic side of the circle. It's about being as close to the center as possible. You can almost hear the wheels turning in her head as she creates this new definition of success for herself.

Suddenly she blurts out, "Here's what success is to me. It's to be so truly peaceful in the center that you can dance within that circle wherever you need to be, whatever works in the moment you're in. Sometimes it's going to be more money. Sometimes it's going to be less money. Sometimes it's going to be adventure. Sometimes it's going to be calm."

She realizes what she's talking about is flexibility. Emotional flexibility. Financial flexibility. Not reacting to events but being able to choose her response; the response that works best for her, the world, and the people she loves. "Success is being able to respond rather than react. Yep, that's it. There you are. For me, success is being able to respond rather than react, and what creates that for me is having resources . . . having the financial resources, having the social resources, and having the spiritual resources. To me that's what success is."

As we end our conversation, Scout seems grateful to have come to this new definition of success for herself.

The Shifting of Success

"People should decide what success means for them, and not be distracted by accepting others' definitions of success."

~Tony Levin, musician

Scout is not alone in her struggle to define success. Everyone I interviewed had come to their own conclusions about what success means and the role it plays in their lives. To some, success is about accomplishment. To others, it's being able to do what they want, when they want—in other words, it's about freedom. Following is a sampling of the varying definitions of success people shared.

It's about achieving goals. It's feeling good about yourself and what you're doing. It's having an abundant life. It's seizing every moment of every day. It's maximizing your potential. It's being able to reach into your pocket and not worry about where that dollar came from or where it's going. It's living life to the fullest. It's a happy family. It's enjoying what you're doing. It's making a difference. It's never having to say "I can't afford it." It's having healthy relationships. It's feeling confident. It's being good at something. It's being known for something. It's generating an income. It's working for yourself and not someone else. It's being satisfied with your quality of life. It's excelling at your pursuits. It's getting good grades. It's being surrounded by friends. It's climbing the corporate ladder. It's doing your work to the best of your ability. It's being happy with the way things are and not worrying about what could have been.

Clearly, defining success is a very personal matter. Yet, it doesn't appear that it's always been so personal. In fact, most people I surveyed shared that the way they define success has changed over the years. Most used to define success in the traditional ways: accomplishment, and what might be called the external symbols of success—a college education, a good job, a successful business, money, a nice house, and a nice car.

However, many people have achieved all of these external symbols of success only to find they still weren't satisfied. They discovered that, despite having all the trappings of success, they still weren't happy in the way they thought they would be. They didn't feel as successful or happy as they anticipated they would feel when they acquired all these things.

If we achieve the success we're striving for and we're still not satisfied when we get it, it begs the question, are we chasing the wrong goal? I would suggest it's not necessarily the goal that's wrong, but rather our expectations of how we'll feel when we achieve the goal. As we'll learn in the next chapter, achievement—an integral part of success—plays an important role in happiness. Therefore, I don't believe we should completely renounce the idea of achievement or striving for success. Perhaps we simply need to make sure we define success more personally and clarify our expectations of what achieving that success will actually do for us.

📷 **Blog Snapshot**

How Do You Spell Success?

Success. It's what we all seek, isn't it? It's the ultimate goal. The proof that all the time, money, or energy we've put into our business, in a pursuit, or in ourselves was a good investment.

We often use it as a measure of comparison. "She's more successful than he is." "Look how successful her business is." "I wish I were having the same success he's having."

Success is what nearly every self-help expert, coach, and business mentor is selling. But what is success, really? So often, marketing tells us success is measured in financial terms or by volume or quantity: a large number of clients, a big e-mail list, a six- or seven-figure business, a lifestyle that enables us to live in a beautiful house, drive a nice car, take fancy vacations . . . live the good life.

That may be how marketers define success, but after surveying more than five hundred people, I've discovered it's not how most of us do, at least not anymore.

When I asked people to rate various factors in terms of the role each plays in their definition of success, both five years ago and today, some interesting trends emerged. The two biggest increases were seen in "your contribution to society and the world" and "your level of happiness." There was at least a ten-point gain for each, indicating that today people consider these to be much greater indicators of success than they did five years ago. They also rated the following indicators higher today than five years ago: "friendships," "how much you enjoy what you do for a living," and "how much money you have in the bank."

In the past five years, "friendships" and "family" both moved ahead of "how much money you make per year" as indicators of success. At the bottom of the list, each decreasing over the past five years were: "level of education," "grades," "the size of house you live in," "your job title or position," and "the kind of car you drive."

Our priorities and the way we measure success have definitely shifted. Yes, having money in the bank is still considered a measure of success. That's not surprising considering the impact of The Great Recession on so many people. We want to feel secure, and having a nest egg contributes to that security.

Interestingly, "freedom to do what you want, when you want" was at the top of the list, both five years ago and today.

Perhaps our definition of success has shifted because many of us spent years working hard to accomplish success in the traditional terms and still found something was missing. We had acquired all the trappings of success, but, in many ways, a trap is exactly what it felt like. We found ourselves saddled by giant mortgages, second mortgages, expensive car leases, and jobs or businesses that were burning us out. We had money and things, but we did not have the one thing we value most: freedom.

I have realized that the traditional status symbols no longer define success for me either. The money, the material possessions . . . yes, they made me look successful, but they never made me *feel* successful. There was always a higher level of success to be achieved. There was always someone else who was more successful and made more money. It was a game I couldn't win no matter how hard I tried or how long I played.

So I chose to redefine success. I believe success is best measured by how you feel about what you've accomplished. It's not about accomplishing someone else's goals. It's about identifying what's important to you and working toward that. It's feeling good about the effort you've put forth more than it's about the final outcome, because too often we can't control the outcome. Wrapping up success in something that is out of your control leads only to frustration.

The happiness gleaned from tangible things such as money, houses, or even a successful marketing promotion is fleeting. The happiness that results from celebrating a job done to the best of your ability, sticks. And, it defies comparison because it's personal.

Research actually shows that happiness precedes success, not the other way around. That means we can choose to be happy right where we are, and that act alone will make us more successful.

I encourage you to consider how you define success. Contemplate what makes you feel good. What really makes you happy? Set personal goals based on what's important to you. Then put your full effort into achieving them, and see how good that feels. Every day look for the little successes as well as the big ones, and take the time to celebrate them all!

Source: www.DebbieLaChusa.com/blog

Redefining Success

> *"Try not to become a man of success but rather to become a man of value."*
>
> ~Albert Einstein, physicist

In the October 2011 issue of *SUCCESS Magazine*, publisher Darren Hardy wrote that he wanted to redefine success and potentially rename his magazine. Hardy titled his publisher's letter "I Want to Rename This Magazine" and wrote, "Our society celebrates those who obtain fame, wealth, power and celebrity . . . and we call them successful." He writes about some of the same things we've already discussed in this book, namely that we're taught from an early age to strive for success, most often defined by status, accomplishment, and material possessions. Yet, when we achieve all of these things, many of us still feel empty inside. While we may accomplish all of these traditional trappings of success, we often don't achieve the one thing that is most meaningful: significance. Hardy writes, "We want to know that our lives meant something, that we've had a positive impact on the lives of others. And only significance provides that, success by itself cannot."

It's pretty telling when a magazine entitled *SUCCESS* is grappling with what the word actually means. And I think Hardy is on to something when he talks about seeking significance. I too believe people are seeking meaning over materialism. We want to be happy, and we're realizing the material side of success doesn't necessarily bring us that happiness. In my survey of five hundred people, the two attributes of success that jumped the most in the past five years were "contribution to society and the world" and "level of happiness." The following attributes all dropped from five years ago: "grades," "level of education," "size of house you live in," "job title or position," "kind of car you drive," "how many clients you have," and "how much money you make." These results support the idea that the pursuit of meaning is overtaking the pursuit of materialism.

📷 Blog Snapshot

What Is Success, Anyway?

I was at lunch with several people the other day, and the subject of my book came up. I shared with them that I was writing about money, success, and happiness. One of the women immediately asked me, "So how do you define success?"

My initial response was, "It's a great question, and I'm finding through my research that most people define it differently now than they did a few years ago."

But she persisted, "Yes, but how do YOU define it?"

I struggled to answer her question. Here I am writing a book about success, and I was reaching for the words to define it.

As I reflected on it later, my first thought was, it's not really about success. It's about being happy. Yes, that's it. The goal is happiness, not success. But as I thought further, I realized that's not really how I feel. That's a cop-out. Success *is* important to me. I began to evaluate different parts of my life and ask myself what made me feel successful in each one.

I feel successful in my relationship with my husband. After all, we've been married thirty years. I pondered what it was that made me feel that's a success (outside of society telling me that being married thirty years is a success). I think it's this: We made a commitment to each other thirty years ago, and we've held to it. We've grown together. We've persevered when times were tough. We never gave up. And thirty years later, we are best friends, we still make a great team, and we're happy.

I feel successful when it comes to my children. I've raised two responsible, respectful kids. I think I've taught them how to be good people and give everything their all. Are my kids perfect? Of course not. But I did my best, and I'm proud of the people they turned out to be.

I feel successful when it comes to my work. In all of my jobs, careers, and businesses, I have always given it my all. I've done my best. I've tried to maintain my integrity. I've held true to my convictions. I've always tried to make a contribution. I've held nothing back. As a result, I feel good about the work I have done.

In the past, like many of the people I interviewed for my book, I would have defined success in external, tangible, measurable terms: the thirty-year marriage, two kids who excelled in sports and went to college, the vice president job title or the business that made six figures.

Not anymore. Success for me now is far more personal. It's an internal game. It's about enjoying and appreciating where I am, and at the same time continuing to challenge myself. It's about knowing I've done my best. It's about feeling good about what I've accomplished, even if I don't reach the ultimate goal. It's about setting my own standards and not measuring my accomplishments with someone else's yardstick.

I'm still grappling with putting my definition of success into words—into a sound bite. I may still struggle the next time someone asks me how I define success. And I think that's OK. It's a big question. Maybe it deserves a big, thoughtful answer.

Source: www.DebbieLaChusa.com/blog

Mary's View of Success

Fifty-four-year-old Mary from Pennsylvania defines success as being at a point in your life where you're happy with things how they are, you're not worrying too much about what could have or should have been, and you know you've spent your time wisely and with the people you love. Mary does make a connection between success and money, but only in that success means managing your money well and not having to constantly worry about it. She says, "You can make all the money in the world and not manage it well, and then to me you're not successful."

Mary admits that at a few points in her life she fell into the "keeping up with the Joneses" mentality. "But then I would come to the reality that those Joneses may be in debt up to their eyeballs." She now believes that financial success is more about where you can be rather than what you can have. "You know, if it allows you to live where you want to live and go where you want to go."

Mary believes most people view success as a destination. She doesn't. To her it's about the journey of life. "To say you're successful and just sort of stop and say 'OK, I'm successful,' that wouldn't be where I'd want to be. I'd want to continually make myself a better person. If you're constantly striving to be better, to be able to deal with other people in a positive way, and to continue to grow your faith, that's success to me."

Mary also understands that things and even people are transitory. They're here one day and gone the next. So, naturally, she doesn't wrap up her definition of success or happiness in them. Her perspective on this grew out of a tragic experience in her life: the passing of her husband four years ago. She explains that when he died they were in serious debt and adds that, thankfully, they were smart enough to invest in life insurance coverage that enabled her to pay off the debt after he passed away. She acknowledges this is a big part of the reason that today she is able to appreciate what she has and call it success. Otherwise, she admits she'd probably have a very different perspective and would likely be working two jobs just to make ends meet.

Mary believes that if you can avoid debt, it frees you up to see what's really important in life. It gives you freedom, something she feels she has at this point. Because of her personal experience, she stresses how important it is to be mindful of the future for those we will leave behind when we die. She encourages everyone to think about and plan for that with a will and insurance. She believes because she and her husband did this, she is now able to live in the moment and enjoy life. Ultimately, that is what makes her feel successful.

Success Is Not a Destination

"Focus on the journey, not the destination.
Joy is found not in finishing an activity but in doing it."

~Greg Anderson, athlete

If you define success in terms of achievement, success becomes about arriving at a destination. When you achieve the goal or accomplish what you set out to accomplish, *then* you are successful. As we discussed in chapter 2, this often invokes the "I'll be happy when . . ." mentality. It's easy to become so focused on where you're going that you forget to enjoy where you are. Defining success this way can preclude us from being present and enjoying the moment.

If we are to appreciate where we are and what we have, instead of always wanting for more, doesn't that *require* us to redefine success? Doesn't that mean we need to find a way to view success in the moment—in the journey of life, rather than relegating it to a destination? Lesley, a fifty-seven-year-old mother of six, self-employed artist, and mentor to other aspiring artists, thinks so. While she sees herself as successful, she is quick to point out that, for her, success is an ongoing journey and she still has further to go.

Lesley says that, ever since she was a child, she has felt she was put on this earth to do something important. She spent many years searching for what that was. In her thirties, living just outside of Washington DC, she admits the emphasis was on getting the house in the right neighborhood and all the external things. But once she'd had her fifth child, had acquired all the material possessions, and appeared to have it all, she found herself asking, "Is this all there is?" She realized something was missing, and it wasn't something money could buy.

While she always wanted to be an artist, it wasn't until she was in her forties that she felt compelled to follow that dream. Once she found her creative calling, her goal became clear: to encourage others to tap into their creativity. Now that she's in her fifties, she says it doesn't matter whether or not others think she's made it. She's happy and considers herself successful. She connects that feeling of success more to feedback than to money. If she knows she's making a difference in other people's lives, that is success. Yet, she says even if she didn't get feedback that her work was making a difference, she'd probably still find a way to do it. She has a need to communicate what she's learned—much of it the hard way—and to inspire and encourage others.

A Professional's View of Success

"A successful day: to learn something new; to laugh at least 10 times; to lift someone up; to make progress on a worthy goal; to practice peace and patience; to do something nice for yourself and another; to appreciate and be grateful for all your blessings."

~*Michael Angier, Founder of SuccessNet.org*

Success has been Michael Angier's vocation for thirty-five years. Obviously, I was curious to hear his definition of success. He says his definition represents what he calls a "very balanced" viewpoint. While money is an important part of it, he doesn't believe a person is successful just because he or she has money. (Winning the lottery is not considered success in Michael's book.) At the same time, he recognizes if you can't pay your bills, it's pretty hard to feel successful.

While many people associate success with their careers or jobs, Michael believes we can experience success and accomplishment in every area of life, including health, community, relationships, family, career, and finances. He also believes to be successful we need to be accomplishing something.

After thirty-five years in the business, Michael doesn't think his definition of success has changed, but he does believe it has changed for many people. Up until recently, he saw much more emphasis on career success, money, and material possessions— what he refers to as the trappings of success. He believes that, because of what's happened with the economy and circumstances beyond many people's control, people have discovered they can still be happy without all the money and material possessions. He believes there are many things people thought they needed to be happy that they have now realized they don't need after all. "I think there are more people than ever looking at their lives and saying, 'Is this really what I want to do?' They're actually constructing their lives more than they used to."

He believes things are shifting because people have more choices. He points out that his parents' generation went to work for a company and expected to work for that company for the rest of their lives. No one expects that today. We're a much more mobile society than what existed a generation or two ago. The Internet has opened up a world of information and options. He believes people today have more permission to be introspective about what they want and to make choices that serve them rather than following an expected path.

Pressure to Succeed

> *"'Pressure' is a word that is misused in our vocabulary. When you start thinking of pressure, it's because you've started to think of failure."*
>
> ~*Tommy Lasorda, baseball coach*

We've already talked about the pressure put on today's youth to succeed—pressure to get good grades, pressure to win at sports, pressure from the media and society in general. Kids grow up surrounded by it. One has to wonder how all this pressure affects them once they become adults. Does it create adults who put continuous pressure on themselves to be better? It might. I know that once I was out of school, competitive sports, and my parents' home, I still felt pressure to succeed, but that pressure came from me. I was the only one pushing myself toward greater and greater success. As I talked to others about success, I discovered that when we're raised with pressure, we often carry that pressure with us into adulthood. And, this pressure often is driven by a sense of responsibility.

Fatima, a forty-three-year-old single mother living in Johannesburg, South Africa, feels tremendous pressure to succeed. Most of it appears to be self-induced. With no financial support for her two children from their father, she wants desperately to be successful for her kids. That success is definitely tied to money, but she says it's also about being the best parent she can be. Her life at this point is all about her kids. She wants to be able to give them the best possible education—a formal education from an international school—and that requires money.

She admits she is heavily influenced by external messages about success. She wants the fancy car. She wants the fancy house. She wants to be stylish. In an almost desperate-sounding voice she says, "There's something about me that wants it so badly, but I'm not getting it." When asked why these things are so important to her, she responds, "I've been asking myself that, and I don't get any clear answers. I don't know why I want it so badly." She acknowledges it could have something to do with the way she was raised. She comes from a very poor background. "It's almost like I want to escape the background that I was brought up in. I don't want my children to have to see what that was like."

She shares that, although she and her three younger brothers were all raised in the same poor environment, they are all in different places in terms of money and success. One younger brother is considered very successful because he has a full-time job and makes a lot of money. Yet, her two other brothers don't care about money at all. She believes she and her successful brother chose to follow in their mother's footsteps—she's the breadwinner and has always been the more responsible parent. Her other two brothers—who don't seem to care about money or success—take after their father.

Fatima, currently an unemployed stay-at-home mom living with her parents, has spent the past two years searching the Internet for information and programs to help her become successful. Because she's in South Africa and many programs are based in the United States, she often stays up all hours of the night pursuing her quest for success. She spends much of that time taking free online classes and practicing the techniques she's learning. While she's not sure it's helped her become more successful, she says it has helped her pay off a lot of debt.

While she says between the support of her parents and her own resourcefulness she always seems to come up with the money she needs, she wants more money so she can feel secure. This contrasts with her earlier comments about wanting to be able to afford a fancy car and house. When I ask her about this contradiction, she admits this is the first time she has heard herself talk about money in terms of security. After reflecting on it for a few moments she says, "When I had a job in the IT [information technology] field, it was always for me. I didn't have a husband. I didn't have children. I stayed at home with my parents. All the money I earned was my own. So, I saved half of it and I spent the other half, which was a lot to spend for a single person. The other half that I saved, I saved for years upon years. So it made me feel good just knowing that I had hundreds of thousands in the bank. Right now I'd like that security."

As she reflects on her prosperous years working in the IT field, she talks about a time she was at a leadership camp and stood at the podium and shared the following Ralph Waldo Emerson quote: "To know even one life has breathed easier because you have lived—that is to have succeeded." She adds, "And now, years later, success to me is defined by the amount of money I have, so even to myself that is quite hypocritical."

Yet, she believes it's all a matter of perspective. She's in a very different financial place now than she was back then. Perhaps the point of view that quote represents, of service rather than security, came easier when she had money and felt secure. For now, Fatima will keep trying to make more money and become successful for her children. She plans to put more time toward building her business and financial safety net in a few months when her son turns four and starts preschool. She says then she will have more free time.

Perspective

"One of the saddest realities is that we never know when our lives are at their peak. Only after it is over and we have some kind of perspective do we realize how good we had it a day, a month, five years ago."

~*Jonathan Carroll, author*

When I was chasing success, one of the biggest problems was that my sights were always set on where I was headed. As a result, it precluded me from actually realizing and appreciating where I was. In hindsight, I can see so many accomplishments and things to be grateful for that I missed in the moment. I sometimes kick myself for not being more aware of them at the time. It's unfortunate that, far too often, the only cure for missing the opportunity of being mentally present is regret.

Prior to my seven-year pursuit of higher and higher levels of success, I was actually much more mentally present in my day-to-day life. Yes, I had goals and actively pursued them, but not with the same myopic focus that became my norm during my seven-year success binge. Now that I truly recognize the gift of living in the present moment, I find myself actually having to work on being present. It's not my natural state, as it once was. In many ways, that makes me sad. At the same time, I hope that someday, after enough practice, it will once again become my natural way.

📷 Blog Snapshot

You Can't Go Back

I heard it many times in all of the personal development seminars I attended over the years. Once you shift, change your mindset, or grow, you can't go back to the way things were—or to the way you were. It was promised as a good thing. Growth and transformation were the goal. You work hard for both. It's challenging to change ingrained mindsets and beliefs. So, I always thought, "Cool . . . after all this hard work, I don't want to go back."

Now I'm not so sure.

Maybe it was just the personal development seminars I attended and the teachers I followed, but the focus was always on striving for more. It was always about changing your mindset and busting through limiting beliefs in order to make more money and be more successful. Combine this with a personality that is already driven and prone to constantly strive for more, and the effects are not always good. In some ways, it creates a monster. One that is never satisfied, can't sit still, and has a hard time relaxing and being happy with the way things are.

Why? Because they can always be better!

The gurus were right. You can't go back. But not in the way I imagined. I'm not convinced anymore that's a good thing. There are days when I get really mad about this. While I have grown in many ways that serve me, this is not one of those ways. I sometimes wish I could go back to the way I was.

I long for the me that was naturally present in life. Now, I have to work at staying in the present moment. I feel like I'm always thinking about my goals, my business, what I will be doing next, and how I can grow, live my purpose, and serve the world. I long for the me that just naturally followed inspiration. Now it takes effort and focus and daily practice. I long for the days when I was just happy with my life. When it wasn't always about getting somewhere else.

I'm working hard to retrain my brain back into that more relaxed state. It was healthier for me. My life was more balanced. I was plenty successful, and I was more satisfied.

No, I can't go back. However, I can go forward with a positive attitude. Now that I'm aware of both ways, I can choose the one that suits me best.

Source: www.FollowingInspiration.com

Perspective is something Sharie, a fifty-two-year-old married mother of two teenagers, understands. "I think over the years, as you get older, success continually gets redefined." She admits that, in the past, she equated success with money and material possessions: the fancy house and the big fancy car. She and her family were headed down that material path until about ten years ago. Today she has a very different perspective and views that materialistic definition of success as far too shallow.

What caused her shift in perspective? She says it's the result of her husband losing his job ten years ago and the impact his challenge to find work has had on her family and their financial situation. Dealing with the financial difficulties helped Sharie realize that you can't count on happiness that results from external sources, because those things are often outside your control.

While Sharie admits she'd like to be in a different place financially, she is happy. She has faced her share of difficulties in life, yet her attitude is that you can let it tear you down or you can look at it and know things will get better. She believes that everything happens for a reason. She firmly believes nothing is random. "There's a reason that these things happen, and we may not see it today. We may not see it tomorrow. It may take ten years. You either make lemonade with it or you let it ruin your life."

A Success About-Face

> *"If you do not change direction, you may end up where you are heading."*
>
> *~Lao Tzu, philosopher*

I would say I have experienced an about-face when it comes to how I view and pursue success in my life. My about-face happened when I realized that what I thought I wanted didn't actually make me happy. That caused me to step back and re-evaluate what I was chasing and make some serious changes. Changes that have brought peace into my life where there used to be constant uneasiness. Changes that have replaced consistent striving with content and gratitude.

Kellie, a 34-year-old architect-turned-health-and-wellness-coach, has also experienced an about-face when it comes to how she views and pursues success. In fact, success as she used to define it now makes her cringe. Kellie went to architecture school, and in the competitive world of architecture, she learned that success was defined by achievement, climbing the corporate ladder, and making money. Kellie found this path to be physically and emotionally exhausting and realized it was not a world she wanted to be a part of.

She didn't know what she wanted to do, so she put her life in the hands of fate, taking whatever jobs came her way. Still, she constantly sought success, because that's what she had learned to do. After years of perpetually seeking achievement, she discovered she was miserable. Getting sick and realizing she was burned out provided the perfect exit strategy. Kellie was determined to seek another path.

Today Kellie's definition of success has taken an about-face. She now feels successful if she's able to be present in her day-to-day life.

She feels successful if she's doing work that makes her happy. She feels successful when she has time to give to her family. She feels successful when she has flexibility and balance in her life. She feels successful when she has time to take care of herself.

Kellie believes that, while her original insatiable quest for success was fueled by her years in architecture school, aspects of her childhood may have predisposed her to it. As a child she craved approval and sought it through achievement. Her quest for success was driven by her reliance on external influences— approval and recognition—because those things made her feel good inside. Today she says her drive for success is much more internally motivated. It comes from a place of being centered. She admits the outside influences still come into play, and she is diligent about keeping her focus on what's important to her. Kellie believes that often we change on the inside first and it takes some time for the outside to catch up. That's the place she finds herself today, still trying to catch up to her new definition of success.

The Aging of Success

> *"Aging is an inevitable process. I surely wouldn't want to grow younger. The older you become, the more you know; your bank account of knowledge is much richer."*
>
> ~William M. Holden, author

A common theme I saw through all of my interviews was the tendency to define success differently as we age. As we get older our attitudes shift, and the external, material symbols of success often begin taking a backseat to our internal sense of satisfaction. In some cases this seems to come about after acquiring all of the traditional markers of success and realizing there's still a void, that something is still missing. In other cases it just seems to coincide with the change in perspective that accompanies maturation.

No one summed it up better than Christie, a sixty-eight-year-old writer and tutor living in San Francisco: "When I was younger, success was certainly about acknowledgement and money and being in the right place at the right time and having the right kind of job, the right kind of look. I didn't think about it much, but I realize that I was picking up on all of those markers of success and trying to adopt as many of them as I could."

Now that she's older, Christie says success is much more internally driven. She believes when you get older, things change. As she puts it, "You're no longer the player in quite the same way." To Christie, this means figuring out where she belongs and what she needs has a whole lot more to do with what she can manufacture for herself than it does with her environment telling her what her value is. She laughs and says, "Because if I did that, if I waited for that, I would find at this point in my life that I'm not perceived as having much value."

She believes this aging of success is biologically driven and refers to what she calls the arc of productivity. "It's knowing we have a certain amount of time here and there's something to be done." She also believes whether she is happy and successful in large part relies on her attitude toward both: "It truly is perception and attitude, yes, barring really dramatic things like terrible external hardships or accidents. But generally speaking, how I look at my day and my life . . . I'm the one calling the shots with how it is." She admits this is something she's really come to realize only in the last four to five years.

An Inside Game

"We all talk to ourselves. A major key to success exists in what we say to ourselves, which helps to shape our attitude and mindset."

~Darren L. Johnson, author

Success really is just a mindset. It's what we think it is. We can allow our definition to be influenced by other people and outside factors, or we can choose to define it for ourselves. It's clear that many of us are driven to be successful. Our actions and decisions reflect this drive. However, those actions and decisions are also very much a reflection of how we choose to define success.

If we choose an internally motivated definition of success, our life may look very different from our life if we choose to follow external influences. Those who are pursuing their own personal definition of success are much more likely to be satisfied with their lives, because they have chosen to pursue what *they* deem important, whereas those who allow themselves to be driven by what others define as success may find emptiness when they achieve that success. They just may find that what they were striving for isn't important to them after all and, as a result, does not make them happy. The lesson is to choose your goals carefully. Be true to yourself. In the end, it doesn't matter what your life looks like on the outside, as long as you're happy on the inside.

Donna, a forty-three-year-old self-employed book-writing coach from San Diego, exemplifies this attitude in the way she chooses to live her life, which has included its share of difficulties. Donna shows us that if we want to be happy regardless of what life throws at us, we must make the game of success an inside game.

Donna says success is about seizing every moment of every day to the best of her potential. When she's able to do that in the moment, that's a successful moment. When she's able to string those moments together, they add up to a successful day. Donna shares, "We're only here on this planet earth for so long, and I want to make the most of it. It's always been one of my personal standards of no regrets and wanting to do the best I could."

Donna says her view of success has changed over the years. In fact, she has identified three different phases. She describes the first phase as the time when she was developing into a young adult, and she admits success at that time was outwardly driven. It was about being a good student and getting the grades her parents expected.

That phase was about finding her way in the world, and that way often was influenced by teachers, peers, and outside factors.

When Donna was twenty-four, both of her parents died. This ushered in phase two, which she refers to as "Welcome to Adulthood." With her only sister at school several states away, she was thrust into making her own decisions. "That's when I think I came into my own, depending [on] and honing and developing that internal feeling of 'OK, if we're going to do things, it's for us, for me.'"

Today Donna sees herself embarking on phase three. While she says she is still internally driven, she owns a business now and has other people depending on her, which causes her to be a bit more thoughtful when deciding what action to take. She realizes it's no longer just about her. At the same time, she is still very clear that success is about listening to her inner voice.

Donna admits that money, or lack of it, has played a role in her success. At one point not that long ago, she was ready to declare bankruptcy. She says she worked hard to turn things around, and because of her drive, within ten months she was earning six figures. She says that after she got to that point financially and regained her sense of peace, the money didn't feel so important. It's as if she had reached a certain level and thought, "OK, this is good." Now she says she has a different sort of drive. It's not the desperation she faced previously. She does consider herself successful now, and if she makes a lot of money, she says that would be great, but it's not how she measures success.

The Personal Nature of Success

"If one advances confidently in the direction of his dreams, and endeavors to live the life he has imagined, he will meet with a success unexpected in common hours."

~Henry David Thoreau, author

I began my interviews looking for a universal definition of success. I didn't find one. What I discovered instead was that we all define success differently and that our definitions evolve over time. Age, life experience, circumstances, spirituality, financial situations, and how we choose to deal with all of these factors most certainly influence our definition of success. Fundamentally, success is about setting goals and achieving them. However, goals vary by person. While one person may set a goal to make money, another may set a goal to be happy. Both consider themselves successful when they achieve their respective goals. It might not be that their definitions of success are different; their success just looks different.

Additionally, there appears to be a protective mechanism at work here. If we set a big goal and don't achieve it, rather than labeling ourselves a failure we often choose to rationalize the situation. If we were chasing money and we don't obtain it, we may say we've realized money won't make us happy. If we were chasing material possessions and don't acquire them, or we acquire and then lose them, we rationalize that they didn't really make us happy after all. If we were chasing professional success and didn't reach the pinnacle we were striving for, we console ourselves by saying that we discovered that wasn't what we really wanted and we're thankful we ended up where we are instead. And, while all of these realizations or changes of heart may in fact be true for us in the moment, in some way they still represent a rationalization. Perhaps this is just the way we learn what we do and don't want.

This judgment and redefinition in hindsight also appears to be an element of self-preservation. In the book *Stumbling on Happiness*, Daniel Gilbert refers to this phenomenon as resilience: "Resilience is often the most commonly observed outcome trajectory following exposure to a potentially traumatic event."

According to Gilbert, studies indicate that often people who have survived major trauma claim their lives were enhanced by the experience. While we're not necessarily talking about traumatic experiences in our pursuit of success, what this shows is the human tendency to bounce back. It illustrates that we tend to look for the positive outcomes in our negative experiences. We seek to learn from our failures and mistakes.

Perhaps it's a survival technique, a coping mechanism, or simply the way we grow as human beings. Regardless of what causes it, it became very clear to me in all of my interviews that this very same mechanism is alive and well when it comes to our pursuit of success. Our definitions evolve based on our circumstances and vantage points. We look for definitions that serve and support us. That means there are probably as many definitions of success as there are people. When my father reviewed the first draft of this chapter, he commented that the world population had just hit the seven billion mark and therefore there are probably seven billion definitions of success. He just may be right!

It's clear that to be meaningful, our definitions of success must comprise what we deem important. And, because that may also be different for different people, it further explains why there are so many different viewpoints on success.

Regardless of how you choose to define it, the pursuit of success appears to be a significant part of many people's lives. That's not necessarily a bad thing. It helps bring meaning into our lives. It motivates us. It enables us to live lives of service and contribution as opposed to simply passing the time. The pursuit of success doesn't appear to be the problem. Rather, the problems seem to arise when we allow our definitions of success and subsequent pursuit of it to be influenced by other people and external factors. We face two dangers when we allow this to happen. First, we may find the success we're pursuing is impossible to achieve. Second, if we do achieve it, we may find it's not really what *we* wanted after all.

Spellbound

1. Have you allowed your definition of success to be influenced by other people or external factors?

2. Do you believe there is one, universal definition of success?

3. Have you achieved success in terms of money, accomplishments, or possessions and realized you still are not happy?

4. Have you achieved the success you were striving for and still felt like there was something missing?

5. Have you bought into the traditional markers of success—a great job, a successful business, a nice house, a nice car, and a lot of money—and achieved some or all of these things, but then felt trapped by them?

6. Have you gone into debt trying to become more successful?

7. Have you sacrificed important relationships trying to become more successful?

8. Do you find yourself questioning everything you thought you wanted?

9. Do you feel a sense of competitiveness, believing that to be successful you have to achieve what others have achieved or you have to outdo them?

10. Do you spend all of your time focused on the future and what you're trying to achieve, at the expense of enjoying life and what you have today?

Breaking the Spell

1. Stop looking to other people for their definitions of success. Reflect on what makes you happy, and what goals you would feel good about accomplishing, and redefine success on your terms.

2. Accept there is not one universal definition of success. Success is in the eye of the beholder!

3. If you've determined that money, achievements, and material possessions don't make you happy, spend some time discovering what does, and revamp your life to incorporate more of these things into it.

4. Take some time to reflect on what is most meaningful to you. Look back at times in your life when you felt happy and fulfilled and recall what you were doing or what you had accomplished that resulted in those feelings. Aim to bring more of that back into your life.

5. If you feel trapped by the life you have created, step back and think about how you can simplify. Identify what is making you feel trapped and start working to eliminate it from your life. And remember, it doesn't matter what anyone else thinks.

6. If you're in debt from your quest for success, create a budget or a plan to pay off that debt. Recognize that it may be challenging but that once the debt is gone you will feel a huge sense of relief and freedom.

7. If you've sacrificed important relationships on your quest for success, it's time to mend them. Recognize that success without someone to share it with is empty.

8. If you've been chasing other people's dreams for so long that you don't even know what your own dreams are anymore, take a timeout to reconnect with yourself. Meditate. Create a vision board. Remember, there are no rules. Your heart will tell you what matters to you, but you have to shut out the outside voices and listen so you can hear it.

9. Remember life is not a competition. There will always be people with more accomplishments, more money, and more success. Determine what makes you happy and strive for that. Resist comparing yourself to others.

10. Remember life is a balance of enjoying the moment and achievement. Be happy today, where you are and with what you have. Set goals for the things you would like to achieve and take action toward them. But always remember to maintain a balance. If you find yourself sacrificing today's happiness completely for your future goals, it's time to step back and re-evaluate. Yes, there may be some sacrifices necessary to achieve bigger goals, but you should never be totally miserable trying to get someplace else. If you are, you're missing out on life.

CHAPTER 8

SUCCESS DRIVE

"You've Really Got a Hold on Me."

~Smokey Robinson, 1962 top-10 single by The Miracles

I thought I had freed myself from the hold success had on me. Then I got the news. I didn't win. After being so sure I would be fine whether or not I won, I found myself completely sidelined. As much as I thought I'd released myself from needing external validation for my work, I realized I was still spellbound. The culprit? A book-publishing contest. My entry? A proposal for *this* book. And, even though I had known my book was quite possibly not the type they were looking for, I had entered anyway. It provided me with motivation to begin writing and a deadline to complete the book by. I told myself that was reason enough. Winning would be icing on the cake. Well, it turns out I really like icing!

Understanding Success Drive

"To strive vigorously toward a goal or objective; to work, play, or try wholeheartedly and with determination."

~dictionary definition of "drive"

Like it or not, I've come to accept success is important to me. And I am not alone. Every person I interviewed for this book told me success was important to them. It's important to my clients; they invest considerable time and money to make their businesses more successful. We've established in the previous chapters that from a very early age we're surrounded by messages that condition us to strive for success.

I'm not sure that simply wanting to be successful is a problem. I do, however, think it becomes a problem when we become consumed by our pursuit of success. It becomes a problem when we believe achieving higher and higher levels of success will make us happier. It becomes a problem when we believe the success we're seeking will deliver us to some blissful place where everything is perfect and all our problems are solved. It becomes a problem when we tie our emotional happiness to becoming successful. It becomes a problem when we adopt other people's definitions of success and lose touch with what's most important to us. It becomes a problem when we allow ourselves to believe we need external kudos and recognition to validate our worth or the path we've chosen. It becomes a problem when we become spellbound by our pursuit of success and constantly chase it regardless of the physical, mental, emotional, and financial costs.

We've established some of the societal and cultural reasons we strive for success, but are there also internal factors that drive us? Are some people programmed to seek success more than others? Is it possible, or even probable, for *anyone* to get caught up in the quest for success the way I did? Is there something in my genes that caused it? Was it due to my personality type? Can the pursuit of success become an addiction like gambling or alcohol?

I set out to answer these questions, hoping it would provide further explanation for my behavior as well as what I've seen happening in our world. In the process, I came to the conclusion that there are many factors that play a role in what I call "success drive." In this chapter I present what I found. I share the research, what I learned from the experts, and the conclusions I have drawn from it all.

Personality Type

"Personality is immediately apparent, from birth, and I don't think it really changes."

~Meryl Streep, actress

Before being hired for one of my first full-time jobs after college graduation, I was asked to take a personality test. Apparently they wanted to find out whether I was a good fit for the firm. I wanted the job, so off I went to the testing center. I got the job and stayed for eight years—the longest I've ever worked for anyone other than myself. I don't know whether the personality test was the reason the job turned out to be a good fit. I'll probably never know. However, I do believe our personality traits influence what we are drawn to and what we excel at. Therefore, it seems plausible they could also influence us in terms of how we choose to pursue success or whether we choose to pursue it at all.

We all know people who are driven to succeed and willing to do whatever it takes to accomplish their goals. They bulldoze over obstacles. They don't allow anything to stop them. They never give up. We also all know people who seem quite content with the status quo. They're perfectly happy to sit back and enjoy life exactly as it is, with no obvious motivation to seek more. Clearly, these are two very different types of people. It could be said they represent the two ends of the success drive scale. The question is, why are some people totally driven to strive for more while others are perfectly content with what they have? Are certain personality types more inclined to seek success? Are some personality types more likely to get caught in the web of success or put their happiness on hold until they achieve a certain level of success?

I began my research on personality type by taking several personality tests myself. I wanted to see whether the tests accurately reflected what I know about myself and how I operate in the world.

I wanted to see whether they would explain the choices I've made and help me understand how I got so caught up in the quest for success.

I learned my Myers-Briggs Personality Type is ISTJ (introversion-sensing-thinking-judging). I'm a D/C (dominant-driving-doer/cautious-competent-careful) according to the D-I-S-C System and an equalizer/influencer according to the Strong Life Test. I'm an Enneagram number 3 (the achiever), a gold/backup blue introvert in the Color Q Personality Test, and a seeker in the VisualDNA Personality Test.

It doesn't matter whether you're familiar with all of these personality tests, although you may choose to take some yourself to help you better understand what drives you (many are free, and you'll find links to all of them in the references section). What does matter is that I discovered they all accurately defined my personality, what motivates me, and the way I behave in the world. They helped me understand me! They also explained a lot about why I became so spellbound by success. Perhaps they can do the same for you.

Let's take a closer look at two of the more popular personality testing systems to better understand the connection between personality type and success drive.

Myers-Briggs

The Myers-Briggs Type Indicator is the most widely used personality test. Myers-Briggs contends that our personalities predict patterns of behavior and are defined by four dichotomies, with each person leaning toward one from each of the following pairs:

extraversion vs. introversion
sensing vs. intuition
thinking vs. feeling
judging vs. perceiving

While each of these eight characteristics influences behavior, the Myers-Briggs system involves assigning a combination of four preferences, one from each of the four categories. When I asked Shoya Zichy, a Myers-Briggs expert and the creator of the Color Q Personality System (a derivative of the Myers-Briggs system that has been administered to more than fifty thousand people worldwide) how or whether personality type might influence our pursuit of money and success, her response was, "It's a complicated topic, because money—unlike other areas that we work in, such as leadership, family dynamics, and teams—is something that, A, we have to have in life and, B, much of our attitude [toward] is also very profoundly influenced by our family."

Zichy says there are many factors outside of personality type that influence success drive, such as personal values, how we are raised, how frugal our parents were, whether we had money growing up, and the degree of stress caused by having or not having money. However, she has found several aspects of personality that are connected to our striving for success. Extroverts—people who are outgoing and like to be around other people—are more influenced by the opinions of others. They are tuned in to other people's expectations and want to be liked and respected. Therefore, they may be driven to succeed to impress others. On the other hand, introverts—those who are reflective and reserved and prefer to do things alone or with a small group—don't care all that much what others think. Introverts also might seek success, but they do so to prove something to themselves.

Zichy has also found that, between the thinking and feeling personality characteristics, thinkers tend to see money and success as proof of competence. Therefore, it is much more important to them. "Having a nice house is important to a thinker because it is proof to the community that they have been successful."

When it comes to the Myers-Briggs dichotomy of judging vs. perceiving, Zichy has found that those with a preference toward judging tend to be more driven for money and success. She has also found that people with both the thinking and judging (TJ) preferences have the highest drive for money and success. As a TJ myself, I'm beginning to see why becoming more successful and making more money was so important to me!

This seems to suggest that some personality types may be more driven to succeed than others. However, it also appears that all types may choose to pursue success, but they do so for different reasons. It seems that personality type may influence the way we behave while pursuing success more than it influences whether we choose to pursue success in the first place.

Additionally, according to Zichy, how well you understand your personality type probably does impact whether you get caught up chasing success in an unhealthy way. She believes that when you understand your personality type, it makes you more aware of your preferences, strengths, and weaknesses. That awareness helps you stay grounded, and when you're well grounded, you're less likely to be influenced by other people or advertising messages. Also, how hard we chase money and success ultimately comes down to understanding what motivates us. According to Zichy, if we're in touch with what's most important to us and why we do what we do, we will be less likely to get caught up chasing the wrong things or chasing things for the wrong reasons.

Enneagram

While certainly one of the most popular, Myers-Briggs is just one of many personality testing systems available. The Enneagram, a more spiritually based system with roots dating back thousands of years, is another. There are nine Enneagram personality types, representing nine different perspectives on life and ways of being in the world. Lynda Roberts, a member of The Enneagram Institute Training Faculty, says that, even though we all have all nine types within us, each person has a dominant type. She explains that the system is dynamic and complex and is not about stereotyping or labeling people. Instead, she says knowing your dominant type can help you see some of the traps you tend to fall into.

Roberts said that the Enneagram 3, referred to as "the achiever" (my type!), is probably the one most driven to succeed. The achiever is very sensitive to how he or she is seen by others and wants to be seen as successful. Roberts said the Enneagram 7, the enthusiast, may also be driven, but more because he or she is always seeking experiences and sources of stimulation. She adds that the Enneagram 2 (the helper), 3 (the achiever), and 4 (the individualist) are all part of what's referred to as the image triad, and therefore are sensitive to how others see them. As a result, they all may be driven to succeed; however, they're not driven in the same way or motivated by the same things. While the achiever is oriented toward achievement and success, the helper is oriented toward relationships and the individualist toward needing to feel and be unique. Each type may pursue success relative to his or her orientation. As a result, the pursuit of success and resulting achievement may look different for each.

Roberts says we can use the Enneagram system to become aware of our patterns and understand what triggers us to act in ways that may not be in our best interest. Her perspective agrees with Zichy's (the Myers-Briggs expert): the more we understand ourselves and the more grounded we are, the less likely we are to fall victim to the negative aspects or weaknesses of our personality types or be influenced by other people or external factors.

In my search to uncover whether personality type is a major indicator of success drive, I found clues but no definitive answers. While it appears that some personality types may be more prone to seek success, it is clear personality type alone is not a sole determinant—there are other factors involved. We've already discussed many of the external factors. We'll take a look at some of the other internal factors in the rest of this chapter.

Personal Values

*"Happiness is that state of consciousness which proceeds from
the achievement of one's values."*

~Ayn Rand, writer

Values are deeply rooted beliefs, and according to the personality experts I interviewed, they definitely influence our behavior. In fact, Deidre Sheldon, a certified Myers-Briggs Personality
Inventory Assessment provider, believes personal values always
trump personality type when it comes to behavior.

Our personal values develop from a variety of sources, including our parents, the environment we are raised in, society, and even
the generation we belong to. Sheldon believes our values have a
stronger influence on our pursuit of money and success than our
personality type does. She also believes that, while personality type
may make some people more inclined to follow others, it's one's
beliefs and values that determine which leader or crowd a person
will choose to follow. Additionally, she says the weaker a person's
foundation of personal values, the more readily that person will
look to others for guidance.

Psychologist Jean Twenge shares in her book *Generation Me:
Why Today's Young Americans Are More Confident, Assertive, Entitled—
and More Miserable Than Ever Before*, that people born after 1970
reflect very different values from people of earlier generations.
"GenMe's," as Twenge calls them, were raised in an era focused
on individualism and self-esteem. As a result, they've grown up
with a sense of self-importance that often manifests as materialism. She writes, "In 1967, when boomers were in college, 45% of
freshmen said it was important to be well-off financially. By 2004,
74% embraced this life goal." She admits this may be partly due
to necessities such as housing being more expensive. However,
she points out that members of generation me have always lived

in a time when possessions were valued. It stands to reason this focus on self-importance and material possessions would drive the pursuit of money and success, at least for members of generation me.

Goal Setting

> *"People with clear, written goals accomplish far more in a shorter period of time than people without them could ever imagine."*
>
> ~Brian Tracy, author

Goal setting is a commonly recommended practice for getting what you want. After all, goals can provide direction and motivation. Goal setting proponents advocate putting goals in writing and making sure they're SMART—specific, measurable, achievable, realistic, and time-bound. Mark Victor Hansen, coauthor of the *Chicken Soup for the Soul* book series, advocates setting 101 goals. In fact, when I saw him speak at a conference, he actually pulled his list of 101 goals out of his pocket. Apparently, not only does he advocate writing down goals, he suggests we carry them with us so we're constantly reminded of what we're striving for.

I'm not going to debate the effectiveness or value of goal setting. Rather, my point is to illuminate yet another way we have been taught to focus on the future and strive for more. In fact, it's somewhat expected that we have goals. When my husband and I were dating, I remember my father asking my husband what his goals in life were. I'm sure my dad wanted to make sure I wasn't marrying a deadbeat. I get it. My dad wanted the best for me. It's natural to want the best for our children. In fact, I believe it's natural to want the best for ourselves. Goals show we have an eye on the future, that we're not just wandering aimlessly. As the saying goes, "A man without goals is like a ship without a rudder."

Goals also provide an avenue of measurement. And, as I discovered when I spoke with Carol, a forty-five-year-old mother and preschool teacher from North Dakota, goals also provide validation of our success. To Carol, success literally means achieving her goals. She says she likes to set goals, and if she achieves them she's believes she has set the *right* goals. Her goal setting isn't limited to her career; she also sets goals in her role as a mother. When she achieves these motherhood goals, she feels like a good mom. In addition to feeling successful when she achieves her goals, Carol feels successful when she has enough money to do the things she wants to do and when she feels she has helped others. Carol believes success is a necessary component of happiness.

"I feel like if you're not successful, then how can you be happy?" she says. "When you're not meeting goals, you're not getting ahead, and you're not doing more. I just think that the more you do, the more successful you'll be . . . and that makes you feel happy and fulfilled and successful."

For Beth, a fifty-two-year-old divorced mother of three, success is also about achieving goals. However, Beth says it's also about the sense of achievement she experiences on the way to the goal, not just the culmination of it. She reminisces about preparing for and competing in a bodybuilding competition. She thought she would experience all the glory on the day of the competition and that this glory would be tied to whether she won. As she reflects on that day, she says it actually turned out to be very anti-climactic. "I realized the success came from all the work I did leading up to that day. That was much more meaningful to me than the competition. And I didn't know that before the experience."

She now realizes that success isn't necessarily in achieving the goals she creates, but instead it's found on the path to those goals. Because of this outlook, Beth can feel successful even if she doesn't reach her goals. For her, it's about setting a goal; taking the necessary steps to achieve it; being disciplined, focused, and committed; and feeling joyful about following through. Success is more about the process. She admits she may be disappointed if she doesn't achieve something she sets out to accomplish, but she doesn't view it as failure. It's merely a step along the way, and that step often leads to something else. "If I don't reach that goal, I'll be somewhere else," she says. "And that will be where I should be."

Goals are a very accepted and highly promoted way of accomplishing what we want in life. It's no wonder so many people advocate and practice goal-setting. However, in his book *Overachievement*, Dr. John Eliot paints a very different picture. In his study of high performers, he has discovered they think differently from most people. The traditional focus on goal setting is not what drives them. He writes:

> It is a myth that success is about setting the right goals and working hard to achieve them. The path to the top is rarely so direct. And the most inspired stories (coincidentally belonging to the happiest people) are about achievements that stemmed from unexpected career twists, events, and discoveries of people open to all the possibilities that life may offer them.

Does goal setting influence success drive? Absolutely. Goals involve focusing on what you want to accomplish in the future. They're about achieving more. It's not that goal setting is bad, it's just another example of the way we've been conditioned to always seek more. I know I was a victim of relentless goal setting for years. I'd set a goal, achieve it, and immediately set a new goal. I was so busy looking toward the next mountain to climb that I never stopped long enough to celebrate my achievements. That constant focus on the future caused me to burn out. It was also at the root of much frustration, because I was never satisfied with where I was.

I no longer set goals. Instead, I have a vision of what I'd like to achieve, but I leave the specifics open. I have found this allows me to be more present while still being open to growth. I don't become so attached to specific outcomes that I drive myself crazy trying to achieve them. Yes, a vision is harder to measure than specific goals, but given my personality type, I've found it to be a much healthier way to manage my success drive.

Programmed for Success

> *"Just Do It."*
>
> ~*Nike advertising slogan*

We've established that society and environmental conditions play a role in success drive. Personality type, values, and goal setting also contribute. But does it go deeper than that? Are we wired to want more? Are our brains programmed to achieve? It turns out they may be.

Dr. Srikumar S. Rao is an expert on success and happiness and the author of *Happiness at Work: Be Resilient, Motivated and Successful—No Matter What,* in which he writes:

> When you get what you want—what you have striven mightily for—there is a thrill of satisfaction. For a moment you are on a peak, and the vista is gorgeous. You feel like an emperor. This euphoria does not last. There is always another thing that you suddenly need. And another. And another.

Sound familiar? Rao writes that underneath this need to achieve is the fact that most people are not happy, even those who appear to have it all. Instead, they are plagued by anxiety and stress. Never-ending to-do lists and a constant feeling that there is too much to do and not enough time to do it rule their lives. Rao suggests that happiness is in fact our innate nature but we have spent our entire lives learning to be unhappy. As we discussed in chapter 2, we have been conditioned to believe that we have to be, do, or have more to be happy. So naturally we keep striving for more. Rao writes that this if-then mentality (if I get this, then I'll be happy) prevents us from experiencing our innate happiness. The more we get caught up in the if-then model, the more happiness eludes us. Rao doesn't advocate that we stop setting goals or striving for more. He simply advises us to acknowledge that our success or failure has no bearing whatsoever on our well-being.

In his book *Flow*, psychologist Mihaly Csikszentmihalyi investigates what he calls "optimal experience" or a state of deep enjoyment, creativity, and total involvement with life. Csikszentmihalyi calls this state "flow." You may know it as "being in the zone." Flow is the state of being so engaged in what you're doing that you lose track of time. Through his research, Csikszentmihalyi discovered that no matter who we are, where we live, or what we're doing, we describe optimal experience exactly the same way. He also discovered that optimal experience can be achieved through a wide variety of activities, however, it always involves activities that provide a challenge and require skill.

Apparently we don't find sitting around and doing nothing nearly as enjoyable as pushing ourselves, competing, and achieving our goals. Getting lost in an activity (the definition of flow) happens most often when we are achieving something, and according to Csikszentmihalyi, clear goals and feedback are an important part of that process. If optimal experience, or flow, is where we find ultimate happiness, and one of the primary requirements is undertaking a challenge, perhaps our brains are wired to pursue achievement. When I spoke with Edna, a thirty-five-year-old coach, personal trainer, and new mom, she told me that is exactly how she's wired.

It's important to Edna to excel at the things she pursues. If she's doing well at something, she knows she's going to be successful, and that makes her feel good, "If I feel successful at something, I think I'm going to be very happy," she says. Conversely, Edna says if she's not achieving her goals, if things aren't going her way, or she's not learning lessons along the way, she's not going to feel successful and therefore won't feel happy.

For Sheree, a forty-three-year-old mother and academic advisor from Chicago, success is also about achievement. She says it's a big reason she wanted to work at a university. It gives her the opportunity to help college graduates celebrate their accomplishments. Sheree says college graduation is the epitome of the work the students have put in. They're able to see the results of all of their efforts, even if it wasn't easy, and she points out that in many cases it is not. She tells her students they are not just getting the degree for themselves—it's about passing on what they have learned to someone else. She is overwhelmed with gratitude at the opportunity to be a part of this celebration with the students. You get a sense this is exactly why she chose to work at a university, because she gets to celebrate achievement regularly.

Looking Successful

"We have become a culture that places more importance on the appearance of success than actual success."

~Jean Twenge, author and psychology professor

In their book, *The Narcissism Epidemic: Living in the Age of Entitlement*, Jean Twenge and W. Keith Campbell suggest the recession, recent political scandals, the national debt crisis, grade inflation, reality television, and materialism are all the result of an increase in narcissism. Narcissism is defined as excessive self-love or vanity. It's one thing to have self-esteem or feel good about yourself, but narcissism is feeling superior or believing you're superior when you're really not. Twenge and Campbell write, "Not only are there more narcissists than ever, but non-narcissistic people are seduced by the increasing emphasis on material wealth, physical appearance, celebrity worship, and attention seeking."

That means the focus on looking successful and feeling superior is a cultural trend that could very well be responsible, at least in part, for the pursuit of money and success. Twenge and Campbell cite materialism as one of the more obvious examples of narcissism in America because it's all about buying things that communicate status and importance—expensive cars, jewelry, clothing, a nice house. They also claim this new materialism has infected many people who are not otherwise narcissistic by nature. This provides a solid explanation for why so many people seem to be seeking more money, success, and material possessions.

Something to Prove

"I've been in a hurry all my life. I've been in a hurry to succeed, and in a hurry to prove myself."

~Henry Kravis, businessman

A deep-seeded need to constantly prove oneself can lead to continually seeking higher and higher levels of success. In my case, I realized in my forties that I had spent twenty years trying to prove myself to my father. After dropping out of college and getting married at nineteen, I spent years creating success after success to prove I hadn't made a mistake.

Recently, I was watching an episode of *60 Minutes* that featured an interview with country/pop music sensation Taylor Swift. While I was quite impressed with the maturity and level head on this twenty-one-year-old superstar, I was also a bit surprised to hear someone who has achieved such stellar success talk about feeling a need to continually prove herself. When Leslie Stahl asked Swift, "What's it like to achieve your dream so early?" Swift replied candidly, "It's great." She then added, "It just means I have a lot of time to figure out how I'm going to prove myself over and over and over again." At twenty-one, Swift had already sold more than fifty million albums, yet apparently she still felt a need to prove herself.

We Are What We Do

"Beware, so long as you live, of judging men by their outward appearance."

~Jean de La Fontaine, poet

When we meet someone, the question is never "Who are you?" Rather, it's "What do you do?" We've been conditioned to define ourselves by our vocations. And, like it or not, we tend to judge others by what they do. We instinctively admire someone who replies, "I'm a doctor" more than someone who responds, "I'm a janitor." Never mind the doctor may be miserable in her job and the janitor completely fulfilled. We view the doctor as successful because we know becoming a doctor requires extensive schooling, excellent grades, dedication, and commitment. These are traits we've been taught to admire. They are traits that signal success.

On the other hand, we probably view the janitor as someone who didn't possess the intellectual qualities, personal drive, or financial resources to pursue higher education. We assume he is financially inferior. We don't see him as someone who is making a big impact on the world. We don't necessarily perceive that as bad, but at the same time, we probably don't aspire to be like him. And, we certainly don't want our children to grow up to be janitors.

This entire judgment process goes on inside our heads in a matter of seconds. It doesn't sound terribly politically correct, compassionate, or considerate. It *is* very judgmental, and I think some of us would deny we ever think like this. Yet, if we're being honest, we must admit we've all thought this way at one time or another. Additionally, if you ask yourself who you would rather be—or who you would rather your children grow up to be—my guess is your answer would *not* be the janitor. Do you think this conditioning might impact our success drive? It's hard to imagine it doesn't.

Addicted to Success?

*"Every form of addiction is bad, no matter whether the
narcotic be alcohol or morphine or idealism."*

~*Carl Jung, psychologist*

According to a February 2009 *Wall Street Journal* article, "You
Might as Well Face It: You're Addicted to Success," professional
success can induce the same feelings of ecstasy as a drug, and it
can have addictive qualities: "Recapturing that feeling can require
greater and greater feats, a phenomenon that—more than simple
greed—explains the drive for ever larger bonuses and conquests."
The article goes on to quote a passage from the book *Feeling Good,*
written by David Burns, a Stanford University psychiatrist: "With
riches, success and fame . . . you find that greater and greater
doses of your 'upper' are needed to become 'high.'"

In "Addicted to Success?" an article published in *Psychology
Today,* Dr. Susanne Babbel refers to people who "have become
'addicted' to the stimulation that comes with the stress of trying
to excessively achieve high goals." Babbel says there are many
reasons a person may be constantly unsatisfied with his or her
achievements and constantly striving for more. She's found this
behavior to be rooted in unconscious biomechanical systems of
the brain. She says these patients are subconsciously compelled to
seek out adrenaline-producing activities. Adrenaline has a stimulating effect on the body, and she therefore suggests it could be
addictive: "When adrenaline rush is coupled with the experience
of habitually succeeding or excelling while operating in a stress-
filled way, it becomes apparent how one might seek to constantly
perpetuate that sort of behavior."

The Painful Reality of Adrenaline Addiction by Patrick Lencioni
suggests that adrenaline can become addictive. Lencioni, president of a San Francisco Bay area management consulting firm and

a best-selling author who has worked with hundreds of CEOs and executive teams, writes:

> Einstein once said that the definition of stupidity is doing the same thing over and over again and expecting different results. Sometimes, however, it isn't stupidity that causes this behavior, but something far more insidious and painful: addiction. Many of the leaders I've worked with struggle with an addiction that hurts their organizations, their families, and their job satisfaction. I'm not talking about the need for drugs or alcohol, but rather another chemical of sorts: adrenaline.

📷 Blog Snapshot

Success: Could It Be an Addiction?

I spent most of the past week working on my book manuscript. I have a deadline of July 31 to submit my book proposal into a contest in which I have the opportunity to win a publishing contract or one of a handful of other prizes that could help my book be more successful.

Of course, because of my predisposition to want to succeed at everything I do, I have my sights set on the publishing contract. With the deadline and big goal looming over me, I found myself writing from my head. I kept telling myself, "This book has to be great, and it has to capture the judges' attention."

The more I wrote, and then read back what I wrote, the more frustrated I became. It's next to impossible to follow inspiration when you're stuck in your head.

When I realized I was back to my *old* ways and sat down late one night when I was tired (probably too tired to think!) and just wrote what I was inspired to write, the words flowed. I got up the next morning and kept writing from my heart—telling the story I want to tell and not worrying about whether it's going to win the contest. When I read back what I had written, it was SO much better. It flowed. It shared the message I want to share.

This morning, as I was writing in my journal and reflecting back on the week, I realized the irony of the situation. Here I am, writing a book about getting caught up in the constant pursuit of success, and once again I'm getting caught up! It certainly shows how seductive success can be. And it makes me wonder, could it actually be an addiction? Could we be addicted to the high we get when we succeed, so much so that we keep seeking more of it? Definitely something I plan to research more as I'm writing this book.

In the meantime, I'm going to keep striving to write from an inspired place and let go of my attachment to winning the contest. Because I know a better book will be born.
Source: www.FollowingInspiration.com

Soft Addictions

"Soft addictions are those seemingly harmless habits like over-shopping, overeating, watching too much TV, endlessly surfing the Internet, procrastinating—that actually keep us from the life we want."

~Judith Wright, author

Judith Wright, author of *The Soft Addiction Solution,* says 91 percent of Americans admit to having soft addictions. She suggests these seemingly harmless habits cost us time and money, drain our energy, and numb our feelings. She offers the following questions to help us determine whether our behavior is merely a habit or is indeed a soft addiction:

1. Do you hide the behavior? Would you be embarrassed if people found out about it?
2. Do you zone out while you're doing it?
3. Do you say, "I know, I know" when teased about the behavior, but still don't do anything about it?
4. Do you feel better or worse after doing it? If you feel a little foggy or numb, Wright says it's a soft addiction.

When I consider how I might have answered these questions during my seven-year pursuit of money and success, I can imagine myself answering yes to them all. I know I would have been embarrassed for anyone to know how much money I had invested in my quest to make more money. Admitting the dollar figure in this book took a lot of courage. I was worried about what people would think. There were times at success conferences when I found myself running to the back of the room to invest in another "incredible offer." I realize in hindsight that I was very likely caught up in the excitement of the event and the promises of success and riches.

Was I zoned out, as Wright suggests? I may very well have been. Those events can be very seductive. If anyone had questioned how much time and money I was investing compared to the financial results I was getting in return, I can imagine myself acknowledging that perhaps the equation was a bit upside-down, but I would rationalize it by saying I was building success and that takes time. Then I would continue to invest. And, while my pursuit of success felt good in the moment, after all was said and done seven years into it, I definitely felt worse. I regretted all the money spent, and, looking back I can hardly believe I allowed it to go on for so long.

Perhaps for me and others constantly pursuing success, it is indeed a form of soft addiction, or a professional addiction fueled by the rush of accomplishment. But could it be an actual, medically diagnosed addiction? I interviewed two addiction experts to find out.

The Cycle of Addiction

> *"Before you can break out of prison, you must first realize you're locked up."*
>
> *~anonymous*

Dr. Rita Bernadette DeShields has been working since the 1970s with people suffering from addiction. She believes we can be addicted to anything, but at the root of all addiction is some unfinished business in our past that creates tension or emotion such as anger, loneliness, or angst. A person who becomes addicted has learned that his or her addictive behavior assuages or calms the negative emotion. It fills a void, at least temporarily. She believes it is possible to become addicted to success and suggests the underlying emotion of such an addiction is probably low self-esteem.

DeShields says that, with substances or physical addictions, there is actually a chemical reaction in the body that creates a state of relaxation and calms the negative emotions. With success, it's not a physical addiction, but we still experience an endorphin release in the brain that tells us we're OK and keeps the underlying emotion at bay. According to DeShields, until we fully understand the underlying emotion, we'll keep repeating the behavior to soothe ourselves. She describes this as the "cycle of addiction." She says when people spend beyond their means and rack up credit card debt trying to achieve more material possessions or to look or feel successful, they're really trying to fill a void—an empty hole inside—that is really about loneliness. "When you go buy the new coat or get a new job or a new car or new carpet, you're filling that empty hole just like the alcoholic. It is very common. People are just not awake to it."

Compulsions

> *"A strong, usually irresistible impulse to perform an act,*
> *especially one that is irrational or contrary to one's will."*
>
> *~dictionary definition of "compulsion"*

On the other hand, Lance Dodes, a medical doctor and author of *The Heart of Addiction* and *Breaking Addiction: A 7-Step Handbook for Ending Any Addiction*, doesn't believe people can become addicted to things, including success. "It's not that things magnetically draw us, so success has no capacity to induce an addiction any more than alcohol or shopping does," he says.

Like DeShields, Dodes believes that people use certain behaviors to address internal feelings, but he prefers the word "compulsion" to "addiction."

Compulsion represents an issue inside the person that compels him or her to act.

"I would be very hesitant to ever say that one could be addicted to success, because I think the whole language of that is off. But certainly people do sometimes act compulsively or feel compulsively driven to achieve in some way, which has deeper roots, and because it has deeper roots, it's compelled." Dodes says the deeper-rooted compulsion keeps people striving for more, regardless of the success they achieve. He says these people feel a deep need to keep proving themselves.

Dodes describes success, alcohol, and gambling as *objects* of addiction rather than addictions. It's a subtle difference but an important one. Therefore, Dodes suggests that instead of asking if it is possible to be addicted to success, we instead consider what makes people feel compelled to seek success. He says that people who constantly strive for higher and higher levels of success may have serious self-doubts or inferior feelings, which they feel a need to manage or try to overcome.

He also says their relentless pursuit of success may be driven by competition. Someone may be compelled to be more physically fit, be a better athlete, or make more money, and this may actually be fueled by competition rather than a need to feel worthy. He also says that, while we may be fully aware that we are striving for more or trying to *best* a competitor, we may be unaware of the deeper reasons we're doing it. To illustrate this point, Dodes describes someone who is climbing the corporate ladder to gain more presence in the company or make more money yet may be quite unaware of the fact that what he's really doing is building a bigger sandcastle than his brother, with whom he's always competed.

Something else that may impact the compulsion for success is the fact that because success is usually encouraged and rewarded, it may be more invisible than other compulsions, such as gambling or alcohol. As a result, the person suffering from the compulsion may not even recognize there is a problem. As Dodes points out, on the outside the person is admired, but, unfortunately, what we don't see is the pain on the inside that is driving the compulsion.

Additionally, if we're being rewarded through our compulsion—we're achieving more success, more money, and more recognition (the things we're craving)—we are more likely to continue the compulsive behavior. "It's not unusual to see highly successful people, what we call 'successful' people, in treatment who are absolutely miserable and unhappy in their lives," Dodes says.

Dodes disagrees that success compulsion is due to adrenaline addiction, and he makes a very convincing case, rooted in both psychology and science. He points out that adrenaline is a normal chemical in the body and is not physically addictive. He says if a person is chasing the thrill that comes with success, you have to explain why he or she keeps seeking that thrill. Dodes says there is always a psychology behind it; it has nothing to do with chemistry. "If I shot you up with adrenaline, you'd get all the chemical signs of it. You'd be excited. Your blood pressure would go up. Your pulse would race. You'd have all the effects of having it in your body. It wouldn't turn you into an adrenaline addict, because there's no reason to keep doing it."

Dodes points to a story from his book *The Heart of Addiction* about soldiers in Vietnam who became addicted to heroin. Heroin is supposed to be an addictive substance, and many soldiers were indeed physically addicted to it while in Vietnam. Yet, Dodes points out that when they left Vietnam, they stopped using the drug. "So the whole idea that being physically exposed to something turns you into an addict is simply untrue. Alcohol is another great example, because practically every adult in our culture drinks . . . yet, although there are plenty of alcoholics, it's still a very small minority of all the people in the country." He argues that if the substance alone were the cause of addiction, everyone who drank would be an alcoholic. Dodes says this proves the adrenaline theory just doesn't hold up.

His argument makes a lot of sense if you think about it in terms of success addiction. We've all experienced success to some degree in our lives. We've gotten promotions and pay raises or accomplished big goals and felt the rush that comes with those achievements. Yet not everyone keeps seeking to recreate that rush. Some people are quite content where they are. While they enjoy those little moments of success, those moments don't turn them into someone who constantly chases more. Therefore, there must be an underlying psychological reason that compels some people to keep striving for more. The idea of low self-esteem, a need to prove oneself, or compete (even if we're not aware we're competing) makes sense.

Dodes admits the chemical addiction argument is true for rats, and that is the reason so many studies come to the conclusion it must also be true for humans. However, he adds, "But what they're forgetting is that even though rats and people react to heroin the same way—we get high—people have an enormous brain, which rats don't have, and our enormous brain gives us psychology. We're much more complicated than rats."

Dodes also points out that just because a behavior is repetitive or excessive doesn't necessarily mean it's a compulsion or an addiction. It can also be the result of trying to fit in or go along with a group. In response to the question, "If you do something too much, is it an addiction?" Dodes writes on his blog, "If everybody is doing it, then you may do it too, against your better judgment."

This begs the question, how do you diagnose true addictions? According to Dodes, it's not enough that the behavior is destructive. Many repetitive, non-addictive behaviors are destructive. He shares the example of drinking and driving. It can still kill you even if you're not an alcoholic. Additionally, even though addictions always cause trouble for the people who suffer from them, the trouble may be small enough to go unnoticed. He shares a story about a man who gambled millions of dollars compulsively on the lottery but never lost enough money to make much of a financial difference in his life. Therefore, Dodes says if you can't reliably diagnose addictions from their outwardly observable effects, then they must be diagnosed from the inside out. As such, in his professional opinion, addictions must be rooted in our psychology. He says they are emotional mechanisms used to manage feelings of helplessness, and to diagnose them you have to know the underlying reasons for the behavior.

Clearly, the idea that success can be a compulsion, or that underlying feelings of self-doubt, competitiveness, or helplessness can lead one to pursue success in ways that mirror addiction, has merit. While neither I nor this book are qualified to diagnose addiction or even compulsion, my hope is this discussion may prompt you to look deeper if you believe you may have an unhealthy obsession with the pursuit of money, success, and happiness.

In the meantime, you may want to heed some of the advice that DeShields and Dodes share. First, DeShields suggests honestly evaluating how your behavior is working in your life. If you realize it is having negative consequences, be open to investigating what's driving the behavior. What is the underlying feeling that is causing you to continually seek success? DeShields also suggests education: reading books, attending workshops, and learning more about these issues. Dodes agrees that the first step is recognizing the behavior is not working for you or is having negative consequences, and he says the next step is making a commitment to find out what's driving the behavior. He believes in most cases it's probably low self-esteem, and the solution is to get into a treatment program that can address the underlying issue.

This advice worked for me. While I never sought professional treatment, it was my awareness that my behavior was no longer serving my business, my finances, or me—and in fact it was negatively impacting all three—that finally put a stop to my overactive success drive. Once I became aware and began reflecting on why I was continually pursuing success, it became very clear I was trying to prove something. I realized my self-worth was indeed wrapped up in how successful I was.

I made a commitment to "unplug" and not spend another dime trying to improve my business or financial situation. I put myself into a self-imposed "no buy zone" until I could pay off my debt and better understand how and why I had gotten so caught up in the first place. I sought the assistance of a mind re-patterning expert who helped me work on the self-worth issue and break the pattern of constantly feeling a need to prove myself. Additionally, in my research for this book I have read countless books, conducted many interviews, and consulted various research studies, all which have helped me better understand the problem and heal myself. I hope reading this book will do the same for you.

Clearly there are many factors that contribute to success drive. Society. Our environment. The generation we belong to. Personality type. Personal values. Goal setting. And compulsive behavior, addiction, and their underlying psychological roots. I believe the answer to why I got so caught up in continually pursuing success is that I lost myself somewhere along the way, and what may have started as a healthy pursuit of success turned into a compulsion. I became ungrounded and began looking outside myself for answers. As a result, I fell victim to some of the negative aspects of my own personality. I traded in my beliefs for the beliefs of others. I adopted other people's definitions of success and began pursuing them.

The good news is, as soon as I recognized this and turned off all the outside noise and chatter, I quickly found myself again. That means you can do the same. While it may require outside help, ultimately I believe the antidote lies within. It lies in knowing yourself, staying true to who you are, honoring your values and beliefs, and never letting anyone tell you that you need to be, do, or have more to be considered successful.

Spellbound

1. Have you let other people's values and beliefs override your own?

2. Are you constantly setting new goals and not enjoying the present moment or being grateful for what you already have?

3. Do you believe you have to achieve more to be happy?

4. Are you more focused on looking successful to others than actually accomplishing something you can personally feel good about?

5. Even though you've already achieved many goals or become successful, do you still feel the need to prove yourself?

6. Do you judge others (and yourself) based on career, income, professional success, or material possessions, instead of who they (or you) are as a person?

7. Are you more focused on accomplishment than being happy?

8. Are you spending more money to become successful than you're reaping from your efforts (i.e., financially upside-down in your quest for success)?

9. Are you spending money you don't have and going into debt to finance your quest for success?

10. Would you be embarrassed if anyone knew how much time and money you've invested to make more money or become more successful?

Breaking the Spell

1. Get back in touch with *your* values and beliefs and begin living your life accordingly. Consider taking a values test such as the one at www.make-it-fly.com/a0601.htm.

2. Setting goals is fine, but be sure to celebrate when you achieve them (don't just immediately set a new, higher goal). Additionally, take time to appreciate where you are currently and be grateful for what you already have. It's not always about getting *more*.

3. Make a decision to be happy exactly where you are right now. Happiness is a choice and a state of mind. It is not contingent on achieving something or getting more. There's nothing wrong with setting goals or trying to achieve more in your life, just be careful not to put your happiness on hold in the meantime.

4. Stop worrying about how successful you look to others. Focus instead on living your life in a way that is fulfilling and satisfying to you.

5. Recognize you are worthy even if you never accomplish another goal. You don't need to prove anything to yourself or others. Instead, focus on living your life in a way that makes you happy and serves others.

6. Remember that appearances can be deceiving. Just because someone looks successful or appears to be financially well off doesn't mean he or she is. Rather than judging people by outward appearances or what they do for a living, get to know them and judge them for *who* they are as people.

7. Focus on what makes you happy right now, exactly where you are. You can still strive for more, but don't get so caught up in where you're headed that you forget to enjoy today.

8. Honestly assess your income and expenses. Make sure when you invest in something you receive a solid return. Investments should pay dividends, not put you in debt. Additionally, thoroughly evaluate future opportunities before committing. It's easy to get caught up in the excitement of big promises of fame and fortune and make decisions from a purely emotional place. Vow to make balanced, well-thought-out decisions, considering both emotion and logic. Don't allow yourself to be pressured to make an instant decision just to get a good deal; make sure you have given the opportunity adequate thought and *you* are ready to commit.

9. Vow to get out of debt and to not continue investing in things you do not already have the money to pay for, or at least the current income to pay off. If you really want to invest in something and you don't currently have the money, make a commitment to earn the money first.

10. Honestly evaluate the time and money you've invested in your quest for success and the results you've achieved. If you'd be embarrassed to share your findings with a friend, family member, or coach, it's time to curb your habit. Additionally, be sure to follow suggestion #8 above.

CHAPTER 9

THE PURSUIT OF HAPPINESS

*"Now and then it's good to pause in our pursuit of happiness
and just be happy."*

~Guillaume Apollinaire, novelist

When I originally titled this book, and this chapter, I expected this section to be the bright light amidst some of the more disconcerting evidence I found in my research. This chapter was, after all, to be about happiness. Isn't that really the purpose of life? To be happy? Instead of focusing on accruing money, success, and material possessions, shouldn't we just pursue happiness? The answer is yes and no. I've learned the *pursuit* of happiness can be just as much of a detractor from true happiness as too much focus on money and success. Therefore, I'd like you to consider how happy *you are* instead of how happy you are *trying to be*.

I have realized that during my seven-year quest for success I was considerably more focused on doing all the things I believed would make me happy than I was on just *being* happy. As a result, I often sacrificed current happiness for the hope of future happiness. As you'll discover in this chapter, the problem with that is, often, what we believe will make us happy, doesn't. It's simply the way our minds, memories, and imaginations work.

According to the dictionary, "pursuit" means an effort to secure or attain. That means we don't currently possess the object of our pursuit. In the case of happiness, pursuit implies that we believe we have to achieve or obtain something to be happy. But the truth is, we don't. As we will discuss in this chapter, happiness is largely a choice. While Anthony, from chapter 1, says he needs $46 million to be happy, he really needs it only if he *believes* he needs it. He can choose to be happy right now with what he has. He may still choose to strive for the $46 million, but if he believes he can only be happy once he acquires it, what happens if he never does? Does that mean he never gets to be happy? Additionally, substantial research indicates that even if he were to acquire the $46 million, he may find it's not all he expected it to be. That's right. Anthony may get rich and still not be happy.

Remembering What Happiness Is

> *"When I was five years old, my mother always told me that happiness was the key to life. When I went to school, they asked me what I wanted to be when I grew up. I wrote down 'happy.' They told me I didn't understand the assignment. I told them they didn't understand life."*
>
> ~John Lennon, singer-songwriter

To stop chasing happiness and start being happy, we first need to know what makes us happy. I'm not talking about all the things you may currently *think* make you happy, such as money, success, and material possessions. While some or even all of those things may make you happy, I'm willing to bet there are plenty of other things that also make you happy that you've lost touch with. I encourage you to refer back to the list you created in chapter 1 of the top twenty things you enjoy doing. When creating that list, you focused on things you like to *do* because research shows that experiences yield lasting happiness while material items more often yield fleeting happiness.

When I made my list, I was surprised at how many things on it had nothing to do with money, possessions, or my business. Topping my list were simple pleasures such as hanging out with my daughter, being outside in the sunshine, and hugging my dogs. Yes, accomplishing things makes me happy, but it didn't make my top twenty list. Having a lot of money was nowhere on my list either. That doesn't mean money isn't important. It is. It's a necessary part of life, but in and of itself, it doesn't generate happiness.

As a site nurse who cares for people in their homes, Susan, a fifty-year-old married mother of four, has seen firsthand that not everyone who has money and material possessions is happy. "I go into very rich homes. I go into millionaire's homes, and they're depressed. They're not happy. It could be for a number of reasons, maybe a hormonal imbalance, a chemical imbalance, or . . . their lives are too complicated, and that brings them unhappiness. So, money doesn't always bring happiness."

Susan has been poor, and she's had money. She says some of the most fun times in her life were when she was the poorest, perhaps because she was too young to know any different. She describes a little one-room apartment she lived in as the best house she's ever had, adding that she has also lived in a mansion. "I've had it both ways, to the extreme both ways, and I see it every day. I go into the poorest of poor homes, sometimes in trailers, and I'll tell you these people are happy. Why? They're living their life the way they want. They live there. That's their castle even though it's an old, broken-down trailer. It's amazing, because even I look and think, 'How can they be happy living like this?'"

She realizes it works for them, and what's good for them might not be good for her. She contrasts these people with another one of her patients, who lived very extravagantly in a "Hollywood-movie-star-type neighborhood" yet was suffering from depression and anxiety, explaining that money sometimes helps but sometimes just makes things worse.

The good news is, most of us haven't always been so focused on money and the idea of buying happiness. That means if we can remember where true happiness comes from, we have the ability to recapture it. As children, most of us were in touch with our innate happiness. We found happiness in simple pleasures. How many times have you watched a child have more fun playing with the box a present came in than the present itself? MasterCard even created a TV commercial in its "Priceless" campaign that features a toddler playing with a box instead of the expensive toys that came in it, saying, "Hand crafted toys . . . the softest bear on the web . . . a new bedtime story added to cart . . . watching her play with the box instead: priceless."

Children don't understand the concept of money. They don't know they're *supposed* to covet the expensive toys and leave the box. They simply do what feels good to them. When my daughter was a toddler, she found endless enjoyment playing in the plastic bowl cupboard in my kitchen. She did the same thing at Grandma's house, despite having a living room full of toys.

Children also don't worry about what other people think. They don't set goals. Instead, they experience life moment to moment. They are happy when what they are doing makes them happy, and they are sad when they don't get their way. Children know how to experience and express unbridled happiness (and sadness, too— we've all seen the child throwing a temper tantrum in public, oblivious to all the people gawking). Clearly, as adults, it behooves us to exercise some control over how and where we show our emotions, but we could learn a few things from the emotional authenticity children exhibit.

Lou, a fifty-year-old federal government employee, believes happiness that lasts doesn't come from external things. He says it comes from within. "Otherwise, you're just going to be going from one thing to the next, looking for that happiness or looking for that next high, and there's nothing permanent about that. It's always just a mirage or just out of your reach. What you find is that once you learn to embrace yourself and love yourself, you become happier."

At the same time, Lou recognizes that many of us are brought up to look for happiness externally. "We're brought up in a culture of 'The American Dream,' which is to own a big house, own a couple of cars, surround yourself with stuff. You're bombarded with commercials on TV, prints ads, you know, it's capitalism." But he points out that when there's an economic crisis, what you're left with is yourself. He says at that point you realize what's really important, and it's not things, it's relationships.

Lou hasn't had an easy life. He has suffered from a gambling problem and depression. He has been bankrupt and nearly homeless. While those experiences were difficult, he says the lessons he learned were priceless. As a result, he believes it's not necessarily bad for people to go through these types of things. He says it's not what happens to them that matters, it's how they react to what happens to them.

He also says that when he was in the middle of his gambling spree, he thought he was happy. One day, after winning a fairly large sum, he realized the money wasn't making him happy. It was just providing a high and allowing him to avoid his life situation. He admits he didn't stop gambling right away. It took another six weeks of living the high life. When did he stop? When the money ran out. At that point he told himself, "You've got to take responsibility for this."

Lou shares that a big part of turning his life around involved looking inward, beginning a path of self-exploration, and studying Eastern philosophies. He wants to stress to others how important it is to not give away your power to other people. "Don't let them define how you should think about the experiences in your life. Go within and find your grandest vision of yourself and live that vision." With that he also shares that he sees our world changing;

people are shifting their perspective from acquiring things to embracing experience. He adds enthusiastically, "One of these days, we're going to hit critical mass, and it's going to be like a tidal wave, and it's going to transform the world."

Somewhere between childhood and adulthood, many of us lose our ability to find happiness in life's simple pleasures. Granted, life is more complicated for adults. We have responsibilities such as jobs, bills, and children. But, far too often, we let these responsibilities squelch our innate happiness. We begin to believe that happiness, or the lack of it, is based on what we do or what we have. We recognize that we experience joy when we get a promotion, a new car, or a new client, and we begin attributing happiness to these things. Often, without realizing it, we begin comparing ourselves to others. They seem happy and have things we don't—therefore, we assume if only we had what they have, we'd be happy too. We become so wrapped up in what we don't have or don't like about our lives that we begin believing we can't be happy *until* we get that promotion, new car, or new client. Or, like Anthony until we have $46 million. It's not that we can't derive joy from all of these things, and perhaps that's where the confusion begins. Accomplishments, material possessions, and money *can* make us happy, but that happiness usually doesn't last.

Kellie, the wellness coach (and former architect) we met in chapter 7, has realized this and now chooses to focus on finding happiness in the day-to-day moments of her life. When asked if she is happy today, Kellie hesitates and responds that she has a hard time with that question. She has joy in her life. Yet her perspective is so different now. She sees nothing as good or bad—it just is. Happiness is fleeting. It is found in those moments of being a mom, going on a field trip with her son's class, taking care of herself, spending time with people she cares about, and having balance in her life.

Still, Kellie doesn't agree with the statement "Money can't buy happiness." She says money does matter. She wouldn't want to be in a situation of financial hardship. She's clear that would create stress and would negatively impact her level of happiness. She believes there is an in-between place when it comes to money and happiness. She doesn't need unlimited amounts of money, but she does need some—enough to provide for her family. After that, she says it doesn't matter so much.

Don't Worry, Be Happy

> *"Don't take life too seriously; you'll never get out alive."*
>
> *~Bugs Bunny*

So if you've gotten caught up in the materialistic pursuit of happiness and true happiness is still eluding you, how do you get back on track? How do you start simply *being* happy? First, you realize the past is the past and you can't change it. There is no sense beating yourself up over decisions you cannot undue. Instead, make a decision to begin living your life differently from this point on and start taking steps to right your ship, just as I did. Begin incorporating activities from your top twenty list into your daily life. Doing something every day that brings you joy can make a huge difference in your level of happiness. When you realize you can be happy just sitting outside in the sunshine, going for a walk, or playing with your dogs or children, it begins to put everything else in your life into perspective.

You can continue to have a vision for the future, set goals, and pursue dreams, just make sure you're enjoying the *pursuit.* In his book *The Happiness Hypothesis,* Jonathan Haidt writes about the fleeting nature of happiness derived from achieving goals. He refers to a concept he calls "the progress principle," which suggests we gain more pleasure from the pursuit of our goals than the actual achievement of them. According to Haidt, when we constantly dream about how happy we'll be when we achieve a goal, once we finally do succeed, the euphoria is very often fleeting. Because of this, we strive to recreate that euphoria by immediately setting a new goal. Therefore, if we want to be happy and not just chasing fleeting spurts of happiness, our focus should be on enjoying the journey to our goals.

If you are a goal setter, ask yourself if you are pursuing your goals for the happiness you expect to feel when you achieve them or if the pursuit itself brings you happiness. If the pursuit doesn't make you happy, reconsider how important the goals are. Ask yourself why you are pursuing them. If your goals are not about happiness but are important to you, pursue them if you choose. Just be aware of what you're doing and why.

Predicting Happiness

"Happiness is the easiest emotion to feel, the most difficult to define, and the hardest to create intentionally."

~Norman Cousins, writer and editor

In *The Happiness Advantage*, Achor writes, "The chief engine of happiness is positive emotions." Achor references the ten most common positive emotions as "joy, gratitude, serenity, interest, hope, pride, amusement, inspiration, awe, and love." While we often feel as though we are at the mercy of our emotions, we do in fact control them. That means happiness is a choice—a choice we can make moment to moment, in reaction to, or in spite of, our circumstances.

In fact, according to the book *Stumbling on Happiness* by Daniel Gilbert, we are better off assessing our happiness in the moment than trying to predict what will make us happy in the future. Based on a concept Gilbert refers to as "presentism," we have a difficult time trying to imagine a future that is much different from our current situation. He says we find it difficult to imagine thinking, wanting, or feeling differently than we do presently. Additionally, because our brains are unable to retain all of the details of what happens in our memory, it retains pieces of our experiences, and when we recall a memory, our brain fills in the holes, using our current situation as a reference. As a result, we often wrongly predict future emotions or feelings.

Additionally, when we dream of something, we tend to build it up in our minds so much that, by the time it actually happens, the culmination may be anticlimactic. Recall Beth's story from chapter 8 about the bodybuilding competition. She discovered the event day didn't measure up to her expectations and that the glory was not all wrapped up in winning, as she expected it would be. Instead, she found her true sense of achievement in the process of preparing for the competition (a great example of "the progress principle" discussed in chapter 8). Gilbert says the fact our brains perform this filling-in trick is a good thing, writing that, without it, we wouldn't have clear memories or a vivid imagination. But we must be aware that it colors our vision for the future and proceed cautiously with our predictions of what we believe will make us happy.

The other challenge with predicting happiness is that we wrongly assume positive events will always make us happy and negative events will always make us sad. In his book *The Happiness Hypothesis,* Jonathan Haidt explains this common misjudgment is due to "the adaptation principle." When we think about all the good things that could happen to us, or all the bad things, we predict how we believe we will feel if those things happen. Not surprisingly, we predict we will be happy if good things happen and sad if bad things happen. However, studies show this is not necessarily so. Haidt writes that, regardless of what happens, we tend to adapt. He points out that lottery winners and those who suffer accidents resulting in paraplegia both pretty much return to their baseline level of happiness within one year. That means we adjust to our new situation and the luster, or the pain, diminishes. This could explain why we keep striving for more. It may be an effort to sustain our happiness at that higher, yet fleeting, level.

This resilience may not be the only reason we tend to return to our baseline level of happiness regardless of what happens in our lives. It may also be tied to something known as "the happiness set point."

Where Happiness Comes From

"Happiness is not a goal; it is a byproduct."

~*Eleanor Roosevelt, former first lady*

Several of the books on happiness that I read referred to something called the "happiness set point." Research indicates 50 percent of our happiness is genetic; 40 percent is determined by our thoughts, feelings, and actions; and 10 percent is a result of our circumstances—things such as money, marital status, our job, and even winning the lottery or being injured in an accident. That means that, while half of our potential for happiness is set, we can control the other half. And, the majority of that second half—a full 40 percent of the total—involves how we choose to think and feel about things, not the things themselves.

So, if things or circumstances don't make us happier, why do so many of us spend our time looking for happiness in them? I believe the answer lies in what has already been presented in this book. Advertising paints a rosy picture of our future with new products and services in it. Reality TV spotlights the rich and famous living "the good life" with all their extravagances. The personal development industry goads us to be, do, and have more. Schools and youth sports foster competition. We find ourselves trying to keep up with the Joneses because the Joneses seem happier. Social media enable our friends to brag about their lives and showcase their accomplishments, and we walk away feeling inferior in comparison. Never mind that what is being portrayed in social media or reality television may not be reality.

All the while, we want to be happy, and if we're not, we take cues from everything around us. Add it all up, and it's no wonder so many of us have become spellbound!

Experiencing Happiness

"Enjoy the little things, for one day you may look back and realize they were the big things."

~Robert Brault, writer

If we want to be happy, rather than striving for money and material possessions, one study suggests we should pursue experiences. The article, "Buying Experiences, Not Possessions, Leads to Greater Happiness," published in 2009 in *Science Daily*, cites a study conducted by an assistant professor of psychology at San Francisco State University that found when we purchase items such as a meal in a restaurant or theater tickets, we experience greater well-being than when we purchase material items. This is reportedly because these experiential purchases satisfy our need for social connectedness. Achor echoes this in *The Happiness Advantage*, citing a study in which researchers interviewed more than 150 people about recent purchases and discovered more pleasure was derived from experiential purchases than material purchases.

In my research, I discovered that people are waking up to the fact that happiness can't be bought, and this is encouraging. Here are some of the comments shared by respondents to my money, success, and happiness survey:

"Money has been the vehicle for freedom but not for happiness. Happiness and security have come from the freedom money has provided. The real happiness has come from not having to worry about money, and that gives permission to focus on relationships, friendships, and being fully present in each and every activity in your life. There is a link between money, success, and happiness; however, I believe it is in the definitions of those priorities, not in the money itself. All the money in the world cannot buy happiness if you are not already a happy person."

❧

"*I make half of what I have made in the past, and I have never had more peace, joy, and happiness in my day-to-day life.*"

❧

"*More and more, I am learning that inner contentment comes first, and then, often, the money follows the inner happiness.*"

❧

"*Once you figure out that happiness only relates to money because it reduces your stress, and that true happiness comes from what you do and contribute to your world around you, life gets better.*"

❧

"*Over the years, I think a lot of people have been learning to not correlate happiness with money. After losing our home to foreclosure, being laid off, and being on the edge of bankruptcy, we learned that happiness is about spending time with family and doing the things we've always wanted to do. So in December 2010, we sold all our stuff, packed our cars, and drove from Maryland to sunny San Diego to start over. Our story officially starts here.*"

❧

*"I took your survey today . . . and then was going to sleep
and kept thinking about the correlation between money and
success and was surprised by some thoughts. I grew up in the
highlands of Scotland without much of anything. We lived
in a small cottage, we had a small coal stove for heat, we had
running water, but not hot water. We had to boil water for
washing our hands or taking baths. But if you look at the few
pictures we have from that time, my parents, my brother, and
I were always smiling and laughing. All I remember from that
time was fun. We took a lot of walks. We didn't have many
books. Instead my parents told us stories. Robbie the Racecar
stories for my brother. Abbie the Airplane stories for me. With
those stories, my parents gave me creativity. A creativity that I
wouldn't have gotten if I were playing store-bought games or
watching television. I remember my dad cutting a sword out
of cardboard and wrapping tinfoil around the end of it so it
looked like metal. My brother and I pretended we were pirates
for days.*

*Then we moved to the States, and my dad started a
business, and it slowly grew. He spent more time at the
office. My mom got her master's degree and a great job. My
brother and I attended different schools (me public because I
could handle it, him private because he needed more help).
We were apart. Financially, we were well off, bought a lake
home, had nice cars, the best clothes, a housekeeper. But I
would say we were much less successful than when we lived
in that small stone cottage in Scotland, because we had lost
each other.*

*Thanks for making me stop and think and be proud of what
I'm now giving my kids—lots of Abbie the Airplane stories
and a few cut-out tin foil swords."*

📷 Blog Snapshot

The Spell Is Broken

I struggled with whether to write this post. In my heart, I knew I should. I have an important message to share. In my head, I had concerns. What would people think, particularly my clients or prospective clients?

In the end, my heart won. I'm in a place in my life where I'm experiencing great change, change I know will make my next fifty years much more peaceful and fulfilling than the last fifty. I've grown so much this year that I can't imagine living another day in my old mindset. I feel compelled to share what I've learned with others so they too can benefit (that's the main reason I'm writing my book, too).

So here goes . . .

As you may know, for the past six months I've been researching and writing my latest book, *Breaking the Spell.* What you may not know is that I've basically been on sabbatical from my business during that time. I made a choice to stop marketing my services and pursuing clients so I could focus on my book. It felt right, albeit a little bit scary. I've always made a good living. In fact, for as long as I can remember, I've earned more than my husband. And, as I've learned in the process of writing my book, my self-worth has been tightly connected to my level of success and the amount of money I make (money has been a form of measurement).

I'm guessing you can imagine what happens when you stop marketing and, more importantly, when you make a decision you don't want any new clients. Not surprisingly, you stop getting clients and the money flow stops. As a result, my business income has all but dried up.

One of my biggest fears has manifested. And you know what? It's OK. The world didn't end. I'm not homeless, and I'm nowhere near becoming homeless. I don't feel like a fraud.

I don't feel unworthy. All of the fears that I had previously connected with not making a six-figure income did NOT materialize. In fact, something amazing has happened instead.

I feel FREE! I feel HAPPY. Happier than I've been in a long time. Not because I'm not making money. In fact, it has absolutely nothing to do with money. I feel happier because I'm doing work I feel inspired to do and I'm not so focused on the money side of the equation. I'm just doing the work and thoroughly enjoying it. And, from the feedback I'm receiving, I'm making an impact on others, which is something that's very important to me.

It's not that I'm not working. I'm working every day, doing research and writing. And it's very challenging work. The difference between now and how I've worked in the past is that my motivation is coming from a different place.

Don't get me wrong—I'm not ready to quit my business or give up trying to make money or be successful. But at the same time, I'm no longer driven by the pursuit of money and success. Instead, I'm driven by my purpose and what makes me happy. It's a very different place for me. I admit there have been plenty of times over the last six months that I've found myself worrying about the future, and I've had to stop myself from going back into "create a business and make money" mode. It was tempting as I saw the income start disappearing. I *know* how to do that. It's been my go-to mentality for years.

However, I can honestly say that's just not my priority right now. And I feel totally at peace when I say that. That is a big shift for me! For the first time in probably close to thirty years, I feel like I have truly broken the spell that money and success had cast on me.

I knew when I set out to write *Breaking the Spell* I would likely have to fully experience the process in order to finish writing the book. I can now say that I have fully experienced it. I have broken free. And, not surprisingly, just in time to finish writing the book. All the more reason to trust the universe. The timing is always perfect!

In the last few months, plenty of ideas for where to take my business in the future have surfaced. I am just beginning to plan for and implement some of those ideas now.

I'm also very grateful for the clients who did choose to work with me this year and for the big chunk of last year's income that I had put into my savings account. Both enabled me to continue supporting my family while taking this sabbatical. I'm also very grateful for my supportive husband, who has encouraged me to do what I need to do and not worry about the money. He's kept me going when I've felt like it might just be easier to go back to business. Of course, he knew better!

This experience has also caused me to consider more carefully what I'm spending money on. I've re-evaluated our family's spending and have cut unnecessary expenses that, quite frankly, I probably would have continued to mindlessly incur had I not gone through this experience. And we're not even noticing the difference! I know I will be much more mindful of my spending going forward, regardless of how much money I'm making.

I have a very strong sense that next year is going to be amazing. I know I'll start earning money again, perhaps even a lot of it. But it's no longer how I plan to keep score. I have changed, and I know I will never run my business, or my life, the same way again.

For that transformation I will be eternally grateful. The decision to begin following inspiration a year ago is the best decision I could have made. In many ways, it saved me. It's been scary and challenging, but I have grown as a person. And I don't plan to ever go back to my old way. It's far too peaceful and exciting here. Now my mission is to invite others to join me!

Source: www.FollowingInspiration.com

Whistle While You Work

"Real success is finding your lifework in the work that you love."

~David McCullough, biographer and historian

In chapter 8 we discussed the judgment we often make based on what people do for a living, recognizing it's easy to admire the doctor and look down on the janitor. We often assume that those who make more money are happier, just as we often assume we will be happier if we are richer. However, just as we have been wrong about the connection between money and happiness, we are also wrong in believing happiness is contingent on the type of job we hold.

Recall in chapter 4 the study that found people view their work in one of three ways: as a job, a career, or a calling. And, people who view their work as a calling find it more rewarding than those who view it as a job or career. The surprising fact is that how people view their work actually has very little to do with what kind of work they are doing. There are doctors who view their work as a job and janitors who view their work as a calling. Once again we see that it's much more about how we look at things than the things themselves.

In an article for the *Harvard Business Review,* Daniel Gulati, coauthor of *Passion and Purpose: Stories from the Best and Brightest Young Business Leaders,* paints a picture of today's young leaders— those he describes as "rockstar twenty-somethings who command high six figure salaries, are in stable relationships, and have all the career options in the world"—as a shining example of the fact that money and success do not buy happiness. Gulati interviewed hundreds of young successful leaders and found a consistent theme: they weren't happy.

He cites three reasons: First, they no longer see their jobs as secure. The financial crisis, recession, and resulting job cuts have seriously impacted employment stability. Second, as we discussed in chapter 5, the prevalence of social media opens up a world of constant comparison and competition with their peers, often leading them to feel inferior. And third, they have more career choices than ever. While that may sound like a good thing, it actually brings with it a lot of pressure to make the *right* choice. To find happiness, Gulati advises these young leaders to focus their careers around their passions more than prestige, and pursue meaningful work instead of money.

While she may not be a twenty-something young leader, reaching the top of her career field is also important to Carol, a forty-five-year-old mother from North Dakota. She says she actually achieved that goal four years ago. However, due to life's circumstances—her eldest daughter was killed in a motorcycle accident and Carol went into hiding for a few years—she now finds herself starting over. Carol says that, before her daughter's accident, she was recognized as someone who was up-and-coming in her field, someone who was making a difference. She wants very much to get back to the top of her game, saying, "I aspire to be that shiny penny I felt like I was."

Ironically, Carol admits she's probably happier now than she was four years ago, at the height of her success. Yet, she admits there is a nagging voice inside that says she can always be better. She wonders when she will be happy, because she doesn't really know what her end goal is. She feels a need to be at the top of her field. She feels pressure to continue her education so she can have all the letters after her name but then wonders if "the alphabet soup" will make her happy. "Do I need to get up to that level to be happy?" she wonders. Carol seems unsure about what will make her happy. I hang up the phone at the end of our interview wondering if she ever will be.

Controlling Our Happiness

"The most successful people, in work and in life, are those who have what psychologists call an 'internal locus of control,' the belief that their actions have a direct effect on their outcomes."

~Shawn Achor, in his book The Happiness Advantage

According to Stefan Klein in *The Science of Happiness*, feeling a sense of control over our own fate is a key ingredient in happiness. In *The Happiness Advantage*, Achor agrees, writing that one of the strongest drivers of well-being is a feeling of control. Achor writes that students who feel in control are happier, get higher grades, and are more motivated to pursue the careers they really want. Employees who feel they are in control are also happier and do better in their jobs. Achor references a 2002 study of nearly three thousand employees that found those with greater feelings of control at work were more satisfied with nearly every aspect of their lives. However, he adds that it isn't necessarily how much control we actually have but rather how much control we *think* we have.

Kimberly Englot, founder of The Center for Authentic Self Development, came to the same conclusion. Before writing her book *The Now of Happiness,* she believed she would be happy when she found the perfect job or made a certain amount of money. But she kept achieving those goals and happiness still eluded her. Kimberly then discovered for herself exactly what the research suggests, that happiness is about feeling in control. She realized she has control over how she views the world, the people she surrounds herself with, and the stories and limiting beliefs in her head. When she exercised this control, she finally found happiness. She's quick to point out that money and success came *after* the happiness.

For Kimberly, being successful and happy has a lot more to do with having freedom than it does with having money. She shares that when she was promoting her book, her tagline was about being happy now *and* striving for better. She asks, "Why does it have to be one way or the other? Why do you have to be satisfied where you are? No striving allowed, live in the moment only, and don't focus on the future."

"There's definitely nothing wrong with having goals or dreams," Kimberly continues. "Just don't let them completely take over. I think it's a bit of harmony between focusing on being happy in the moment and not beating yourself up too much over the fact that you don't have all of the physical things or even as much freedom as you'd like. But also, don't spend your entire life striving for more, because I did that, too, and it just feels empty once you get there."

Tina, a forty-four-year-old small-business coach from Michigan, admits that when she was younger she did all of the things she thought she was supposed to do, and while she probably looked like she had it all, she wasn't happy. She went to college, graduate school, and law school and even traveled to Europe, but none of it made her happy. She explains that, while in law school, she was a witness in a murder investigation. "I'm learning about criminal law, and I'm a witness in a murder case," she recalls. "But what happened was, I recognized that here's a woman who had been killed who was just a few years older than me . . . and my life just was not happy. It might look good, but I wasn't happy."

This prompted Tina to begin searching for what would make her happy. "I read all the gurus' [books], and I did all the programs. I worked with coaches, too, and I always felt there was a piece missing. Like OK, I'm feeling good, I'm pretty happy, but I think I could feel even better. I was always striving for that higher level of happiness as a measure of success for myself." She wonders whether there was a part of her that believed she didn't deserve ultimate happiness and perhaps that's why she couldn't seem to find it. She believes there may have been an element of self-sabotage due to these worthiness issues. Once she identified this, she began making daily choices to love herself more. Ultimately, she found this self-love to be the key to her happiness.

Tina shares that in some ways she wishes she were more driven by money or success. "Maybe I'd make more money because, you know, the Law of Attraction . . . if I'm not asking for money, well it's not going to come." She says it's a dilemma because, to have the freedom to do the things she wants, she needs money. But she feels like if she's doing what she loves and she's happy, the money and freedom will follow. She realizes as we're talking that she is making some discoveries about herself and is looking at success, money, and happiness differently than she has in the past. She comments that perhaps that's why people get confused and find themselves searching for more—they aren't quite sure what the connection is between money, success, and happiness. She shares her own frustration over the years: "I was always looking for that next level of happiness, but I wasn't sure what I was missing, because I'd have up and down levels of success, and I'd have up and down levels of happiness, and it was always this sort of roller coaster."

Tina says she has come to the realization that the answer to this confusion is love. "No matter what people are looking for, if they're looking for more success, if they're looking for more happiness, if they're looking for whatever, I think you'll find it when you just go within and you truly love yourself as you are and accept where you are."

The Happiness Formula

"Happiness is when what you think, what you say, and what you do are in harmony."

~Mahatma Gandhi

So, how do we achieve that state of happiness we desire? Do we just decide to be happy? Perhaps, although that's probably easier said than done, especially if we're accustomed to looking for happiness as the result of action or acquisition. However, I do believe choosing to be happy is the first step. It may require making the choice minute-by-minute until it becomes a habit. For some people, starting a gratitude journal and writing down three things each day that they are grateful for is a simple way to change their focus from what they *don't* have to what they *do*. The good news is, the more you begin focusing on being happy in the moment, the more you begin to see things in your life to be happy for.

The truth is, someone will always have more than you have, and you can always strive for more, but neither should stop you from being happy today. If achievement is important to you—and, as we have learned, it is an integral part of happiness—by all means, set goals and create a vision and a dream. And pursue those goals, vision, and dream to your heart's content. But always remember to maintain a balance. As I often tell my clients when counseling them about their businesses, you want to keep one eye on the future and your feet firmly planted in the present. That's good advice for life, too.

No Regrets

> *"Learn as if you were going to live forever. Live as if you were going to die tomorrow."*
>
> ~Mahatma Gandhi

As I look back over the past seven years, I admit I have some regrets. I spent a lot of time and money chasing something I believed would make me happy that, in the end, did not. Instead, I ended up frustrated and in debt. While I understand that everything we go through makes us who we are and that I wouldn't be where I am today without all of those experiences, I'd be lying if I said I'd do it all again. There are so many positive things I could have done with the $200,000 I invested in my quest for success. I could have helped my children more with their college expenses so they wouldn't have had to incur student loans. I could have bought my daughter a car so when she moved across the country to attend graduate school (which she is paying for herself), she wouldn't have had to worry about how to get from home to work and school. I could have nearly paid off my mortgage so our financial burden would be less as my husband and I head into our retirement years. I could have put away more for retirement so that at age fifty I could feel more prepared for that stage of life.

I could have done many things with that money. Instead, it's gone, and while I have plenty of experiences and wisdom to show for it, I don't have the million dollars or the wildly successful business I was seeking. I'm sure I am not alone in my regrets. I'm sure people who are trying to dig their way out of massive debt wish they had been a little more cautious with their spending. I imagine those who lost homes to foreclosure wish they could turn back time and do things differently. I'm guessing those who have been forced to file for bankruptcy are re-evaluating their financial decisions and wondering how it might have been avoided. I also imagine there are others who are getting by just fine but who look back and agree they too may have been a little too fast and loose with their spending and it's time to make some changes before it's too late.

In the end, if happiness is your goal, and I would suggest it ought to be, I encourage you to step back, evaluate your life, your actions, your spending, and your attitude, and ask yourself if the way you have been living supports that goal. You may also want to keep the following in mind. It's a great reminder, from the end of the road, to live each day to the fullest.

After years working in palliative care, tending to people who were dying, Bronnie Ware wrote an article titled *Regrets of the Dying*, which three million people read in its first year. She has since written and published a book on the same subject that I've included in the references section in case you would like to check it out. Ware's article shared the five common regrets among the dying patients she cared for:

1. I wish I'd had the courage to live a life true to myself, not the life others expected of me.
2. I wish I didn't work so hard.
3. I wish I'd had the courage to express my feelings.
4. I wish I had stayed in touch with my friends.
5. I wish I had let myself be happier.

I encourage you to take these regrets to heart and not make them yours. Stop working so hard trying to be happy. Stop looking for happiness in things. Stop chasing success and money in the hopes they will bring you happiness. Stop *pursuing* happiness. Instead, simply choose to be happy.

Spellbound

1. Are you spending your time pursuing happiness or things you believe will make you happy, instead of just being happy?

2. Have you lost touch with some of the simpler pleasures in life that used to make you happy?

3. Do you find yourself trying to buy happiness with material possessions?

4. Do you believe you'll be happy when you acquire a large sum of money?

5. Have you noticed that you set goals and that when you achieve them you're not as happy as you expected to be, or the happiness you experience is fleeting?

6. Do you find yourself constantly setting new goals, trying to recreate the brief euphoria associated with accomplishing them?

7. Are you unhappy because bad things have happened to you or you've suffered unfortunate circumstances?

8. Does happiness always feel like it's out there in the future somewhere?

9. Do you believe you can be happy only if you find a different job or if you or your business become more successful?

10. If you were to die tomorrow, would you find yourself with regrets, wishing you had spent more time enjoying friends, family, and life?

Breaking the Spell

1. Stop pursuing happiness through the acquisition of money, success, or material possessions. Make a decision to be happy right where you are.

2. Reflect back on your life and make a list of twenty things that make you happy, focusing on experiences rather than material possessions. Commit to incorporating these activities back into your daily life.

3. Recognize that material possessions provide fleeting happiness at best, and stop looking for true, lasting happiness in them.

4. Recognize that, while money can make life easier, more money does not always equal more happiness.

5. When setting goals, make sure you are setting goals for which you will enjoy the pursuit. Avoid setting goals where all the glory is in the accomplishment. Stop putting your happiness on hold until you get "there."

6. Strike a happiness balance between what you have and what you are pursuing. Keep one eye on the future and both feet planted firmly in the present.

7. Recognize that everyone eventually moves past bad or unfortunate experiences and the key to doing so is attitude. Look for the blessings in failures, mistakes, or misfortune, and focus on moving forward. You can find happiness again if you choose to.

8. Recognize happiness is not "out there." Choose to be happy today, even if you have to make that choice on a moment-to-moment basis until it becomes a habit.

9. Find things to be happy for in your current job or business. It's fine to strive for more, but realize that you can be happy right where you are in the meantime, simply with a change of attitude.

10. Live your life to the fullest. Focus on people and experiences more than "stuff" to avoid having regrets when you get to the end.

CHAPTER 10

BREAKING THE SPELL

"It does not do to dwell on dreams and forget to live."

~from the book Harry Potter and the Sorcerer's Stone

Hope for the Flowers is a wonderful children's story about a caterpillar that decides there must be more to life than eating leaves. On his quest for more, he decides to follow the other caterpillars, which spend their days climbing to the top of a pillar reaching high into the sky, even though none of them seem to know what is at the top. The caterpillar leaves behind love and companionship only to find when he gets to the top there is nothing there. In the end, he discovers climbing the pillar is not the answer to his search for more. Instead, he realizes the answer lies in following his heart, letting go of life as he knows it, and transforming into a beautiful butterfly.

I love *Hope for the Flowers*, because, even though it's a children's story, it carries several very important messages. And perhaps one of the reasons I do love it so much is the fact that it *is* a simple children's story. It conveys some of the core, foundational concepts in life that I fear too many people—myself included—have lost sight of in our increasingly materialistic and success-oriented world. The story illustrates that just because others are pursuing what they define as success doesn't mean it's the right choice for you. Following the pack is not always in our best interest, and I would argue that following blindly is *never* in our best interest.

It also clearly demonstrates that there is almost always more than one way to accomplish a goal and that the best course of action often requires faith in the unknown and is not the most obvious solution. I believe this story shares an excellent example of what is possible when you stop allowing yourself to get caught up in what everyone else is doing and instead choose to follow your heart and trust your own internal guidance system. I call that "following inspiration."

The Power to Change

"Change the way you look at things, and the things you look at change."

~Wayne Dyer, psychologist

We've all heard the clichés about change: Change is hard. Change is the only constant. People resist change. I would like to suggest you consider another perspective: change is simply how you choose to look at it. It can be hard if you choose to view it as hard. It can feel scary if you allow yourself to be frightened by the unknown. However, you can just as easily choose to be excited and curious about the possibilities. And, the reality is, if you're not happy with your life, change is the only remedy.

I've gone through tremendous change over the past year in my process of breaking the spell. While it has been challenging, it has also been one of the most exciting and liberating experiences of my life, and I continue to look toward the future with enthusiasm. Ironically, by letting go of my attachment to controlling how I thought things needed to be, I feel much more in control. I have shifted from trying to control my results in the outside world—which most often is outside of our control anyway—to focusing on controlling how I respond to what happens.

The truth is, all we really can control is our reaction to events. We choose our thoughts. We are the ones who label events as good or bad, successes or failures. It is within our power to adopt an attitude of acceptance and gratitude for everything that occurs. While it's not necessarily easy, particularly if we've grown accustomed to feeling like victims of our circumstances, it is possible if we put our minds to it. And, the rewards are many.

In their book *Switch: How to Change Things When Change Is Hard*, Chip and Dan Heath say successful change involves doing three things. First, you must change your situation. Second, you must get both your heart and mind on board. Third, you must be absolutely clear and specific about what you want to change. I can attest that this is exactly the process I followed to break the spell and change my life. By declaring myself in a "no buy zone" and refusing to invest any more time or money trying to become more successful, I changed my situation. By focusing my attention inward, I was able to get back in touch with what is most important to me and stop being so strongly influenced by other people.

Additionally, realizing I had always been "led by my head," I made the decision to begin following my heart and embarked on my Following Inspiration Experiment (to learn more, visit www. FollowingInspiration.com). I made a commitment to stop setting and striving after left-brained financial and business goals and to instead allow my actions to be driven by my heart. I made the decision to do what felt good and made me happy instead of what looked good to the outside world. By getting more in touch with my heart, I was able to begin living a more peaceful life. As an achievement-oriented person, this was a huge shift for me. Yes, I still use my head to logically evaluate situations and make decisions, however, I practice a much better balance between heart and mind.

Lastly, I became very clear about what my goals were, and they were no longer about making more money or becoming more successful. Instead, my goals were to be happy and do the work my heart was calling me to do. This led me to taking a six-month sabbatical from my business to focus on researching and writing this book. Once I quieted all the outside noises and other people's voices, my inner voice came through loud and clear. It told me I needed to make a change if I truly wanted to be happy. I realized I needed to shift my mindset and learn some new things to change my situation. In the process of researching, reading books, interviewing many people, and journaling extensively, I learned what I needed to dramatically transform my life. It didn't happen overnight; it was a yearlong process. It took a lot of inner work. It required me to change the way I thought about life, money, and success. It was challenging—after all, I was attempting to change mindsets and a way of being that had very much become *who* I was, or at least who I *thought* I was.

In the end, it was well worth the effort. I am now happier, healthier, and wealthier than I have ever been. If you recall, I shared in the introduction that the word "wealthy" is derived from the Old English word *wela,* which means well-being. Well-being isn't defined by money or success. Well-being means leading a rich, satisfying, and happy life. After years of pursuing a wealthy life, I have finally found mine. It's a place of contentment, and while I previously viewed contentment as settling—and settling was not a good thing in the world of "there's always more to be, do, and have"—I now see that it's a very peaceful and satisfying place. I also recognize I will not stand still in this place. I will continue to grow and learn for the sake of growing and learning and to help me better understand myself, others, life in general, and the world. My knowledge seeking is no longer purely an effort to become richer or more successful or to prove something to myself or anyone else.

Awakening

"Each one has to find his peace from within. And peace to be real must be unaffected by outside circumstances."

~*Mahatma Gandhi*

I have referred to the state I was in, and the state many people in this world also seem to be in, as "spellbound." I view the process I went through and the process I am encouraging you to embark on as "breaking the spell." Yet in many ways, this change I'm talking about is also an awakening of sorts. Breaking the spell is about getting back in touch with your soul and your purpose and remembering what life is truly about. As I hope I've made abundantly clear in this book, life is not about all the "stuff." While money, material possessions, and increasing levels of success can make you momentarily happy, research conclusively shows these things do not lead to lasting happiness. The good news is, when you accept this fact and choose to wake up, you have the opportunity to finally achieve the happiness you've been searching for.

In their book *Loyalty to Your Soul: The Heart of Spiritual Psychology*, Dr. H. Ronald Hulnick and Dr. Mary R. Hulnick suggest this awakening is actually a spiritual awakening: "There are many people—their eyes still bleary from sleep—looking around and wondering what to do now that they've discovered that there are aspects to human existence vastly more valuable than material success."

Yes, you may feel a bit lost after waking up. You will need to learn how to approach your life differently, leave old habits behind, and adopt a few new ones. You will need to change your mindset and decision-making processes. You may even need to change your job, your business, or your friends. But as Mark, a fifty-six-year-old former television producer from Hawaii, discovered, making these changes can lead to a much deeper satisfaction with life.

Mark admits that when he was younger, success meant money and material possessions. But around the age of forty he began to realize the material side of success was fleeting. He discovered that type of happiness only lasted for a moment, and he needed more than just a moment. He believes people's perception of the world changes around age forty—while you're physically closer to the grave, you are also closer to God. This perspective shifted Mark's view of success; it became less about money and material possessions and more spiritually centered.

So, after spending twenty-six years working as a TV producer, Mark realized there was more to life than work and made the decision to leave broadcasting. He began spending more time with his family. He joined the ministry. He travelled. He got involved with crusades and began making documentaries, which gave him the chance to use his broadcasting skills in a new and more meaningful way.

Mark says he understands why success is often externally driven, pointing out that when you go to a reunion, you ask people what they're doing with their lives. Did they go to college? What kind of job do they have? Do they have a family? Still, Mark believes success ultimately is an internal game. He believes you have to feel satisfied with what you've done with your life. You have to ask yourself, "Am I where I'm supposed to be?" He speaks of a spiritual longing many of us seek to fill, what he refers to as a "hole in our heart." He believes that, in our younger years, we attempt to fill that hole with external accomplishments and material things. That changes as we grow older and wiser. We become more spiritual and internally driven. In the end, Mark believes achieving success and happiness is about personal choice. "You have to decide what you value and live your life for that," he says.

Creating Your Own Reality

"Our intention creates our reality."

~Wayne Dyer, psychologist

In essence, when we break the spell, or awaken to a purpose greater than striving for material wealth and traditional success, we are required to step off the beaten path and forge our own. We must become leaders of our own lives rather than followers of others. We must decide what is most important, define success in a manner that suits us, and very often embark on a path that is unfamiliar. However, I believe it is this personal path that leads to peace and true happiness. In fact, in my experience, once you make the mindset shift, and before you *do* anything else, you immediately experience more peace and happiness. You realize happiness is a choice, and when you make the decision to be happy, your life immediately improves.

While in the past you may have chosen to be unhappy with your lot in life, envy those who have more, and strive for different circumstances to be happy, you no longer have to make these choices. You can instead choose to be grateful for what you have and be happy right where you are. It's simply a matter of recognizing that how you view things is an inside game that you control. It is not controlled by other people or by outside circumstances unless you allow it to be.

Jennifer Urezzio is the founder and spiritual director of Know Soul's Language. She teaches people how to access their own intuitive guidance so they can positively transform and expand every aspect of their lives. She believes personal transformation work is part and parcel to becoming successful and happy. "I think that in order to get whatever you want, it takes inner work, because the same level of consciousness that created the problem can't solve it," she says. "Inner awareness, inner conversation, inner dialogue has to take place so you can make a different choice and do something differently so you can get a different outcome."

She also believes there must be a balance between doing the internal work and taking action in the external world: "It's a combination of both that allows for success and happiness." She says it's easy for people to get caught up doing too much spiritual work and become ungrounded, and we need to be grounded to manifest what we want in life.

Go Your Own Way

> "Everything's waiting for you. You can go your own way!"
>
> ~from the song "Go Your Own Way" by Fleetwood Mac

When I counsel my clients about the best way to design a business, I encourage them to go their own way—to design a business around their desired lifestyle and goals as well as one that represents their personal beliefs and unique point of view. It's not about modeling others. It's not about copying someone else's success system. I believe this approach applies to life just as much as it applies to business. The challenge is, it's often easier to follow others than to forge our own path. After all, their path is already laid out and appears to have worked for them. Why not just hop on and follow along? Won't it lead you to the same place it led them?

Because you are *not* them—your circumstances, life experience, and personality are likely different—chances are, even if you take the exact same steps they took, you will end up in a different place. While you can always learn from other people's experiences, it is important to evaluate how that learning can best be applied to your life. Be willing to keep the practices that *fit* you and discard the rest. Take what you learn from others and create your own customized approach to life—one that serves you, those you care about, and the world. It really is about being an individual and living your own life—a life that does not need to look like anyone else's.

Forging your own path requires you to have clarity about what *you* want and what is important to you. It requires you to have confidence in yourself and not be concerned about what others think. It requires a commitment to keep going when the going gets tough, because challenges and obstacles always arise. It requires faith, because you often can't see where the path is leading. However, if you choose to trust your inner guidance system and follow your own path, you will be happier and may actually be more successful too.

If you look at history, you realize great leaders are rarely followers. As Dr. John Eliot points out in his book *Overachievement*, great leaders and those who change the world are exceptional and unconventional thinkers. He says great performers don't worry about what others think about them: "Their sense of self never depends on the feedback—positive or negative—they get from their environment." They often are seen as strange or crazy, but ultimately we define them as geniuses. So, ironically, while many people seek success by following others, those who achieve greatness generally don't follow. They go their own way.

Breaking the Chain

"If a link is broken, the entire chain breaks."

~*Yiddish proverb*

It seems that whether you want to be successful or simply want to be happy, the solution is not found in following other people or chasing their ideals or definitions of success. Rather, it's found in following your own internal guidance system. When we are able to do this, we can break the chain that has held us hostage to the idea that happiness is found outside of ourselves in money, achievement, and material possessions. We will no longer be seduced by guru promises or marketing campaigns. We will become immune to the false reality that is often portrayed on television and see it for what it is—packaged entertainment. We will begin to see that social media represents a limited view of people's lives and will stop trying to measure up to these rosy representations. We will stop focusing so much on others and what they think of us and instead will discover a place of peace and happiness within ourselves. We will accept who we are and where we are. We will create our own vision for the future. And we will strike a healthier balance between enjoying the present moment and pursuing our dreams.

Breaking the spell is absolutely an internal process. All of the external influences we have discussed in this book will likely continue to exist. But their hold on us doesn't have to persist. When we are able to break the spell, we can peacefully coexist with these external influences. They will no longer have a grip on us. And perhaps if enough people endeavor to make this shift, we just might be able to change the world. Imagine the impact this change of focus could have on future generations. If we start living this new way, consider the example we will be setting for our children. Consider their potential for happiness if they can learn to adopt this new mindset. We are talking about a shift—a shift that begins one person at a time and has the potential to spread like a virus around the globe.

Make no mistake, our world is changing. All you have to do is look around—the evidence is everywhere. Globally, we have been on a path that has resulted in some serious implications, many of which I have discussed in this book. While we are influenced by these happenings, we have also contributed to them. The good news is, we have the power to begin moving our world in a more positive direction. But to do so, we must first change ourselves. It's a challenging time to be alive, yet it's also an exciting one. We each have the opportunity to be a part of a global awakening. My hope is that you will choose to embrace this opportunity and will help lead others to do the same. Reading this book is a great first step. Changing your mindset and beginning to make changes in your life is the next. If you'd like to join others who are committed to this change, I invite you to join my free *Breaking the Spell* Tribe at www.BreakingTheSpellBook.com/bonuses.

Kirsty, the thirty-six-year-old Aussie we met in chapter 4, chose to make this commitment and shared with me the impact it has had on her family's life: "Our life has changed dramatically in the last five years, where we have gone from being a military family on one wage to self-employed business owners with all the challenges that brings. James and I have been on our own personal journeys with money this year, and it has been incredibly challenging for us. In all of it though, I can honestly say that I am happier now than I have ever been, with way less material possessions and less money, but NO debt! Nowadays I regularly have those moments of pure joy. I have worked a lot with trust this year, around abundance and money, and it is really paying off for me and my family."

Clearly, breaking the spell is a journey. It doesn't happen overnight. It will likely take time to change your habits and begin living in this new way. But it all starts with a decision, with simply making a choice. My wish is that you will make that decision, as I did and as Kirsty has done. Stop following the crowd and doing what you think you're supposed to be doing. Stop expecting your happiness to be found in money, success, and material possessions. Stop looking outside for your happiness. Stop chasing it in achievements. Recognize you can indeed choose to be happy exactly where you. Begin following your heart. And, like the caterpillar in *Hope for the Flowers,* be willing to let go of the life you know and discover a better, happier, more peaceful one.

RECOMMENDED RESOURCES

I invite you to continue your *Breaking the Spell* journey with the following free bonuses available at www.BreakingTheSpellBook. com/bonuses:

- Join the *Breaking the Spell* movement by becoming a member of the free *Breaking the Spell* Tribe.
- Access full recordings and transcripts of the interviews featured in the book.
- Review a full summary of the "Money, Success, Happiness" survey results.
- Print copies of the "Spellbound" and "Breaking the Spell" lists featured at the end of each chapter.
- Access a complete listing, with live links, of all the resources referenced in the book.

Here are more free resources:

- Visit www.MoneySuccessHappiness.com to read the author's ongoing thoughts and commentary and to share your opinions.
- Learn more about the author's Following Inspiration Experiment and follow her journey at www. FollowingInspiration.com.

ACKNOWLEDGEMENTS

I would like to thank my father. While he was the first to admit this is not the type of book he would normally read, he faithfully reviewed and provided feedback on each and every chapter. His objective evaluation helped improve the clarity, organization, and flow of ideas. I am also grateful for the weekly discussions we had about money, success, happiness, history, and culture that each chapter stimulated. I got to know my dad better through the writing of this book, an unanticipated but welcome bonus.

I would also like to thank my husband, Louie, for encouraging me to stick with this project when it became challenging and I wanted to quit. And for supporting our family when my income was declining, all the while telling me not to worry about the money.

Lastly, I'd like to thank the members of my *Breaking the Spell* Tribe for sharing their support and feedback throughout the writing and publishing process. They ensured that I never felt alone on this journey and provided a regular reminder about the power of the written word in helping people grow and shift.

REFERENCES

Introduction
1. Catherine Rampell, "Great Recession: A Brief Etymology," *New York Times*, March 11, 2009, http://economix.blogs.nytimes.com/2009/03/11/great-recession-a-brief-etymology.
2. Neil Irwin, "It's official: The Great Recession ended last summer," *The Washington Post*, September 20, 2010, http://voices.washingtonpost.com/political-economy/2010/09/its_official_the_great_recessi.html.
3. "Late-2000s recession," *Wikipedia*, http://en.wikipedia.org/wiki/Late-2000s_recession.
4. Congressional Research Service: Savings Rates in the United States, September 14, 2010, http://www.fas.org/sgp/crs/misc/RS21480.pdf.
5. Foreclosure statistics:
   - http://www.stopforeclosurefraud.com
   - http://stopforeclosurefraud.com/2010/06/04/graphed-u-s-foreclosures-and-home-repossessions-2005-to-2010
   - http://www.homeguide411.com/housing-crisis.html
6. Bankruptcy statistics:
   - http://www.uscourts.gov/Statistics/BankruptcyStatistics.aspx
   - http://www.bankruptcyaction.com/USbankstats.htm
7. Personal development industry:
   - Marketdata Enterprises, http://www.marketdataenterprises.com.
   - Steve Salerno, *SHAM: How the Self-Help Movement Made American Helpless* (New York: Three Rivers Press, 2005).
8. https://www.facebook.com/press/info.php?statistics

Chapter 1

1. Lynne Twist, *The Soul of Money: Reclaiming the Wealth of Our Inner Resources* (New York: W.W. Norton & Company, 2003).

2. Barbara Stanny, *Secrets of Six-Figure Women: Surprising Strategies to Up Your Earnings and Change Your Life* (New York: Harper Business, 2004).

3. J.K. Rowling/Harry Potter:
   - "Harry Potter Franchise Crosses the $7B Mark at Global Box Office," *International Business Times*, July 23, 2011, http://www.ibtimes.com/articles/185600/20110723/harry-potter-7-billion-global-box-office.htm.
   - Luisa Kroll, "The World's Richest Self-Made Women," *Forbes*, June 14, 2010, http://www.forbes.com/2010/06/14/richest-women-entrepreneur-billionaire-whitman-oprah-rowling.html.
   - "The World's Billionaires," *Forbes*, March 10, 2010, http://www.forbes.com/lists/2010/10/billionaires-2010_The-Worlds-Billionaires_Rank_40.html.
   - "The World's Billionaires," *Forbes*, March 9, 2011, http://www.forbes.com/wealth/billionaires#p_116_s_arank_-1__-1.

4. *Secret Millionaire*, ABC, http://abc.go.com/shows/secret-millionaire.

5. Maslow's Hierarchy of Needs:
   - Kendra Cherry, "Hierarchy of Needs: The Five Levels of Maslow's Hierarchy of Needs," *About.com*, http://psychology.about.com/od/theoriesofpersonality/a/hierarchyneeds.htm.
   - "Maslow's Hierarchy of Needs," *Wikipedia*, http://en.wikipedia.org/wiki/Maslow%27s_hierarchy_of_needs.
   - Rob Stein, "Money can buy one form of happiness, massive global study concludes," *The Washington Post*, July 1, 2010, http://www.washingtonpost.com/wp-dyn/content/article/2010/07/01/AR2010070100039.html.

- Eric Quinones, "Link between income and happiness is mainly an illusion," *News at Princeton*, June 29, 2006, http://www.princeton.edu/main/news/archive/S15/15/09S18/index.xml?section=topstories.
- Belinda Luscombe, "Do We Need $75,000 a Year to Be Happy?," *Time*, September 6, 2010, http://www.time.com/time/magazine/article/0,9171,2019628,00.html.
- 2011 Money, Success & Happiness Survey, http://www.breakthespellbook.com/bonuses.
- Barbara Sher, *Wishcraft: How to Get What You Really Want* (New York: Ballantine Books, 2009).
- Timothy Ferriss, *The 4-Hour Workweek: Escape 9-5, Live Anywhere, and Join the New Rich* (New York: Crown Publishers, 2007).

Chapter 2

1. No Child Left Behind:
   - Greg Toppo, "How Bush education law has changed our schools," *USA TODAY*, January 8, 2007, http://www.usatoday.com/news/education/2007-01-07-no-child_x.htm.
   - "What are Some Criticisms of No Child Left Behind?" *Wisegeek*, http://www.wisegeek.com/what-are-some-criticisms-of-no-child-left-behind.htm.
2. The cost of college:
   - "College Tuition Continues to Climb But Record Grant Aid Helps Many Students and Families," *CollegeBoard.com*, October 28, 2010, http://press.collegeboard.org/releases/2010/college-tuition-continues-climb-record-grant-aid-helps-many-students-and-families.
   - "Poll: Few Parents Ready to Pay for Kids' College" *ABC News*, February 10, 2007, http://abcnews.go.com/WNT/LifeStages/story?id=2865943&page=1.
3. Teen ethics poll:

- "Teen Ethics Poll: 44% Feel Intense Pressure To Succeed, No Matter the Cost," Metrics2.com, http://www.metrics2. com/blog/2006/12/06/teen_ethics_poll_44_feel_ intense_pressure_to_succe.html.
- Denise Reynolds, "Teens Today Feel Overwhelming Pressure to Succeed," *EmaxHealth*, March 12, 2010, http:// www.emaxhealth.com/1506/20/36018/teens-today-feel-overwhelming-pressure-succeed.html.

4. Teen suicide:
   - "National Suicide Statistics at a Glance: Percentage* of U.S. High School Students Reporting Considering, Planning, or Attempting Suicide in the Past 12 Months, by Sex, United States, 2007," Centers for Disease Control, http://www.cdc. gov/ViolencePrevention/suicide/statistics/youth_risk.html.
   - "What are the leading causes of death for teenagers?," Centers for Disease Control, http://www.cdc.gov/nchs/ data/databriefs/db37.htm#leading.
   - "Suicide Facts at a Glance, Summer 2010," Centers for Disease Control, http://www.cdc.gov/ViolencePrevention/ suicide/index.html.
   - "Suicide and suicidal behavior," *MedlinePlus*, http://www. nlm.nih.gov/medlineplus/ency/article/001554.htm.

5. Courtney E. Martin, *Perfect Girls, Starving Daughters: How the Quest for Perfection is Harming Young Women* (New York: Berkley Books, 2007).

6. Jennifer Delahunty Britz, "To All the Girls I've Rejected," *The New York Times*, March 23, 2006, http://www.nytimes. com/2006/03/23/opinion/23britz.html.

7. Debbi Baker and Kristina Davis, "Friends mourn deaths of mother, daughter in Rancho Peñasquitos," *San Diego News*, July 18, 2011, http://www.signonsandiego.com/news/2011/ jul/18/police-investigating-doulbe-homicide-rancho-penasq.

8. P.K. Daniel, "Slain Teammate Remains in our Hearts," *San Diego News*, July 27, 2011, http://www.signonsandiego.com/ news/2011/jul/27/slain-teammate-remains-in-our-hearts.

9. Elizabeth Landau, "Study: Experiences make us happier than possessions," *CNN.com*, February 10, 2009, http://edition.cnn.com/2009/HEALTH/02/10/happiness.possessions.

10. http://www.authentichappiness.sas.upenn.edu

11. Eudaimonia, *Wikipedia*, http://en.wikipedia.org/wiki/Eudaimonia.

12. Robert Kiyosaki and Emi Kiyosaki, *Rich Brother Rich Sister: Two Different Paths to God, Money and Happiness* (New York: Vanguard Books, 2009).

13. Shawn Achor, *The Happiness Advantage: The Seven Principles of Positive Psychology That Fuel Success and Performance at Work* (New York: Crown Business, 2010).

Chapter 3

1. Salerno, *SHAM.*

2. Cults:
   - http://www.howcultswork.com
   - http://cultresearch.org
   - International Cultic Studies Association, http://www.csj.org and http://www.icsahome.com.
   - Steven Alan Hassan and the Freedom of Mind Center, http://freedomofmind.com.

3. MJ DeMarco, *The Millionaire Fastlane: Crack the Code to Wealth and Live Rich for a Lifetime!* (Phoenix: Viperion Publishing, 2010).

4. "Self-Improvement Market Shifts to Digital, Audio & Online," *Marketdata Enterprises*, November 23, 2010, *www.marketdataenterprises.com/pressreleases/SIMkt2010PR.pdf.*

5. Reality TV:
   - Feifei Sun, "Teen Moms Are Taking over Reality TV. Is That a Good Thing?," *Time*, July 10, 2011, http://www.time.com/time/magazine/article/0,9171,2081928,00.html.
   - "Lifestyles of the Rich and Famous," *The Internet Movie Database*, http://www.imdb.com/title/tt0086750.
   - "Lifestyles of the Rich and Famous," *Wikipedia*, http://en.wikipedia.org/wiki/Lifestyles_of_the_Rich_and_Famous.

- "MTV Cribs," *The Internet Movie Database,* http://www.imdb.com/title/tt0276656/episodes.
- "MTV Cribs," *Wikipedia,* http://en.wikipedia.org/wiki/MTV_Cribs.
- "The Real Housewives," *Bravo TV,* http://www.bravotv.com/shows.
- James Hibberd, "Ratings: How every broadcast show ranked this season," *Entertainment Weekly,* May 25, 2011, http://insidetv.ew.com/2011/05/25/2010-11-season-tv-ratings.
- James Poniewozik, "Reality TV at 10: How It's Changed Television—And Us," *Time,* February 22, 2010, http://www.time.com/time/magazine/article/0,9171,1963739,00.html.
- Eric Jaffe, "Reality Check," *Observer,* http://www.psychologicalscience.org/observer/getArticle.cfm?id=1742.
- "Survivor," *Wikipedia,* http://en.wikipedia.org/wiki/Survivor_%28TV_series%29.
- "Real Housewives' Suicide: What Really Happened?," *ABC News,* August 17, 2011, http://abcnews.go.com/GMA/video/russell-armstrong-suicide-real-housewives-beverly-hills-taylor-armstrong-husband-14322545.
- Jeff Labrecque, "Russell Armstrong to mother before suicide: 'They're just going to crucify me this season,'" *Entertainment Weekly,* August 18, 2011, http://insidetv.ew.com/2011/08/18/russell-armstrong-mother.
- J. Ryan Stradel, "Unscripted does not mean Unwritten," *Writers Guild of America, West,* http://www.wga.org/organizesub.aspx?id=1096.

6. Sarah Z. Wexler, *Living Large: From SUVs to Double Ds, Why Going Big Isn't Going Better,* (New York: St. Martin's Press, 2010).
7. Weddings and divorces:
   - "Latest Wedding Statistics, Trends & Facts," *The Wedding Report,* http://www.theweddingreport.com.

- "Kim Kardashian's $10 Million Wedding!" *OK! Magazine,* June 22, 2011, http://www.okmagazine.com/2011/06/cover-story-kim-kardashians-10-million-wedding.
- Rebecca Ford and Lauren Schutte, "Kim Kardashian Divorce: 10 Signs the Marriage Was One Big Hoax All Along" *The Hollywood Reporter,* October 31, 2011, http://www.hollywoodreporter.com/news/kim-kardashian-divorce-kris-humphries-media-publicity-255371.
- "National Marriage and Divorce Rate Trends," Centers for Disease Control and Prevention, http://www.cdc.gov/nchs/nvss/marriage_divorce_tables.htm.
- "Census: Divorces Decline In United States," *The Huffington Post,* May 18, 2022, http://www.huffingtonpost.com/2011/05/18/census-divorces-decline-i_n_863639.html

8. "Cultivation Theory," *Wikipedia,* http://en.wikipedia.org/wiki/Cultivation_theory.

9. "Make Up For Ever Prints First Unretouched Makeup Ad," *The Huffington Post,* March 14, 2011; http://www.huffingtonpost.com/2011/03/14/make-up-for-ever-prints-unretouched-beauty-ad_n_835278.html.

10. Myrna Blyth, *Spin Sisters: How the Women of the Media Sell Unhappiness—and Liberalism—to the Women of America* (New York: St. Martin's Griffin, 2005).

11. Myrna Blyth: http://www.cblpi.org/programs/bio.cfm?ID=16&Type=Speaker.

12. Twitter:
   - Mary Ann Georgantopoulos, "Top 10 Celebrities with the Most Twitter Followers," *International Business Times,* March 7, 2011, http://www.ibtimes.com/articles/119721/20110307/celebrities-twitter-followers-following-social-network-charlie-sheen-lady-gaga-ashton-kutcher-tweet.htm.
   - "Kim's $weet tweets," *New York Post,* December 30, 2009, http://www.nypost.com/p/entertainment/tv/kim_weet_tweets_DaJ73tUIqAcpDXZzkmN0aJ.

13. "Demi Moore's Plastic Surgery Confession," *Plastic Surgery Portal*, http://www.plasticsurgeryportal.com/articles/demi-moore-plastic-surgery-confession/140.

14. Amy Winehouse:
   - "Amy Winehouse Dead: Singer Found Dead At London Home," *The Huffington Post*, July 23, 2011, http://www.huffingtonpost.com/2011/07/23/amy-winehouse-dead-singer_n_907753.html#s314557&title=Rehab.
   - Sarah Bull, "Amy Winehouse, 27, found dead at her London flat after suspected 'drug overdose,'" *Mail Online*, July 26, 2011, http://www.dailymail.co.uk/tvshowbiz/article-2018020/Amy-Winehouse-dead-London-flat-drug-overdose.html.
   - Luchina Fisher, "If Not Drugs, What Killed Amy Winehouse?," *ABC News*, August 24, 2011, http://abcnews.go.com/Entertainment/drugs-killed-amy-winehouse/story?id=14364250.

15. The 27 Club:
   - "27 Club," *Wikipedia*, http://en.wikipedia.org/wiki/27_Club.
   - Kiri Blakeley, "Amy Winehouse Joins Unfortunate '27 Club,'" *Forbes*, July 23, 2011, http://www.forbes.com/sites/kiriblakeley/2011/07/23/amy-winehouse-joins-unfortunate-27-club.

16. Olympic suicide and falls from grace:
   - Lana Bandoim, "Jeret Peterson not the first Olympic athlete to commit suicide," *Yahoo Sports*, July 29, 2011, http://sports.yahoo.com/olympics/news?slug=ycn-8881723.
   - Tony Manfred, "Olympic Silver Medalist Commits Suicide in Utah," *Business Insider*, July 27, 2011, http://www.businessinsider.com/jeret-peterson-olympic-medalist-suicide-2011-7.
   - Tim Nudd, "Jeret Peterson, Olympic Skier, Commits Suicide," *People*, July 27, 2011, http://www.people.com/people/article/0,,20513232,00.html.

- <u>Dan Childs,</u> "Phelps' 'Mistake': De-Stressing or Chasing a Thrill?," *ABC News,* http://abcnews.go.com/Health/MindMoodNews/story?id=6787832&page=1.

Chapter 4

1. *The Secret,* www.thesecret.tv.
2. History of the self-help industry:
   - "Self-Help," *Wikipedia,* http://en.wikipedia.org/wiki/Self-help.
   - "Samuel Smiles," *Wikipedia,* http://en.wikipedia.org/wiki/Samuel_Smiles.
   - Benjamin Franklin, *Poor Richard's Almanac,* see http://www.richhall.com/poor_richard.htm.
   - "I'm OK, You're OK," *Wikipedia,* http://en.wikipedia.org/wiki/I%27m_OK,_You%27re_OK.
3. "Information Age," *Wikipedia,* http://en.wikipedia.org/wiki/Information_Age.
4. "The 2012 Statistical Abstract," U.S. Census Bureau, http://www.census.gov/compendia/statab/cats/income_expenditures_poverty_wealth.html.
5. Information marketing:
   - Entrepreneur Press, *Start Your Own Information Marketing Business* (Irvine, CA: Entrepreneur Press, 2008).
   - Information Marketing Association, http://www.info-marketing.org.
6. Personal coaching:
   - Marketdata Enterprises press releases, http://www.marketdataenterprises.com:
     - "Self Improvement Market Grows 50% Since 2000: Personal Coaching and Infomercials Soar," February 2004.
     - "Self-Improvement Market Grows 25% in Last Two Years: Personal Coaching, Infomercials Do Best," September 12, 2006.

○   "Self-Improvement Market Slows, as Recession Takes Toll Consumers Await the Next Big Thing," October 14, 2008.

○   "Self-Improvement Market Shifts to Digital, Audio & Online Oprah's OWN Network to Be the "Next Big Thing," November 23, 2010.

•   iCoachAcademy, http://www.icoachacademy.com/en/faq/coaching-industry.

•   International Coach Federation, http://www.coachfederation.org.

7. James Arthur Ray:

•   "James Arthur Ray guilty in Ariz. sweat lodge deaths," *CBS News*, June 22, 2011, http://www.cbsnews.com/8301-504083_162-20073489-504083.html.

•   Daisy Nguyen and Felicia Fonseca, "James Arthur Ray: Guru Says He's Being Tested By Sweat Lodge Deaths," *The Huffington Post*, October 14, 2009, http://www.huffingtonpost.com/2009/10/14/james-arthur-ray-guru-say_n_320067.html.

•   Terry Greene Sterling, "Sweat-Lodge Guru's Homicide Verdict," *The Daily Beast*" June 22, 2011, http://www.thedailybeast.com/articles/2011/06/22/sweat-lodge-trial-guru-james-arthur-ray-s-homicide-verdict.html.

•   Howard Breuer, "James Arthur Ray Sentenced to Two Years in Prison for Sweat Lodge Deaths," *People*, November 18, 2011, http://www.people.com/people/article/0,,20546783,00.html.

•   *Tragedy in Sedona: My Life in James Arthur Ray's Inner Circle* by Connie Joy (Transformation Media Books, 2010).

•   "Tragedy in Sedona" *San Diego Living*, August 20, 2010, http://www.youtube.com/watch?v=PnuWNufFc0w&feature=player_embedded.

8. Nightingale Conant, http://www.nightingale.com.

9. Robert   Allen,   http://www.robertgallen.com/informationmarketing.php.

10. DeMarco, *The Millionaire Fastlane*.
11. "IRS Statistics of Income 2008," Internal Revenue Service, http://www.irs.gov/taxstats/index.html.
12. Achor, *The Happiness Advantage*.
13. Paul Damien *Help: Debunking the Outrageous Claims of Self-Help Gurus* (St. George, UT: Synergy Books, 2008).

Chapter 5

1. "The Grand Illusion Album," *Wikipedia*, http://en.wikipedia. org/wiki/The_Grand_Illusion_%28album%29.
2. Social networking:
   - Fast Company Blog, "The History of Social Networking," blog entry by JD Rucker, January 24, 2011, http://www.fast-company.com/1720374/the-history-of-social-networking.
   - Christopher Nickson, "The History of Social Networking," *Digital Trends*, January 21, 2009, http://www.digitaltrends. com/features/the-history-of-social-networking.
   - Facebook statistics, https://www.facebook.com/press/info. php?statistics.
   - Twitter blog, http://blog.twitter.com/2011/03/numbers. html.
   - "About Us," LinkedIn Press Center, http://press.linkedin. com/about.
   - Nicholas Carlson, "Chart of the Day: How Many Users Does Twitter REALLY Have?," *Business Insider*, March 31, 2011, http://www.businessinsider.com/chart-of-the-day-how-many-users-does-twitter-really-have-2011-3.
   - Aaron Smith, "Twitter Update 2011," *Pew Research Center Publications*, http://pewresearch.org/pubs/2007/twitter-users-cell-phone-2011-demographics.
   - "2011 Social Media Marketing Industry Report" *Social Media Examiner*, http://www.socialmediaexaminer.com.
   - Tom Yencho, "Researcher: Workers more prone to lie in e-mail," Lehigh University Website, September 23,

2008, http://www3.lehigh.edu/News/V2news_story. asp?iNewsID=2892.

- Jennifer Van Grove, "Study: Social Media Is for Narcissists," *Mashable* August 25, 2009, http://mashable. com/2009/08/25/gen-y-social-media-study.

- Jean M. Twenge and W. Keith Campbell, *The Narcissism Epidemic: Living in the Age of Entitlement* (New York: Free Press, 2009).

- "Most Facebook users have low self esteem: Study," *NDTV*, September 9, 2010, http://www.ndtv.com/article/world/ most-facebook-users-have-low-self-esteem-study-50935.

- Brendan Sasso, "Facebook use correlates with narcissism in teens," *The Hill*, August 8, 2011, http://thehill.com/blogs/ hillicon-valley/technology/175949-study-facebook-use-cor-related-with-narcissism-in-teenagers.

- Jennifer Van Grove, "Study: 80% of Twitter Users Are All About Me," *Mashable*, September 29, 2009, http://twitoaster.com/country-us/mashable/ study-80-of-twitter-users-are-all-about-me.

- Achor, *The Happiness Advantage*.

- Sharon Gaudin, "Facebook cuts productivity at work," *Computerworld*, July 22, 2009, http://www.computerworld. com/s/article/9135795/Study_Facebook_use_cuts_ productivity_at_work.

- "Why People Are Better At Lying Online Than Telling A Lie Face-to-face," *ScienceDaily*, May 5, 2009, 2011, http:// www.sciencedaily.com/releases/2009/05/090503203738. htm.

- Kimberly Englot, The Center for Authentic Self Development, http://kimberlyenglot.com.

- Cristen Conger, "Do People Lie More Online?," *Discovery News*, March 4, 2011, http://news.discovery.com/tech/do-people-lie-more-online-110304.html?print=true.

3. The Internet and World Wide Web:
    *   "History of the Internet," *Wikipedia*, http://en.wikipedia. org/wiki/History_of_the_Internet.
    *   "History of the World Wide Web," *Wikipedia*, http:// en.wikipedia.org/wiki/History_of_the_World_Wide_Web.
    *   "SixDegrees.com," *Wikipedia*, http://en.wikipedia.org/ wiki/SixDegrees.com.
    *   "Six degrees of separation," *Wikipedia*, http://en.wikipedia. org/wiki/Six_degrees_of_separation.
    *   "The World Population and the Top Ten Countries with the Highest Population," *Internet World Stats*, http://www. internetworldstats.com/stats8.htm.
    *   Matt Rosenberg, "Most Populous Countries Today," *About. com*, May 11, 2011, http://geography.about.com/cs/ worldpopulation/a/mostpopulous.htm.
4. Facebook and Mark Zuckerberg:
    *   "Facebook," *Wikipedia*, http://en.wikipedia.org/wiki/Facebook.
    *   Bobbie Johnson, "Privacy no longer a social norm, says Facebook founder," *The Guardian*, January 10, 2010, http://www.guardian.co.uk/technology/2010/jan/11/ facebook-privacy.
    *   Emma Barnett, "Facebook's Mark Zuckerberg says privacy is no longer a 'social norm,'" *The Telegraph*, January 22, 2010, http://www.telegraph.co.uk/technology/facebook/ 6966628/Facebooks-Mark-Zuckerberg-says-privacy-is-no- longer-a-social-norm.html.
5. Generation Y:
    *   "Generation Y," *Wikipedia*, http://en.wikipedia.org/wiki/ Generation_Y.
    *   Suzanna Choney, "Privacy schmivacy—Gen Y will keep on sharing," *MSN.com*, July 9, 2010, http://www.msnbc.msn. com/id/38165531/ns/technology_and_science-tech_ and_gadgets/t/privacy-schmivacy-gen-y-will-keep-sharing.

- Pew Research Center, "Millennials: Confident. Connected. Open to Change," Pew Research Center website, February 24, 2010, http://pewsocialtrends.org/2010/02/24/millennials-confident-connected-open-to-change.

6. "The Truth About College—And Life by Amy," *StyleSubstanceSoul*, September 15, 2011, http://stylesubstancesoul.com/2011/09/the-truth-about-college-and-life-by-amy.

Chapter 6

1. Erin Sherbert, "Generation Debt," *MetroSantaCruz.com*, July 30, 2008, http://www.metrosantacruz.com/bohemian/07.30.08/cover-0831.html.

2. "Comparison of Prices Over 70 Years," *The People History*, http://www.thepeoplehistory.com/70yearsofpricechange.html.

3. Mary Gallagher, "Historical Home Appreciation Rates," *SF Gate/San Francisco Chronicle*, http://homeguides.sfgate.com/historical-home-appreciation-rates-2984.html.

4. "Historical Census of Housing Tables, 1940–2000," U.S. Census Bureau website, http://www.census.gov/hhes/www/housing/census/historic/values.html.

5. Generations:
    - "Generation," *Wikipedia*, http://en.wikipedia.org/wiki/Generation.
    - Matt Rosenberg, "Names of Generations" *About.com*, http://geography.about.com/od/populationgeography/qt/generations.htm.
    - Alan Fram, "One In Four Working Baby Boomers Say They'll Never Retire, Survey Finds," *The Huffington Post*, April 5, 2011, http://www.huffingtonpost.com/2011/04/05/baby-boomers-retirement-fears_n_844957.html.

6. "Saving Rates in the United States: Calculation and Comparison" *Congressional Research Service*, September 14, 2010.

7. Wexler, *Living Large*.

8. Phill Grove, "Housing Trend; Does Size Still Matter?," REI Maverick, February 16, 2011, http://www.reimaverick.com/housing-trend-does-size-still-matter.
9. HELOCs, cash out refinances, subprime mortgage crisis, foreclosures:
    *   "Home equity loans in California still over $600 billion . . . ," *Dr.HousingBubble,* February 20, 2011, http://www.doctorhousingbubble.com/home-equity-loans-in-california-over-600-billion-pasadena-short-sale-pasadena-real-estate-auction.
    *   "Equifax Data Show U.S. Consumer Payment Trends Continue to Deteriorate," *PR Newswire,* http://www.prnewswire.com/news-releases/equifax-data-show-us-consumer-payment-trends-continue-to-deteriorate-79885077.html.
    *   Carrie Bay, "Mortgage Delinquencies Drop for Fourth Consecutive Month: Equifax," *dsnews.com,* July 1, 2010, http://www.dsnews.com/articles/mortgage-delinquencies-drop-for-fourth-consecutive-month-equifax-2010-07-01.
    *   Krista Franks, "Mortgage Fraud Suspicion Rises 88% Since Last Year," *dsnews.com,* http://www.dsnews.com/articles/index/mortgage-fraud-suspicion-rises-88-since-last-year-2011-09-28.
    *   Bob Willis, "Americans Tap $8.3 Billion in Home Equity, Least in a Decade," *Bloomberg,* September 28, 2011, http://www.bloomberg.com/news/2010-07-28/americans-use-of-8-3-billion-in-home-equity-last-quarter-least-in-decade.html.
    *   "Freddie Mac," *Wikipedia,* http://en.wikipedia.org/wiki/Freddie_Mac.
    *   Vikas Bajaj and Ron Nixon, "Re-Refinancing and Putting Off Mortgage Pain," *The New York Times,* July 23, 2006, http://www.nytimes.com/2006/07/23/business/23mortgage.html?_r=1&pagewanted=1.
    *   "Subprime Mortgage Crisis," *Wikipedia,* http://en.wikipedia.org/wiki/Subprime_mortgage_crisis.

- "Graphed: U.S. Foreclosures and Home Repossessions, 2005 to 2010," *StopForeclosureFraud.com,* June 4, 2010, http://stopforeclosurefraud.com/2010/06/04/graphed-u-s-foreclosures-and-home-repossessions-2005-to-2010.
- "Graphed: U.S. Foreclosures and Home Repossessions, 2005 to 2010," *The Awl,* June 3, 2010; http://www.theawl.com/2010/06/graphed-u-s-foreclosures-and-home-repossessions-2005-to-2010.
- "Timeline of the United States housing bubble," *Wikipedia,* http://en.wikipedia.org/wiki/Timeline_of_the_United_States_housing_bubble.

Chapter 7

1. Darren Hardy, "I Want To Rename This Magazine," *SUCCESS Magazine,* October 2011.
2. Daniel Gilbert, *Stumbling on Happiness* (New York: Vintage Books, 2005).

Chapter 8

1. Personality tests:
   - Myers-Briggs MBTI Complete, https://www.mbticomplete.com/en/index.aspx
   - Free Myers-Briggs Test (this is not the official Myers-Briggs Type Indicator), http://www.personalitypathways.com/type_inventory.html.
   - The DISC System, http://www.personalityinsights.com.
   - The Strong Life Test, http://stronglifetest.com.
   - Free Enneagram Sampler Test, http://www.enneagramin-stitute.com/dis_sample_36.asp?discover.
   - Color Q Personality Test, http://www.colorqpersonalities.com/colorqcoaching.
   - Visual DNA Personality Test, http://personality.visualdna.com/1/index.php.

2. Myers-Briggs:
   - "Myers-Briggs Type Indicator," *Wikipedia*, http://en.wikipedia. org/wiki/Myers-Briggs_Type_Indicator.
   - The Myers-Brigg Foundation, http://www.myersbriggs.org.
   - "High Level Description of Sixteen Personality Types," http://www.personalitypage.com/high-level.html.
   - Deborah Geering, "Playing Against Type," *Portfolio*, November 26, 2007, http://www.portfolio.com/careers/ features/2007/11/26/Myers-Briggs-Personality-Types.
   - "Common Careers for Personality Types," http://www.per- sonalitypage.com/careers.html.
   - Shoya Zichy, http://www. http://colorqpersonalities.com.
   - Shoya Zichy, "Type and Money," *MBTI Type Today*, http:// www.mbtitoday.org/articles/article02.html.
   - Ms. Dee, "Your Life Purpose by MBTI Personality Type," *HubPages*, http://ms-dee.hubpages.com/_3r3z6j6h0kore/ hub/16-Key-Life-Purposes-Driven-by-Personality-Type.
   - The Myers & Briggs Foundation, "Extraversion or Introversion," The Myers & Briggs Foundation website, http://www.myersbriggs.org/my-mbti-personality-type/ mbti-basics/extraversion-or-introversion.asp.
   - The Myers & Briggs Foundation, "Sensing or Intuition," The Myers & Briggs Foundation website, http://www.mye- rsbriggs.org/my-mbti-personality-type/mbti-basics/sens- ing-or-intuition.asp.
3. The Enneagram:
   - The Enneagram Institute, http://www.enneagraminstitute. com.
   - Don Richard Riso and Russ Hudson, *The Wisdom of The Enneagram: The Complete Guide to Psychological and Spiritual Growth for the Nine Personality Types* (New York: Bantam Books, 1999).
   - Lynda Roberts, Faculty of The Enneagram Institute, Project Management Professional (PMP), Secretary to the Board of

the International Enneagram Association (IEA), Certified and Authorized Riso-Hudson Enneagram Teacher and Consultant, http://www.enneagramhorizons.com.

4. Core values:
   - Deidre Sheldon, certified Myers-Briggs Personality Inventory Assessment provider, http://ms-dee.hubpages.com.
   - Core values exercise, http://www.make-it-fly.com/a0601. htm.
   - Jean Twenge, *Generation Me: Why Today's Young Americans Are More Confident, Assertive, Entitled—and More Miserable Than Ever Before* (New York: Free Press, 2006).

5. John Eliot, *Overachievement: The New Science of Working Less to Accomplish More* (New York: Portfolio, 2006).

6. Programmed for success:
   - Srikumar S. Rao, *Happiness at Work: Be Resilient, Motivated, and Successful—No Matter What* (New York: McGraw-Hill, 2010).
   - Mihaly Csikszentmihalyi, *Flow: The Psychology of Optimal Experience* (Harper Perennial, 1990).

7. Looking successful:
   - Maureen Cavanaugh, Hank Crook, and Rachel Goetz, "Is Perception of Success More Important Than Actual Success Nowadays?," *KPBS,* June 29, 2011, http://www.kpbs.org/news/2011/jun/29/perception-sucess-more-important-actual-success-no.
   - Twenge and Campbell, *The Narcissism Epidemic.*
   - Jean M. Twenge, *Generation Me.*
   - Ms. Dee, "Your Life Purpose by MBTI Personality Type," *HubPages,* http://ms-dee.hubpages.com/hub/16-Key-Life-Purposes-Driven-by-Personality-Type.

8. "Taylor Swift: A Young Singer's Meteoric Rise," *60 Minutes,* November 20, 2011, http://www.cbsnews.com/video/watch/?id=7389010n&tag=re1.channel.

9. Addiction:

- The National Center on Addiction and Substance Abuse at Columbia University, "Califano Calls for Fundamental Shift in Attitudes and Policies About Substance Abuse and Addiction," CASA website, http://www.casacolumbia.org/templates/PressReleases.aspx?articleid=487&zoneid=65.
- "Dr. Judith Wright Talks About Soft Addictions on The CBS Early Show," *World News*, http://wn.com/Dr_Judith_Wright_talks_about_soft_addictions_on_the_CBS_Early_Show.
- "Behavioral Addiction," *Wikipedia*, http://en.wikipedia.org/wiki/Behavioral_addiction.
- Kevin Helliker, "You Might as Well Face It: You're Addicted to Success," *The Wall Street Journal*, February 12, 2009, http://online.wsj.com/article/SB123423234983566171.html.
- Susanne Babbel, "Addicted to Success," *Psychology Today*, January 19, 2011, http://www.psychologytoday.com/blog/somatic-psychology/201101/addicted-success.
- Patrick Lencioni, "The Painful Reality of Adrenaline Addiction," Patrick Lencioni, Leadership Preview website, http://www.leadershippreview.org/2005winter/LencioniArticle.pdf.
- Bill Urell, "Addiction: Is It Caused By An Addictive Personality Or Genetic Factors And Predisposition?," Addiction Recovery Basics website, http://addictionrecoverybasics.com/addiction-is-it-caused-by-an-addictive-personality-or-genetic-factors-and-predisposition-part-1-of-2.
- "Addiction," Wikipedia, http://en.wikipedia.org/wiki/Addiction.
- "R 31 Gambling Disorder," American Psychiatric Association DSM-5 Development website, http://www.dsm5.org/ProposedRevisions/Pages/proposedrevision.aspx?rid=210.

- Dr. Rita Bernadette DeShields, addictions specialist, transpersonal health, author, *Freedom to Frolic*, oilspot444@gmail.com.
- Lance Dodes, MD, training and supervising analyst with the Boston Psychoanalytic Society and Institute and assistant clinical professor of psychiatry at Harvard Medical School. Author of *The Heart of Addiction* (New York: HarperCollins, 2002) and *Breaking Addiction: A 7-Step Handbook for Ending Any Addiction* (New York: HarperCollins, 2011). www.lance-dodes.com.

Chapter 9

1. MasterCard TV Commercial, "Child Playing In Box," http://www.youtube.com/watch?v=j-S1DAhQ0YA.
2. Achor, *The Happiness Advantage*.
3. Sonja Lyubomirsky, *The How of Happiness: A New Approach to Getting the Life You Want* (New York: Penguin Books, 2008).
4. Gilbert, *Stumbling on Happiness*.
5. Jonathan Haidt, *The Happiness Hypotheses: Finding Modern Truth in Ancient Wisdom* (New York: Basic Books, 2006).
6. Kimberly Englot, The Center for Authentic Self Development, http://kimberlyenglot.com.
7. Stefan Klein, *The Science of Happiness: How Our Brains Make Us Happy—and What We Can Do to Get Happier* (Cambridge, MA: Marlowe & Company, 2002).
8. Marci Shimoff with Carol Kline, *Happy for No Reason: 7 Steps to Being Happy from the Inside Out* (New York: Free Press, 2008).
9. "Buying Experiences, Not Possessions, Leads To Greater Happiness," *Science Daily*, February 7, 2009, http://www.sciencedaily.com/releases/2009/02/090207150518.htm.
10. *Harvard Business Review Blog*; "Three Ways to Overcome Career Anxiety," blog entry by Daniel Gulati, November 30, 2011.

11. Bronnie Ware, "Regrets of the Dying," *Inspiration and Chai,* http://www.inspirationandchai.com/Regrets-of-the-Dying.html.

Chapter 10
1. Trina Paulus, *Hope For The Flowers* (New York: Paulist Press, 1972).
2. Chip Heath and Dan Heath, *Switch: How to Change Things When Change Is Hard* (New York: Broadway Books, 2010).
3. *Loyalty To Your Soul: The Heart of Spiritual Psychology* by H. Ronald Hulnick Ph.D. and Mary R. Hulnick Ph.D. (Carlsbad, CA: Hay House, 2011).
4. John Eliot, *Overachievement.*
5. Jennifer Urezzio, http://www.knowsoulslanguage.net.

ABOUT THE AUTHOR

Debbie LaChusa is the author of three books: *Twin Connections: Stories that Celebrate the Mysterious Bond Between Twins*; *The Career-at-Home Mom: Secrets for Earning a Six-Figure Income While Having Time for Your Family*; *and Breaking the Spell: The Truth about Money, Success, and the Pursuit of Happiness.* She is also a business and marketing consultant and speaker who shares her experience and expertise frequently on teleclasses, the stage, and in the media. Debbie and her businesses have been featured in *Entrepreneur Magazine* and *Home Business Magazine* and on Forbes.com, CNBC.com, Inc.com, and Yahoo! Finance. She was also chosen as one of five expert bloggers for the Yahoo! Small Business blog.

Debbie earned a degree in business and marketing from San Diego State University in 1985 and has spent the last twenty-seven years working in the marketing and advertising field. Since 1998 she has run her own marketing consulting business. She is known as The Business Stylist, because she specializes in helping service professionals design businesses, brands, and marketing that *fit* them, resulting in businesses that are more enjoyable, successful, and profitable.

You can learn more about Debbie's writing, speaking, and consulting services at www.DebbieLaChusa.com. To read more of her thoughts about money, success, and happiness, visit her blog at www.MoneySuccessHappiness.com.

You may contact Debbie about business, writing or speaking opportunities at:
Debbie LaChusa
DLC Marketing, Inc.
PMB 310, 9625 Mission Gorge Road, Suite B2
Santee, CA 92071
619-334-8590
debbie@debbielachusa.com